FALLING INTO GRACE:

THE FICTION OF ANDREW GREELEY

R. W. Carstens

All my best
RWCarstens
3-9-14

iUniverse, Inc.
New York Bloomington

To all the Dominican ghosts haunting the air
and educating me still,
especially
Sister Thomas Albert Corbett OP

"… lest the cross of Christ be emptied of its power."
1 Corinthians 1:17

Contents

Foreword

I am asked questions about my stories. Each question normally involves an attack of the sort that a prosecutor would ask a witness already presumed guilty.

Question: Why do you write novels?
 Answer: Because I believe that stories are an excellent way to talk about religion, maybe the best way. My stories are about God's love. Like all storytellers, I enjoy telling stories.

Question: Why do people bother reading them?
 Answer: I've never been able to figure that out. Every time I begin a story, I do so with some fear that it will not appeal to readers. So far, that fear is wrong. Still, I'm never sure. I speculate that they like my characters. I like them too. It's fun writing about Chuck O'Malley, Blackie Ryan, and Nuala Anne McGrail.

Question: What about the real life people on whom your characters are based? Is it not wrong to hurt their feelings?
 Answer: Only two characters are based on real people, Monsieur Muggsy Brannigan and Father Ace. Both are pleased with the portraits. As for the others who see themselves in my stories, they should be so lucky.

Question: There are no real life versions of Chuck and Blackie and Nuala Anne?
 Answer: Alas no. The world would be a better place if there were.

Question: How many novels have you written? Don't you think it is time you retire?
 Answer: No way.

Question: What do you do with your money?
 Answer: That is probably none of your business, but it may be only a venial sin to ask. Anyway, since I'm a priest I have to answer. I pay my taxes and I give most of it away. Do you want to see my income tax returns?

Question: How much trouble do you have with the church because of your books?

Answer: No one in authority has ever complained. My fellow priests don't like me very much. My cardinal has even said nice things about my stories on the public record.

Question: What is your spiritual orientation?

Answer: West Side Chicago Irish Catholicism.

Question: Do you get many complaints from readers?

Answer: Not much any more. Mostly from Republicans.

Question: Why is there so much sex in your stories?

Answer: I don't think there is that much saves for those who are prurient. There is a lot more sex in human life, however. Sexual love, anyway, is a sacrament of God's love for us. Consult St. Paul and Benedict XVI on that.

Question: You don't expect your stories to last, do you?

Answer: That's not a sinful question but a silly one. If a storyteller worries about that, he'll never finish a story. (Incidentally, the stories have lasted for thirty years and my publisher is issuing a new edition of my novels, beginning with *The Magic Cup* and *The Cardinal Sins*.)

Question: Why did you let Professor Carstens write a book about your novels?

Answer: Because he seemed to be a man who had the courage and intelligence not to be bothered by questions like these. He's done a fine job.

Andrew Greeley
Tucson
Fourth week in Lent 2008

Preface

Grace abounds; we are immersed in it. Neither magic nor sign, grace is evidence of the divine. Grace sustains us, unites us, comforts us, and sometimes overwhelms us. It is evidence of our freedom. Paradoxically, falling from it is also our falling into it. Such is the message of Andrew Greeley's fiction.

Greeley's characters and the world in which they live and have their being are not the same as the persons or things in God's world (as Greeley would put it); but they could and might be like each other, at least in our imaginations. This is the didactic message of Greeley's fiction. As such, that message depends upon the unique and shared experiences of his readers. Stories are the ways we, ourselves, are who we are. All great storytellers know this, and Father Andrew Greeley is a great storyteller.

This book is the result of hearing great stories about God—and God is always the main character in Greeley's fiction. It marks my attempt to explain the power of his fiction and to connect that fiction to a tradition. To the extent that I have done so, this book presents Greeley's novels as evidence of a set of ancient values, values that are needed today more than ever. Specifically, Greeley's fiction illustrates a particular understanding of several key ideas, the most important being the political ideas of authority and freedom. In part, that fiction represents a mode of political thought which, when taken seriously, offers an understanding of politics, our means of creating a world worthy of human beings, rather than the exercise of violence or power. More pointedly, Greeley's fiction helps us confront the diminishment of freedom and the abuse of authority by government, church, and corporate hierarchies while offering alternative ways of being responsible participants in our communities. It teaches us about the plurality of creation, thus helping those alienated from monistic religious institutions, especially the Roman Catholic Church, and it argues against the disenfranchisement of so many from the social institutions of the American polity. In the end, Greeley's fiction is a way to go home, not to a nostalgic utopian past, but to images that appeal to the best in us, and therefore tell us what might be. His stories portray life as a comedy rather than a tragedy. Collectively, Greeley's novels are contemporary acts of faith, hope, and love that convince some of us that God is alive and well in the world and that show us how to deal with the general drift toward more authoritarian institutions of social control, both at home and abroad.

As in all the good stories I have been told, I have come to appreciate that accomplishment, here or anywhere else, is never singular. As some of Greeley's best characters come to know, I have come to understand that who I am and what I have done results from interconnecting sets of relationships, which I call my family, my church, my students, my university, my country, and my world. They are mine because they have been given to me, and as a steward, I am expected to give them back as the future. Thus, to the many that compose my relationships, I owe a great debt, because their inspiration and support have taught me that I owe everything to Grace.

In what sense? First, I owe a great intellectual debt to Father Andrew Greeley, who probably does not know for how long I have carried this debt. Certainly this book indicates a following of sorts in that I, like so very many, read his books, whether fiction or sociology. This book attests to my judgment about his fiction, but it must also be said that his sociology has confirmed in me the importance of counting and remembering. As a first-class sociologist, Greeley has given his academic life to the idea that we ought not to act either in or on the world without knowing, as best we can, how that world is constituted. In an age that becomes ever faster an age of sound bites, contending opinions, and moral relativism, we ought to thank Greeley and people like him for reminding us that what once was called the life of the mind is necessarily tethered to the practical world.

Yet there is more. Nearly thirty years ago, I attended a meeting of political scientists and sociologists at which Father Andrew Greeley was to present a paper. By this time, he had combined his priestly life with the study of sociology in response to the Second Vatican Council's teaching that we should read the "signs of the time" so that as members of the church we might help bring the Gospel into the world: become leaven in the lump, so to speak. As we all would learn, this was not always appreciated, and he was often criticized because as the messenger he brought serious and sometime somber news. So he had a bit of a reputation. Thus, like geese, political scientists and sociologists flocked to his session; there was standing room only. Greeley began by briefly outlining the project to be discussed, introduced a graduate student as the primary author, and then sat down to let her shine. No matter how the audience tried, they could not get Greeley to displace his student. Although I do not recall the substance of the talk, I do remember that I left the room with the notion that his putting his student before all else was a model of good teaching. That notion became an ideal in my academic life, and its success has given effect to some very fine students.

To them I also owe a great debt. They have given my life a professional meaning that has taken me to the subject of this book. They have been and are grace to me. All of them helped me see that there can be no good teaching, nor much learning, without love. Four of these students deserve special thanks, Clinton Dick, Matt Madej, Wes Page, and Matt King made demands upon the university and me such that, as is not always the case, education worked. Their time at Ohio Dominican was one of extraordinary change and not a little upset. Like my students before and after them, these four extraordinary individuals reminded me when I needed it most that more than a profession, I had a vocation, and part of this vocation was to pass on the life of the mind and the intellectual tradition that sustains it. They cannot know fully how much that has meant to me.

Lastly and most importantly, to Noreen, in whose care is my heart and my soul, and to Finnian and Liam, who carry that care into this world, I say thank you for showing me how amazing Grace truly is. Their lives and constant support testify to the truths embedded in Greeley's fiction, in the theology of story, and in Catholic social teaching. Without these three, I very well might have missed what it means to be swimming in grace.

These are the people, living in God's world, who deserve thanks. But, as we learn from Greeley's fiction, there is more to reality than meets the eye, no matter how loving or important that reality may be. As his novels attest, there is a Reality behind the real. Suspecting this as I do, I am obligated to acknowledge my debt to it. This Reality hides in the everyday, lurks everywhere, and is often missed. So, perhaps, the best way to perceive it is to tell a story.

Once upon a time, in the last half of the twentieth century, in a land brimming with resources and good luck, people began to wonder about why they believed what they did and why they acted as they did. In this land and in the world, most people were good most of the time, and when they failed, it was usually because of ignorance or weakness, or a little bad luck. Those few who seemed to have sided with the worst in this world, often did so because they were confused, or because they had become ill in body and in soul. And there may have been a very few who liked to be bad, but I have never known one of these people, so I cannot comment on them.

One day, almost without warning—except for a very few persons who studied these kinds of things but failed to tell anyone but themselves about their studies—the whole world seemed to come apart. The tools people had hoped to use for their betterment were used to kill and to harm just about everyone everywhere. There was a long Depression and then a terrible war, followed by almost fifty years of terror. People appealed to reason, but most were too afraid to make that choice. They tried to use power and violence as a method of making sure that they were safe from those who had sided with the worst, and they prayed, in their own ways, that no one would blow up this world, or kill whole groups of people, or take their lands, or enslave their children. But it seemed there was no answer. Many began to doubt the goodness of this world, and this, in turn, began a great deal of criticism of one by the other. It seemed that nobody liked each other anymore.

What could be done? Many did not know and gave up thinking about it. Some became cynical and did not get out of bed in the morning—after all, there was nothing they could do, so why get up?—while others pretended that everything was going to be all right. But things were not all right, and because their tools were so good, everybody could talk to and visit everybody else. This was only a mixed blessing, however, since some in other parts of this world were very upset because their part of the world seemed to have been harmed much more than any other. Whether or not this was true, nobody could tell. The few who tried were often ignored and hardly ever appreciated.

But there were some, and they set out to see if they could at least make this world a little better and perhaps worthy of their children. Some went into this world and measured things to see if what people thought about the current state really was that way. Others gave their lives to serving others so that everybody had a little love. Most just kept going with the belief that the Reality behind the real would finally be known.

A very few began to talk in a new way about the real. This new way helped a great many to see Reality, and sometimes, even to hear answers to their worries, and this, in turn, helped them keep going. Some even converted and joined with those who served love to everybody.

Such new talk came to be called a theory of imagination that could show people how to see the Reality behind the real. If this theory were the case, perhaps people could help change the world so that many of the bad things that had happened might not trump the good things, and maybe, even make sure that these bad things would not happen again. Perhaps the good really was stronger than the bad.

But there was a problem. They were call the critics, and they came in very many sizes. Some wanted to return to what they called "the good old days," a time when they were in charge and nobody talked back. Some wanted to retreat into a future they had made up without much caring about whether it would be better than this world—even in its present state, and some just wanted to talk among themselves about what they knew. Many of these critics became very mad when others would not act like them.

This was how it went until one man, I think he was Irish and therefore could tell good stories (I think his name was O'Malley), came along and started to write his stories down so everybody could read them. That kind of thing was known as fiction, and most people thought fiction belonged in drugstores either with other unmentionable things or in ancient libraries with other books that are never read. But O'Malley thought that if he made new talk about imagination and the Reality behind the real into interesting fiction (so these stories would not remain in drugstores or libraries, but rather in the minds and hearts of many, many people) then these very many people would be able to see the Reality behind the real from their point of view, that is, through their own imaginations—something that is very important if you want to teach people what you think will help them. Once they saw their reality as related to a larger and best Reality—the one that always hides within the real—they were able to do something about their own lives, and in doing so, they could help others do the same.

What were O'Malley stories about? They were about some good traditions and some bad traditions, and if you can tell the difference, you are way ahead of the game. They especially were about who gets to boss others around and how we might get them to stop it. They were also about how everybody should and does have a real chance to be happy; how happiness is stronger when it is shared with others; how this sharing helps make us free as well as secure; how in becoming ourselves we need other people with us; how it is good to be wise as well as intelligent, and how we can be wise by knowing all traditions, even the bossy ones.

These stories were very popular, and some people did not like them or their popularity. They tried to confuse others by saying things like: a popular story can't be a good story; good stories are very hard to understand and most people can't; O'Malley already has a job and should not be confusing people by writing stories; the stories are about bad things and O'Malley should not scandalize everybody by writing about bad things; and sometimes they even said that the stories were about things they weren't about. These critics did not go away, but O'Malley kept on writing, and you know what? The world became a better place. Not bad for just stories!

I have heard it rumored that Reality and his mother have both looked at some of these stories. Blessedly they are not critics. By the way, I think Reality's true name is Grace.

Chapter 1: Greeley on Imagination

Whenever discussing a writer's method, it is imperative that the critic indicates clearly his or her understanding of not only what the story is about, but also of how that critic approaches the subject. A discussion of the characters and storylines in a set of novels would seem to require a simple method of analysis, a discussion of what the author means. Yet, any work of art is at the same time it is art, also a work of human imagination. The methodological question behind such an analysis is whether or not an artist's or an author's imaginative work is the same as the artist's or author's meaning, or more problematically, of the artist's or author's self.

This question is important because it takes us to the core of the imaginative problem: how do we say what we mean and is what we intend the same as what we really mean? This problem constitutes, it seems to me, the whole of the artistic or literary process. Whether or not we are dealing with the "narrative imagination," as Martha Nussbaum defines it, or with the "moral imagination," as many ethicists define it, we are dealing with that part of our human being that makes us able to reach across the divide between the self from the world to communicate with others.

To me it seems merely common sense to argue that, given their context, our words mean what they say. Moreover, it seems sensible to suggest that the imagination carries in itself an argument, just as words do. The best we can do in interpreting others, either their words or their imaginative constructs, is to take them at their word, so to speak.

Where there are ambiguities, we have the right to ask for clarification, and we have the duty to take meaning and any such clarifications in their best sense. Otherwise, it seems, words and works can mean anything we impose upon them.

Thus, in this work I mean to interpret fictional characters within the context of the story line and the action that appear in the novels under scrutiny. This is important in a book about Andrew Greeley's novels precisely because he has so often been misconstrued. I think this has been the case through no fault of Father Greeley, but rather, because Andrew Greeley is, in fact, a Catholic priest. That construct itself, "Catholic," and "priest" carry with it an incredible load of judgment and prejudice. Thus, when I speak about Greeley's characters and stories, I am speaking only about these imaginative constructs. Greeley continually asserts that his characters are fictional and do not derive from any particular historical person or from historical events, though he uses his experience as any artist might, perhaps must, and builds from that experience an imaginative world which helps those who read his works better understand the major metaphors of the Christian religion. Hence, I shall only say what Greeley means when I have his words, grammar, syntax, and context to do so. And I shall say such only when I must because I think it essential to intellectual integrity to respect the person and the privacy of the author. An imaginative construct such as a novel is not the same as the author's self or the meaning of the person who writes it.[1]

So, why should a priest write novels? This question should be answered with these two questions: Why should professors write books, or novels or poems? Or why should homemakers, or teachers or safety officers write? The answer is the same in all cases, because it is an essential part of our humanity to comment upon and give meaning to the world we experience. Those who have a particular problem with priests who are artists and authors ought to ask themselves why the vocation to the priesthood should diminish the person who lives that vocation in his right to interpret and to give meaning to his

---

1 The following is derived primarily from Greeley's two autobiographies: *Confessions of a Parish Priest: An Autobiography*. New York: Simon and Schuster, 1986, and *Furthermore! Memories of a Parish Priest*. New York: Doherty Associates Book, 1999.

experience of the world. Indeed, it would seem that priests perhaps more than others, have that right and duty. Speaking as a Catholic, I would think that more imaginative work, more experiences in the arts, and more communication with others, would improve not only the Sunday homily, but also the quality of the priestly ministry. A more liberally educated priesthood and a more widely read laity might go far in making the good news more broadly known. This, however, is merely *ipse dixit*.

Father Greeley says that he is first and last a priest. This is his calling, and all that he has done in his distinguished career as a priest has been in service of the People of God, i.e., the church. That others disagree with this is their right, but we need to understand first the author's point of view. Greeley has had a distinguished career as a teacher and as a social scientist. His work in sociology, particularly the sociology of religion, is debated and respected by those who read it and use it. That he turned to the writing of novels is, it seems to me, a gift to those who do not usually read sociology or any other social science. His turn to imaginative literature involved an insight Greeley derived from his studies in religion. About the same time some American theologians were studying the place of myth and storytelling in the human attempt to understand the noumenal, Greeley came to appreciate how very human storytelling is. He had discovered his theory of the imagination. It is to that theory that we must now turn.

In *Confessions of a Parish Priest*, Greeley notes that his imaginative work on Catholic images presented itself very early in his education. While still a student in high school, his version of what he would later call the Catholic imagination was prompted by his reading of G. K. Chesterton. Greeley writes,

> It was his awe at and admiration of the sacredness and the wonder and the surprise of ordinary life and the sacramentality of the world, which fascinated me. His book on St. Francis of Assisi was the first and still in many ways the most powerful explanation of the Catholic imagination to penetrate my own. "Aha," I found myself saying, "*That's* what it's about. Sure, it all

figures. When God said the world was good, he really meant it was good." (109)

He goes on to question why the nuns and the priest who taught him did not believe in the goodness of all creation, especially the goodness of the body and of human sexuality. Why were they "still on the Manichee side, still refusing to celebrate the epiphany of Being in beings, of God in creatures [...]? I knew beyond all questions that Creation was a sacrament of God and I knew that such an image was at the core of the Catholic tradition" (109).

This image of creation as sacrament would take Greeley on an intellectual journey that eventually would bring him to his theory of imagination and its relationship to Catholic theology and culture. It would be a lonely journey throughout the late 1940s to the Second Vatican Council (1962–65). (In fact, it would be the literary notion of searching for the Holy Grail that would be the subject of his first novel, *The Magic Cup*.[2]) Through this intellectual journey, five "illuminations" would sustain him in his loneliness.

The first is the importance of history. The church is timeless only as a theological abstraction. It has always been rooted in time and in culture and to see it only as it had developed from the Counter-Reformation to the first half of the twentieth century was to miss the pluralism that makes the church universally Catholic (*Confessions of a Parish Priest* 128). The second illumination follows from the first. "Reality is dynamic and changing, not static and timeless" (129). This means that "the way we have always done it" ought to have less significance in the argument about change and pluralism in the church. It also gives new significance to the idea of "the Tradition." "Faith is not merely an act of intellect but rather an act of love by which the whole personality commits itself to an already inviting Lover" (129). (Thus, his novels will illustrate this very point by making God's love for creation the unseen hero in the stories they tell.) It follows then that we recognize that "The Reformation is over; it is time to abandon the garrison posture of the Counter-Reformation Church and begin ecumenical dialogue with Protestants—and with all men and women

---

[2] See Chapter 7, note 136.

of goodwill and good faith" (129). "To adjust to these truths, the Church must be reformed" (129).

These illuminations would make Greeley and others who, like him, found that intellectual integrity demanded similar affirmations, something of a minority. This experience of being the odd man out, when fortified by the clericalism of the time in which he grew up in the American Church, would prompt him to emphasize one of, perhaps the most important after the rejection of Manichaeism, his most perduring themes, that of the destructive power of envy and the mediocrity it produces (135). More on this will be found in a later chapter because of all the vices, envy is the most destructive of the political world; it outclasses all the other cardinal sins. (See 134*ff.* of *Confessions of a Parish Priest.*)

Greeley tells us that his parish work was and is his most loved. He finds that through writing about his past and the world of fiction that he creates in his novels allows him to go home again (165). He discovered that criticism is an essential part of the life of the mind, yet it often can hide the envy of others. It is often said of Greeley, for example, that he writes too much; that the quantity of his work indicates its poor quality. (This is often an assertion of the academic world, which can make any vice a virtue.) About such false criticism, Greeley writes,

> It's a terrible mistake to let the perfect get in the way of the good. If you wait to publish until you have written a great book, you will never publish anything. Great books happen by chance, not by design. The wise writer writes the best he can and leaves it to posterity to decide about greatness. I write [...] to clarify my own thinking and to make available to others, for whatever use it may be to them, these clarifications, I will know that quantity is affecting quality when people stop reading the books and when some fair-minded and honest critic finds notable deficiencies in my work that can be attributed to "writing too much." (178)

In these words, we can find two important themes that run throughout Greeley's novels: the first is the idea of "writing for clarification," and the second is the idea of service through giving something to others that they will use "for whatever use it may be to them...." Embedded in both ideas is an important political qualification. The first entails the notion that no one by himself or herself has the whole truth; rather each of us brings an angle of vision to reality, and it is by sharing these angles of vision that we come to a deeper understanding of the human condition. Unless we clarify what we think by testing it against what others think, there can be no real claim to know the truth. This idea is the foundation of Greeley's intellectual pluralism—that there are many ways to get to the same place. In a democratic society, pluralism is the bedrock of political freedom.

The second notion—that persons should be free to use ideas as they see fit—constitutes a risk involved in being human. If God's infinite love bestows upon us true freedom, then each person has the moral responsibility to respect that freedom, even when that freedom might be used to destroy itself. There is risk in everything we do, and we find in Greeley's novels the conjunction of risk with surprise. This is why he calls his novels comedies of grace, stories that have happy endings! True to the core of the Catholic intellectual tradition, Greeley sides with those who believe that we must trust individuals to get it right. Thus, a politics of the common good would support institutions, political, social, and economic, that are predicated on trusting individuals. This is what is behind those of his characters who are liberals in the older meaning of the term.

It is in this context that we can introduce Greeley's sociology and his commitment to social science. Greeley believes that the plurality of human experience can be understood and used for human betterment. He became a sociologist at the bequest of his Archbishop, Albert Cardinal Meyer (178), because the church of the Second Vatican Council needed men and women who understood the social, economic, political, and psychological experiences of the modern world. Such an understanding would be critical if the church were to read the "signs of the times" (*Gaudium et Spes*) in its process of reforming itself. Sociology, for Greeley, would not displace his role as priest, but rather, enhance it and give it power. His empirical work on the American Church would be foundational in our understanding of the reforms and the failures of the Second Vatican Council.[3] This commitment to testing our experiences of reality using disinterested and scientific methods stands Greeley firmly in the Catholic intellectual tradition's proposition that faith and reason are modes of knowing which cannot contradict each other. This stance is the stance of a person who is not afraid to test faith against reality, as disinterestedly as possible.

"Sociology forced me eventually to become a storyteller," Greeley writes (222). Through the work of Clifford Geertz, "religion as a 'cultural system'" (222), Greeley came to better understand the foundational work of sociology's greats, such as Weber, Durkheim, Parsons, as well as the work of Peter Berger and Luckman (222). Religion as "a person's ultimate world view" (222) must, then, help explain that person's behavior. His agreement with Geertz that religion is a set of symbols that explains the human experiences of reality (223) led him to a synthesis of theology and social sciences: what he calls "a new method of theological thought" (223). Three other writers also have contributed to Greeley's work: Mircea Eliade, Michael Polanyi, and William James (223). From Eliade he learned about universal religious structures of thought (223); from Polanyi he learned that the scientific method was not the paradigm for knowledge it is often thought to be, rather intuitions are often the beginnings of cutting-edge science (224); from James, he learned that "all quest for truth was an exercise in model fitting [...]" (224), and that "[k]nowledge is

---

[3] In 1986 Greeley wrote, "The books my colleagues and I at NORC have done on Catholic education have become the reference manuals for everyone interested in the subject. My book on the papal election of 1978 seems to be in the library of every major newspaper in the world. My *American Catholic: A Social Portrait* is the standard reference volume on the changes in Catholic population in the last twenty-five years. I know of no other works in the field that are so frequently used as my books *Ethnicity of the United States* and the *American Irish*. My volume on the sociology of the paranormal is the only work in the field [as of 1986], and the work that McCready and I have done on ethnicity and alcoholism has also become standard on that subject. My theories in the sociology of religion (contained in *Religion: A Secular Theory, The Religious Imagination*, and *Religious Indicators 1940–1980*) have been hailed by my professional colleagues as a notable breakthrough in the sociology of religion, and my monograph The *Mary Myth* is, as far as I know, the first book to suggest that Mary's functional role in Catholicism is to reflect the womanliness of God." He has gone on to produce other important works in sociology since 1986, and his judgment about the importance of these works seems correct.

an empirical, pragmatic exploration through mystery" (225). Through these insights, along with his reading of the story theology of John Sea and David Tracy (285*ff.*), Greeley came to understand that "Religion was image and story before it was proposition—poetry before it was theology, experience before it was catechism" (357). The stage was set for his theory of imagination.

That theory posits that religion as the ultimate answer a person gives to the most important questions in his or her life is "encoded" in images and in narratives (365).[4] The religious experiences of individuals come from the stories and the images they imply: experience prompts theology. Greeley discovered this in the process of his empirical research (367). He quotes Avery Dulles' *Models of Revelation* on the importance of symbols:

> Symbols by their evocative power arouse the imagination and invite participation. As contrasted with literal discourse, a symbol induces a kind of indwelling in the world of meaning to which it points. Symbols frequently make known a meaning too deep or too comprehensive for clear articulation; they arouse tacit awareness of things too vast, too subtle, or complex to be grasped in an explicit way; they bridge constraints that defy conceptual imagination [...] they exert a dynamic, transforming influence on the consciousness of those who apprehend them. (In *Confessions of a Parish Priest* 376.)

As we shall see, Greeley's novels are multifaceted precisely because of his use of symbols. He continues, noting that his theory, as put forth in *Religion: A Secular Theory,*

> contends that religion emerges from the ordinary experiences of secular life which renew our hope, that these hope-renewing experiences (sometimes but not always ecstatic)

---

[4] Greeley does not deny the importance of doctrine or dogma in theological matters. He writes, "The doctrinal formula is essential as a critique of the story, as a safeguard in its transmission and as an intellectual explanation required by a reflecting animal such as humankind. But in an individual life the story is normally more influential in providing meaning than the schematic and abstract formula" (365).

are encoded in the images or symbols we inherit from our religious traditions, that they are told as stories which correlate with the stories of our tradition, and that they are shared with members of a storytelling community which share the same set of symbols and the same collection of overarching stories. (379)

Revealed in experiential religion are experiences of "Being within beings" (cf. 379). By them and because of them we interpret the fundamental meaning in our lives. In realizing this, Greeley concluded that the best way to serve the People of God would be through storytelling. The storyteller is like us in that he or she develops a narrative out of imagination, just as we do the same out of experience. As our lives are unfinished narratives, we often experience ourselves as confused, since the narrative has yet to be finished. Novels are, as Kathryn Morton writes, the means by which we clarify and intuit the completion of the narrative, which is our life: "I tell you that the only world I know is the world as I know it and I am still learning how to comprehend that" (380).

Later in his *Confessions of a Parish Priest,* Greeley says that he completed his theory of religion when he came to understand that religion's source is secular and ordinary. It is the ordinariness of God's grace that we meet in his novels, and it is this that makes his novels so popular. He writes,

> The paradigm was now clear: the hope-renewal experience (which one could call grace); the memory of that experience set aside in the special category of memories we call symbols because they give direction and purpose to our life (such symbols can be called sacraments because they reveal order and purpose to us); the stories in which we share hope-renewal experiences and images with others, normally by trying to stir up in their imaginations memories of experiences that parallel our own (stories are an attempt of imagination to communicate to other imaginations, bypassing as best it can the barriers of cognitive proposition); and the community, which represents a group of people to whom we can tell our stories because they share our imagery, and whose images in

turn shape our own further hope-renewal experiences and recollections. (433–434)

There are, then, four essential components to Greeley's theory about the relationship of imagination to experiential religion:

- The hope-renewal experience (grace).
- The memory of that experience remembered through symbols that give purpose to life (sacraments).
- These stories are shared with others through the imaginative experiences that parallel our own (what Nussbaum calls the narrative imagination).
- These stories represent a community, a group of people who share our imagery, and in doing so direct us toward further hope-renewal experiences.

Grace, sacrament, solidarity, and community are, then, the marks of Greeley's theory, and they are the marks of what he calls the Catholic imagination. Such an imagination shares several common themes:

- In Catholic experience God is sacramental, meaning that the created world discloses God to us and when it does, we are in the presence of grace—God's life in us. Unlike other religions, God is not wrenched from this world out of fear of a violation of God's monotheism. Indeed, "[t]o banish God from the world and make it a bleak and unsacred place" (435) is to misinterpret completely how God works.
- The Catholic imagination is analogical i.e., it sees in completely different things something of God's life. God is first like us and then, only secondarily, different from us (435). Thus, the Catholic imagination walks a very thin line in its use of sacramental things, which all things are. It can move to the superstitious, making of sacraments and sacramentals talismans and methods of magic; or it can move toward theoretical abstraction to the extent that the hope-renewing event becomes merely

a metaphor and nothing more, which in fact they are not. An analogical imagination is one that sees that "all is grace" (436) and knows how to distinguish grace from magic. (Grace perfects nature, it does not force it, St. Thomas tells us.)

- The Catholic imagination sees life not as a tragedy, where goods are placed in contradictory positions from which only one can be had and with great sorrow at the loss of the opposite good. Though the Catholic imagination does not deny that the world is sometimes a place of tragedy, it sees such tragedies as the result of humankind's misuse of all that is good, i.e., all that is created. Thus, the Catholic imagination is one that sees life as a comedy wherein God's great love always trumps tragedy. Life is always about second chances and even more than second chances (See 436).[5]

- Finally, the world of the Catholic imagination is a world of "dense, complex interrelationships" (437). Persons, not individuals, are the stuff of human community, and they are the result of an interconnecting set of very complex relationships. In this sense, the Catholic understanding of community is organic, and as such, we are not free to walk away from it because as organic beings, we require the organic support of our communities. Thus, in the Catholic imagination, two principles work in tandem: solidarity, the virtue of seeing ourselves as essential parts of the whole, and subsidiarity, the virtue of seeing the personal as the first and best place to begin enacting our duty to ourselves and to others. Context and history will determine the level at which social and personal action is best achieved. Thus, it follows that we are not free *not* to be engaged in community, just as it is imperative always

---

[5] Greeley writes, "The Holy Grail story that we know is a tragic story, a life-denying tale, a Catholic might say a 'Protestant' tale, for Lancelot gets neither Grail nor girl. But the more ancient and more pagan Celtic version of the story ends differently. The Irish Lancelot [Cormac MacDermot in Greeley's *The Magic Cup*] finds the magic cup and gets the magic princess [...]" (436). Indeed, he had them all the time.

and in every case to affirm the transcendent dignity of the human person. The Catholic mind cannot imagine the individual without society, nor society without respect for the individual. Rights and duties, then, are merely different sides to the same reality.

In *Furthermore! Memories of a Parish Priest.* the second of his memoirs, Greeley confirms the first.[6] We learn that his vocation as a priest has and will always be his guiding light, that his study of sociology has been the intellectual means by which he has viewed the world so that he might better serve the church as a priest, and that his fiction is a form of his parish work; through it he preaches the Gospel and ministers to the People of God. Greeley also tells us in these pages what he believes: "I believe in a Giver who is, of all things, not an Accountant, but a Lover; a Lover, as Robert Barron has recently observed, who is caught in the need to love me just as a mother is caught in the need to love her child, a Lover who, according to Irish Dominican poet Paul Murray, would die of sadness if I should cease to exist" (11).

In telling us what he believes, Greeley reveals two important things: First is that he relies upon the work and the kindness of others to discover and to confirm what his life's work has taught him about God. He uses the work of others and graciously acknowledges it because he knows that human beings, no matter what their quest, rely on community. But more importantly, we learn a second thing about him; we learn that he has gone beyond the theology of Accounting, wherein human responsibility is made a means for a God of strict justice to hold human beings to his law. The image of God as Lover is not new to Greeley and his generation; rather, his intellectual and imaginative work rekindles a theology of Love first enunciated in the Gospels. That this Lover would "die of sadness" were she to lose us tells us that his work as a priest involves helping God touch the human heart. This realization goes to the core of every religion worthy of human beings. It begins and ends with a respect for the human person, arguing that justifications of religion (theologies and philosophies) need to respect the integrity of their subjects. If the narratives of our

---

[6] *Confessions of a Parish Priest: An Autobiography.* New York: Simon and Schuster, 1986.

vision of the divine do not fit the human experience we name as religion, then they are narratives that either are ignored or employed with great mischief.

As a sociologist, Greeley has studied religion, especially his own Roman Catholicism, and tries to use the results of this exercise of reason to help people understand what they believe and to interpret how what they believe is institutionalized. His vocation as a priest covers, what he calls, both the Confident Church, in which law and order were of supreme value, and the Confusing Church, which is the current product of the history of religion in the contemporary age (*Furthermore!*... 16–17). Ordained for ten years before the Second Vatican Council, Greeley lived with the people of the Confident Church. The Council was, perhaps, the most important event in his church's history. What his sociology tells us about this event helps us understand its gravity.

> Much of the loss in the transition from Confident to Confusing Catholicism is not the result of the Vatican Council but of the birth control encyclical of 1968 [...]. Most men who leave the priesthood do so not because they want to marry but because they don't like the work. For those who are happy being priests, celibacy is a difficult but not insupportable burden. Two-thirds of the priests in a recent study say that the priesthood is *better* than they expected it would be. Catholic schools are a superb educational bargain and an important capital investment of the Church. There is virtually no decline in belief by Catholics in the major tenets of their faith. Their problems with the leadership are almost entirely in the areas of sex, gender, and authority. The most destructive of the changes from the Confident Church to the Confusing Church are the results of these three dimensions of Catholic teaching and attitude [...]. Catholic laity in six nations by overwhelming numbers want more democratic Church structures (election of bishops, more power to the local churches) and the ordination of married men and [of] women. Moreover, the United States is not the most radical country on these issues. Ireland and Spain are tied for first place on the radicalism scale, Germany is third,

and the United States is fourth. Conservative Catholics are no more than 5 percent of the Catholic population. (17)

These sociological facts should not be read as though they are Greeley's opinion or as his recommendations for how they should be addressed. They are what they are: sociological realities requiring study and response. Over and over again in his work, Father Greeley reminds us that he is the messenger, and he should not be killed because the message is not what we want to hear. Unfortunately, his work has been misjudged or misrepresented and his life as a priest marginalized because he was following one of the clearest teachings of his religion, that God has given us reason and faith as modes of knowing, and that we are to use them both to cooperate in the betterment of the world (service to the common good) and the salvation of all that is.

His sociology has brought him to fiction. What he has learned about religion and its meaning in contemporary society has compelled him to discover ways to make the Gospels resonate in people's lives. In this, he is like the good teacher who continually works at her pedagogy so that students will discover what is true. Greeley's commitment to the "pedagogy of the imagination," his use of the novel as a teaching method, make him one of the most important interpreters of his age. To understand this is to know what religion means to most men and women of our age. *Furthermore!* represents one more attempt on Greeley's part to minister as priest to his people. Important are his understanding of religion as poetry, the "windmills" against which this contemporary Don Quixote flails, and his theory of sociology and fiction.

Religion as poetry. Greeley begins *Furthermore!* ... by wondering why religion is part of every human community and suggests that the answer, as he puts it, "is the result of two incurable diseases from which humankind suffers, life from which we die and hope which hints that there might be more meaning to life than a termination in death" (42).[7] Christianity as a religion addresses this dis-ease by the promise

---

[7] Like our philosophical forebears, Greeley writes, "Humankind in the form in which we know it is the only being of which we are aware that is conscious of its own mortality and is capable of hoping that death is not the final act in human life" 42.

of the resurrection, not resuscitation, not symbolic or natural rebirth; resurrection means that we get our bodies back, that we will be, as Greeley writes elsewhere, young again, and that we shall laugh again. Thus, to the question of why we must die, the Christian answers, not with certainty but with faith that our hope is to be found in our love. As we have loved each other, so have we loved God; and that God, whose life we share through faith, hope, and love, is one who loves us into being, keeps us always in that love, and ultimately is and always will be the very best of friends. This, Greeley affirms, is an experience that most human beings have had![8] Yet, this portrayal of religion depends upon hope and not upon certainty:

> Hope, however, is not certainty. Certainty precludes religion just as despair does. Should there exist somewhere in the cosmos (or in other cosmoses) a mortal being which has absolute certainty that it will be victorious over death, that being will not need religion either. Hope and therefore religion exist only in conditions of uncertainty, of possibility, of relative degrees of probability. Hope, and hence religion, emerge only when the data are inconclusive. Mortality, uncertainty, possibility—these are the triangle of factors out of which religions come. (43)

This "commonality" of hope stands against the forces of our age. The twentieth-century rise of ideologies with their conflicting claims to certainty has transformed religion and its hope into social, economic, and political institutions that oppress in the name of God.

---

[8] "The issue here is not whether every human hopes, much less whether [...] there is a gene, which creates hope even though the situation is hopeless. To explain religion, it is not necessary that every human have experiences which renew hope, nor is it necessary to contend that every human has a religion of some sort. It is enough merely to say that most humans have experiences, which renew their hope and that therefore, humankind, has religion" (43).

Greeley's image of religion stands against this idolatry.[9] For more than a generation, Greeley has used the tools of reason—in his case the methods and measures of sociology—to discern three very important truths:

- Religion does matter in modern society.
- Religious imagery is the most powerful religious predictor variable currently available to us.
- Catholics are different and usually in ways that one would not expect unless one was making a prediction based on [his] theory. Thus, Catholics are more likely to oppose racism, to support environmental reforms, to sympathize with AIDS victims and condemned criminals, and support civil liberties. The differences can be accounted for by different Catholic religious images (52).

Anyone wanting to understand the age in which we live needs to know these three conclusions found in Greeley's *Religion as Poetry*.

Greeley's windmills. In his life as a priest and a sociologist, Greeley has become, by his own admission, identified with five major matters. These are important for Catholics and by extension for everyone because of their underlying value. The first two relate to the issue of democracy as a value in today's society. His study of papal

---

[9] Although it is not my place to defend Father Greeley from his enemies (He does quite well at it himself!), it is important that the reader understand the context of his life so that his ideas might be better understood for what they are. My opinion is that Greeley has had so many enemies not because of his personality, about which I do not know enough to comment and in charity should not even if I do, but because of his message. To tell people that what they have as religion is really a form of political ideology which claims certainty where it cannot is to upset and to make uneasy these same people. Here, Greeley is in very good company: Socrates was killed by the Athenian democracy because he asked it to explain its certainties, and Jesus irritated the Scribes, Pharisees, and political leaders of his day by asking them to show why their version of the Law was better than his. In the case of Jesus, all he left was an empty tomb. What kind of certainty is that?

elections and the story of his confrontations with Cardinal Cody—his archbishop—deal with the foundational value of justice in society. As a human institution,[10] the Roman Catholic Church is required to "read the signs of the time" and to discern how these signs are part of God's providential love. For its first thousand years, the leadership of the church respected the principle that those who are led should have some participatory role to play in choosing their leaders. The absolute monarchy that the papacy has become in the second thousand years represents the historical reality of its political existence. That this second thousand years ended with the principle of democracy as the guard against the principle of absolute power ought to tell us something about how Catholic leaders should be chosen and obeyed. Father Greeley's critique of the current institution of the papacy and of the way dioceses are assigned to men like Cardinal Cody, is only the result of the teaching of the Catholic Church that all authority must first be properly constituted, i. e., its source must be both valid as well as licit and that its exercise must be for the common good. Any other kind of authority is unworthy of human beings (*Furthermore!...* 59–68).

His warnings about the moral damage that reassigning pedophilic priests would cause, again, springs from the requirements of justice. But additionally, Greeley's warnings arose from his profound love for the priesthood and his love for his church. Justice must always be qualified by love if it is to conform to the requirements of the Gospel. Sometimes we are called to witness justice through our love. This has been the role Greeley has played in this matter. Had he been heeded, who can say how much of the damage could have been avoided. Victims, their families, the hierarchy, and the People of God, all would have suffered less had Greeley's truth been known and acted upon (69–90). Thus, his qualification of justice with love also informs his defense of the rights of the laity against the authoritarianism of the best-intentioned parish leaders. One of the common slanders made against Catholics is that they willingly suffer or participate in authoritarian behavior.

---

[10] I am not saying that the church is only a human institution; I am affirming what the church has always taught about itself: Christ and the Holy Spirit are with us through the institution of the church and this institution, like its head, Christ, is both human and divine.

Thus, Catholics in academic life are often suspected as not being able to attend to professional standards of disinterest in their studies, while Catholic voters are still often portrayed as mere minions of their leaders. This nonsense leads to stereotypes about Catholic behavior and every stereotype contains a half-truth. The "neo-authoritarianism" of post-Vatican II parish staff though hardly representative of all Catholics, nonetheless infects the lives and the images of contemporary Catholics. Sister Mary Hitler and Monsignor Mussolini no longer staff the parishes of the American Church, but their lay prototypes do. This, of course, is the result of poor education and poor political means of assigning authority in parish institutions. In pointing out this new authoritarian behavior, Father Greeley is only doing what every Christian is called to do: suffer for the sake of the kingdom. No Catholic may knowingly participate in or condone the unjust diminution of the dignity of the human person. Though, prudence might argue for one mode of opposition over another given certain circumstances, the call to justice and love requires of us a commitment to work for them in the world (100–109). This last observation carries over to Greeley's last windmill, his commitment to and defense of Catholic schools. His work in measuring the effectiveness of Catholic schools may be overlooked only at the risk of getting it wrong. He and his colleagues have demonstrated the empirical importance of Catholic education for (1) those who would become adult members of the Church, (2) those who would be successful in the professional world, and (3) those who must overcome the ill effects of economic and social oppression (110–123).

Roughly the last half of *Furthermore!* is devoted to expanding Greeley's explanation of his use of fiction as a means of teaching the Gospel. Again, what should be evident to anyone reading his fiction, Greeley tells us, is that his novels "are stories of grace" (152), something that should be evident to Catholic readers who know something about the Catholic imagination. To those who are not familiar with Catholic symbols, they are well told stories with a message. His task, he tells us, is "to intrude into your memory with a picture [...]" (152). And as a storyteller, Greeley reveals something of himself to his readers by building a bridge from his imagination to the imaginations of his readers. His success as a novelist is due to his great ability in building bridges of the imagination. That he has seen how this literary task is similar to the counseling task of the priest, testifies to his gifts both as storyteller and as priest. If the narrative imagination is the means by which one person or one culture contacts in immediate ways other persons and cultures, then surely Greeley's fiction is a valid means of preaching the Gospel. His chapter entitled "Stories as Pictures" uses some of his novels and characters to illustrate this use of narrative imagination.

His chapter "Sociology and Fiction—Two Muses or One?" is an exposition of his novels as a means of preaching the Gospel. He admits that his two most predominant myths are that of Ulysses and that of the Holy Grail (163),[11] and he encapsulates for us how these myths are archetypes for him. "Clearly there is a kind of Ulysses theme [...] in my stories. Men and women go away, sometimes it seems, even into the valley of death, and then come back to deal with the problems of winning their Penelope again and routing out those who have taken possession of her" (163). He goes on to say, "[c]learly the symbols of resurrection and second chance, of return and search, of old love lost and found anew, are closely related to one another" (163). Important, however, to Greeley's task is the role his science, sociology, plays in his imagination. It is here that Greeley really matters. He writes,

> I often think that the difference between God and us is that in the former rationality and imagination are combined. Creating a whole poem in a marvelous burst of energy in which rationality and creativity combine to produce the total work is rather like creating a cosmos of your own, a godlike experience. Characters in stories are not the result of carefully engineered construction work in which bits and pieces of people we already know are carefully assembled in conformity with a detailed plan. Rather, Venus-like the character bursts forth, a creature of passion with which to contend as well as love. Is that not what God experienced when She made us? (172)

---

[11] Their Irish versions, however.

Greeley goes on to explain that he thinks his sociology and his fiction derive from the same place, from the "narrative impulse by which we humans strive to make sense of the world around us" (172). In this regard, Greeley is arguing like other contemporary thinkers against the closeting of reason away from the creative act. "The distinction between theory and data with which social scientists are obsessed is a post-hoc reflection and a very inaccurate one on what actually happens in the analytic enterprise. To the extent that the distinction means anything at all, theory and data are merely part of the playful dance which goes on in the creative imagination [...]" (172).[12]

We come, then, finally to Greeley's version of what went wrong and what went right in the transition from what he names the Confident Church to the Confusing Church. In this, we see why he has chosen to use the narrative imagination as his means. In the years immediately after the Second Vatican Council, Greeley detects that the "American Church was caught by surprise" (275). In not understanding the Council's decrees, American romanticism destroyed what it should not have destroyed, e.g., the stripping of the churches of the images and sacramentals that were the physical manifestation of a particular people's religious aesthetic (275). This had the unfortunate effect of throwing the baby out with the bathwater. He writes,

> If one considers that for much of Christian history the population was illiterate and the clergy semiliterate and that authority was far away, one begins to understand that the heritage of most people most of the time was almost entirely story, ritual, ceremony, and eventually art. So it has been for most of human history. So it is, I suggest (and my data backs me up) even today. (281)

But Greeley also knows that God is a God of surprises. Hence, in Greeley's characters and fiction God is always surprising us with his

---

[12] Later on he writes, "What compels me and impels me, what possesses me and obsesses me, is not the interaction of theory and data, but the story I am discovering in the telling, the tale that I am passionately uncovering as my dancing partner maniacally arranges and rearranges the bits and pieces of memory with which she is playing" (178).

ordinary grace: "Catholicism has great stories because at the center of its heritage is 'sacramentalism', the conviction that God discloses Himself in the objects and events and persons of ordinary life" (281).

Greeley's imaginative fiction follows in the tradition of the Catholic understanding of reason and faith as modes of knowing, and of the role art must play in holding both these modes of knowing in balance. "In fact," he writes,

> it is in the poetic, the metaphorical, the experiential dimensions of the personality that religion finds both its origins and raw power. Because we are reflective creatures, we must also reflect on our religious experiences and stories; it is in the (lifelong) interlude of reflection that propositional religion and religious authority become important, indeed indispensable. But then the religiously mature person returns to the imagery, having criticized it, analyzed it, questioned it, to commit the self once more in sophisticated and reflective maturity to the story. (283)

These poetic, metaphorical, experiential dimensions of religion mirror the same dimensions in the human person and save religion from becoming cold, hard dogmas, mental prisons that oppress the soul and body, and create of religion's institutions what Shakespeare call "bare ruin'd choirs/where late the sweet bird sang." Rather, in the best that is the Catholic tradition, Greeley defends a Catholic imagination that "sees God and her grace lurking everywhere," an imagination that "enjoys a more gracious and benign repertory of religious symbols than do most other religions" (283).[13]

---

[13] Lest we think this mere propaganda for his "steamy novels", "Catholics consistently have more 'gracious' images of God: they are more likely than others to picture God as a Mother, a Lover, a Spouse, and a Friend (as opposed to a Father, a Judge, a Master, and a King). The story of the life, death, and resurrection of Jesus is the most 'graceful' story of all—the story of a God who in some fashion took on human form so that He could show us how to live and how to die, a God who went down into the valley of death with us and promised that death would not be the end" (283).

Chapter 2: Locating Greeley's Characters: Two Traditions

Today's echo of a forgotten tradition: At the end of her "Introduction" to *Cultivating Humanity: A Classical Defense of Reform in Liberal Education,* Martha Nussbaum claims that becoming an educated citizen "means learning how to be a human being capable of love and imagination," and that rather than citizens capable of such love and imagination, we are a society populated by "too many [...] who are like Marley's ghost," who, too late for himself, returns to Ebenezer Scrooge to warn him of the inherent unhappiness of individuals more attached to their cashboxes than to each other (14). Nussbaum's task is to argue that a liberal education may be an important corrective to "Marleydom." Very briefly, she argues that any liberal education worthy of its name must accomplish three things: it must help students become self-examining agents of their beliefs, values, and attitudes; it must foster a sense of responsibility to the greater world, which she designates as world citizenship, and it must develop what she calls the sympathetic imagination such that a student can experience in real and immediate ways whatever might be seen as alien.

Critical reasoning and argument are the means to freedom and intellectual strength (29) Nussbaum argues, and she uses this Stoic insight to argue that democratic life can prosper only if citizens are free to understand the reality of their own times and courageous enough to stand for the truth as they see it. In this sense, she argues,

Reason [...] constructs the personality in a very deep way, shaping its motivations as well as its logic. Argument doesn't just provide students with reason for doing thus and so; it helps to make them more likely to act in certain ways, on the basis of certain motives. In this very deep way, it produces people who are responsible for themselves, people whose reasoning and emotion are under their own control. (29–30)

We are free when we have possession of our own thoughts, her argument runs, and thereby we are capable of investigating the thoughts and actions of others. Another way to put this is to say that without truth, people perish as human beings.

If reason is the first step toward freedom—an audacious claim in the contemporary world where freedom most often means license, the second step is more tempering. One of the charges against Socrates was that he had, indeed, corrupted young people by making them smart-mouthed poseurs. Certainly, any critically informed person should be able to detect the closed minds of ideologues. Nussbaum's self-critical reason ought to be coupled to what she calls the imaginative capacity to enter into the lives of others (51), i.e., to be able to *become* what we are not in terms of social, economic, religious, and moral effects. Here her argument is derived from the Stoic notion of *humanitas,* that moral estate into which we place ourselves whenever we seek to do, to have, or to acquire; i.e., whenever we claim a right or have a duty imposed. Again relying on the Stoics, Nussbaum argues that citizenship in the cosmopolitan sense means, "that we should give our first allegiance to *no* mere form of government, no temporal power, but to the moral community made up by the humanity of all human beings" (59). In its simplest form, this means that justice must be the virtue that guides persons in their examination of the many alternatives the world places before them. We must act as though we are legislating for those we love. In the Stoic sense, she writes, to be a "citizen of the world" is to "hold that thinking about humanity as it is realized in the whole world is valuable for self-knowledge." Nussbaum argues that, "we see ourselves and our customs more clearly when we see our own ways in relation to those of other reasonable people," and "we really will be better able to solve our problems if we face them in [a] broader context, our imaginations unconstrained by narrow partisanship" (59–60). But, more importantly, this cosmopolitan citizenship depends on a deeper insight than the above utilitarian reasons may suggest; we see in the diversity of this world the fundamental and unifying principle of *humanitas*.

The question then becomes, how. How is it possible for individuals, living in temporal space with languages of their own and reasoning patterns deeply affected by their histories and mythologies, to enter that moral estate by which human beings connect with others not like themselves? It is here that Nussbaum's argument stands or falls, and it is here that she makes her best defense of education as moral. She argues that students must have experiences that test and develop what she calls their sympathetic imaginations (85). Such imagination "enables us to comprehend the motives and choices of people different from ourselves, seeing them not as forbiddingly alien and other, but as sharing many problems and possibilities with us" (85). This capacity is best developed by what Nussbaum calls the narrative imagination, a sensibility that intuits in others what is present in us and a sense of vulnerability about the world in which we live. Only through compassion can we exist as human beings, and this compassion is developed best by the careful reading of literary and artistic texts. Using Wayne Booth's *The Company We Keep: An Ethics of Fiction*, she quotes his suggestion that such works are friends

> with whom one has chosen to spend one's time. The question now is what does this friendship do to my mind: What does this new friend ask me to notice, to desire, to care about? How does he or she invite me to view my fellow human being? Some novels [...] promote a cheap cynicism about human beings and lead us to see our fellow citizen with disdain. Some lead us to cultivate cheap sensationalistic forms of pleasure and excitement that debase human dignity. Others, by contrast, show what might be called *respect before a soul.* (Booth in Nussbaum 100, my italics.)

Soul-respecting literature and art develop the narrative imagination and lead, finally, to that sympathetic capacity without which reason and truth become instruments of tyranny and abuse.[14]

The Catholic intellectual tradition. It might seem strange to use non-Catholic thinkers like Nussbaum and Booth to introduce the mindset that once was the measure of the Catholic intellectual tradition, but in fact, that tradition has always been open to everyone—its universal character is part of its definition. The strange thing is that those who have had the least experience with the Catholic tradition are sometimes better examples of it than those who have had the direct benefit of a Catholic education, something Greeley's characters often affirm.[15] Nussbaum is an exemplar of the intellectual aptitudes that mark the Catholic intellectual tradition and many of Greeley's characters. That such aptitudes exist beyond Catholic culture is proof of its rootedness in and debt to other cultures, something Catholics treasure and acknowledge. This recognition is the basis of Greeley's intellectual pluralism.

What, then, is the *Catholic* intellectual tradition? Monika Hellwig, one of the most recent American scholars to take up this question, defines the Catholic intellectual tradition in terms of its content—"the classic treasure to be cherished, studied, and handed on"—and in terms of a methodology, a way of doing things—"the outcome of centuries of experience, prayer, action, and critical reflection" ("The Catholic Intellectual Tradition." 3). Like all canons, the Catholic canon of works to be learned is so extensive as to require a lifetime and so fraught with disagreement about which works should have priority in it as to require a lifetime of debate. Certainly this content must involve the greats of antiquity, the Middle Ages—usually ignored in most college curricula—and the minds of modernity who translated these greats.[16] Nevertheless, it seems that the more important element

---

[14] The remainder of Nussbaum's book is an examination of Non-Western Studies, African-American Studies, Women's Studies, Gender Studies, and Religious Studies as means toward the development of self-critical, reasonable, compassionate citizens of the world.

[15] See, for example, Charles O'Malley's experience at Notre Dame in *Younger Than Springtime* (1999).

[16] Whether or not post-modernism is to be included is itself debated, but it will find its proponents included in the tradition at some future point.

in Hellwig's definition is the approach, "the way of doing things," that most informs Greeley's characters and the moral implications of his stories.

Before defining the Catholic intellectual tradition as different or distinct from other traditions, Hellwig points out that the Catholic tradition shares with other traditions several common convictions. She suggests that these involve the insight that life has meaning, which can be known and shared; a respect for moral right and wrong as more than a human invention; an awareness that life's meaning may involve more than the mundane and the temporal, i.e., awareness of the transcendent, and a recognition that this awareness informs how we live with others (6). Yet beyond these first principles the Catholic tradition is rooted in the person of Christ, in whom, as Hellwig puts it, "we have an utterly trustworthy interpretation of the meaning and destiny of human life, of human relationship with God, and of what constitutes a good life" (7). From this faith, she argues, the Catholic intellectual tradition understands education as involving at least six essential components: a continuity between faith and reason; a respect for the whole of the wisdom of the past; a non-elitist, if not egalitarian, approach to life; a continuity between the person and community; the integration of knowledge as the basis of wisdom, and the sacramental imagination (7). Each of these can be found in Greeley's fiction as a premise for action or as a basis for the direction of the plot. (See Chapter 6 for examples.)

Each element would involve a very long discourse in order to do justice to the degree of subtly entailed in each. Perhaps it is the Catholic intellectual tradition's failure to do so that has led so many to believe otherwise about itself. Suffice it to say, however, that each element involves an approach to study and learning that informs it success.[17]

The compatibility of faith and reason: This element of the tradition stands in the face of much modern and post-modern criticism, but it remains essential to the Catholic project. All belief

[17] See the literature on Catholic education's rigor and its success in Greeley's sociology.

and all knowing involve the believer or the knower in some kind of relationship to the truth. The Catholic intellectual tradition merely takes this truism as its starting principle, and as such, this principle has imbued the tradition with long life. What we believe, Catholics argue, cannot contradict what we know to be true, and what we know to be true must be reconciled with belief. There can be no double truth theory in the Catholic mind. This is so because the whole project itself depends on the validity of truth itself. Truth is another name for God in this tradition. Thus, it has become a traditional task of Catholic thinkers to reconcile the work of science with the world of belief. One of the reasons this tradition has persisted for so long is this dynamic, and it is this dynamic between science (knowing broadly defined) and faith (properly construed) which has produced in Catholic institutions a strong dependence on philosophy in their curricula.

Respect for the whole of the wisdom of the past: Because faith and reason cannot validly be at odds, the Catholic intellectual tradition relies on all and every form of knowledge wherever it is found. This means that no intellectual tradition is to be dismissed either because it is non-Christian, or because it may stem from non-Christian sources. All knowledge, every wisdom, is properly respected and investigated for its truth. For this reason, the Catholic library has been the repository of many works which would otherwise have gone without homes.

A non-elitist, perhaps, egalitarian approach to life: Certainly in a church riddled with hierarchy, the claim to be non-elitist and egalitarian seems unusual if not out of place; moreover, the contemporary confusion of hierarchy with patriarchy is everywhere evident in the Catholic Church. It may be argued, however, that this confusion results from a failure to make an important distinction. Patriarchy and matriarchy involve gender as justification for authority; arguments about hierarchy, on the other hand, are about the proper order of authority.[18] Hellwig's point about the non-elitist approach of

---

[18]My purpose here is not to debate, nor defend, the real issue of gender inequality in Catholic thought. The purpose is to make explicit an intellectual tradition, which might itself be the instrument by which gender equality can become real in the church.

the Catholic intellectual tradition is not that it is without hierarchy, but that given that hierarchy, the principle of universality must be respected. Since the church is catholic it belongs to all people in all places and is to be in its ministry servant to all. This means that in its role as teacher—part of which function is invested in the Catholic university—its teaching must be accessible to all. This presents a challenge to Catholic scholars inasmuch as they are duty bound to remain accessible to non-specialist.

Equality seems implicit in the Catholic intellectual tradition. It is implied by the claim that all men and women are children of one God, who, in loving them redeemed them and will judge them. Moreover, the church as the guardian of the transcendent dignity of each person is required to render, as well as teach, social justice, a body of principles, which entail careful consideration of all claims to equality.[19]

The continuity of the person and the community: This continuity, wherein the person and community are considered essential components of each other, regulated by the principles of subsidiarity and solidarity, is perhaps the tradition's greatest contribution to political thought. The human person, gifted with a dignity that transcends human invention, is always considered to be the part of an interconnecting set of relationships, which if not appropriate to that dignity must be changed. Thus, the claims to social justice, which the tradition makes, are claims to personal well being. Thus, the idea of the common good serves as the arbiter of the claims of individuals and those of society.

The integration of knowledge as the basis of wisdom: This is usually something heard in commencement addresses, usually because by such times it has not taken place in any appreciably way and it is too late. Yet the Catholic intellectual tradition takes this integration very seriously because the whole purpose of a Catholic education is

---

[19] See, for example, John Paul II, *Centesimus Annus, Sollicitudo Rei Socialis*, and *Laborem Exercens*.

to create a citizen with a coherent worldview, knowing how to use knowledge well and for the good.

The sacramental imagination: If there is a basic principle from which all others flow in the Catholic intellectual tradition, it is the principle that grace perfects nature.[20] The Catholic imagination derives from the view that nature is the envelope of grace and meaning. No thing is in its nature evil, so no thing is beyond God's life. Hence, the Catholic intellectual tradition trusts memory and imagination as its primary tools. Hellwig says that memory records and imagination arranges what we experience (9). Symbol is the result, and the arrangements of symbols tell the stories that we create and repeat. Thus, the tradition is one of contemplation as well as action inasmuch as it seeks to see the sacred in reality. Students of this tradition are required to study art, literature, music—all the liberal arts—not because they provide a patina of culture or a costume for expertise, but because these intellectual endeavors reveal the truth in ways that are essential to human meaning and purpose. As such, the tradition and the schools that help embody it, are to be countercultural.

Terrence Tilley, arguing that traditions are created as they create, further articulates the above six elements. In *Inventing the Catholic Tradition,* he begins by noting that the Catholic imagination is marked by a peculiar way of approaching the world and its many questions. Contrary to the dialectical mode of either/or, the analogical (sacramental) mind is capable of seeing paired items in terms of both/and. (See Tilley 125.) This is to say that the analogical mind is capable of seeking the unity in difference and of arranging knowledge not in terms of contradictions but in terms of paradoxes. To reason analogically is to seek the connections between ideas, things, and movements. This kind of mind approaches the questions of faith and reason differently than those who begin with the assumption that the two are irreconcilable. The analogical mind begins with the assumption that truth is real and realizable—limited though this might be—and consequently, recognizes diversity as essentially the parts of a whole.

---

[20] See St. Thomas Aquinas, *Summa Theologiae* I II qq 109–114. Hereafter *ST.*

A second rule of Tilley's grammar of the Catholic intellectual tradition, perhaps like Hellwig's second and third points, is "that there is hope for everyone and everything. There is nothing that cannot be or could not have been redeemed" (134). This, I think, is especially important in the dark times in which we live, times made all the more difficult because of a deep cynicism in the general mind. If we are to be individuals who have the means to resist the allurements that chain Christopher Marley to his cash box, if we are to reconcile human expertise with the values that will direct the use of expertise such that we do not become more deeply implicated in the imperialism of our age, then we need to develop this imagination of hope. For implicit in this hopefulness is a recognition of the mindless optimism that has so wretchedly failed and feeds today's cynical general culture. Voltaire has Candide discover that even though this may not be the best of all possible worlds, nonetheless, we can tend our own gardens. Here the plural is important. Candide does not say "my own" garden because he has learned from the school of hard knocks that we sink or swim together. The evils that blight his life and the lives of his companions as the evils that have produced our world, are the result neither of fate nor providence, but of human failure and vice. Hope is the virtue that ties faith to love, and as such, it remains connected to knowledge, justice, and action.

One of the greatest mistakes we discover from the study of political history is that evil is not so much a failure of the good, and thus, an obvious negative, as it is disguised and embodied in personal and social attempts to do something worthwhile. This mistake has led to xenophobia and racism, and to a great extent, has contributed to the chaos of the international system still driven by the claims of nationalism and privilege. Our misconception that evil is something we can root out and kill stems largely from a misunderstanding of hope. The Catholic intellectual tradition of hope is also a tradition that understands evil as the absence of the good, the absence of something essential to the well-being of persons and communities. The conclusion that follows is that no thing or no person is beyond hope. This has implications in how the Catholic mind approaches the study of the social sciences, how it conceives of society's problems and need for justice, and how it judges the intentions of other nations and peoples. Because that mind is a hopeful mind, no one is thought to be incapable of change, and no body is ever too reprobate as to be beyond salvation.

From this follows Tilley's third rule for a grammar of the tradition (136), the inclusive community. It is said that James Joyce was being anti-Catholic when he connected the word "Catholic" with "here comes everyone." Yet in a sense he was correct. The Catholic community is by definition universal, so much so that both the past and the future are thought to belong to all. In its intellectual tradition, it maintains that nothing is ever to be lost. This idea of stewardship has implications in terms of the stands we take and the political choices we make.

And it is on this set of issues that the tradition runs the risk of becoming parochial. "The fourth principle of the Catholic Intellectual Tradition," Tilley tells us, "is an acceptance of the worldliness of the Church in particular and of religion more generally" (139). The claim that follows from this principle is that the church is to be a public church. This means that its members and it leaders have as citizens the obligation to get on the public agenda. Although there is no doubt that this principle could be, and has been, misused, its abuse does not negate its validity. What it does mean is that the values and the good sought in the Catholic agenda have a right to be debated publicly and without scorn. When, for example, the US Catholic bishops debated the use of nuclear weapons in US foreign policy, they argued against the common misunderstanding of the doctrine of the separation of church and state in the first amendment by arguing that as citizens they had every right to engage in that debate, and as moral leaders, they had the obligation to do so.

This right to engage in public debate as religious thinkers involves the intellectual rejection of reductionism. In claiming a public place for religion in the American state, Catholics claim that religion is more than a psychological trait or a social opiate. They claim religion as an essential part of being human and, as such, a critical element in any society. In political matters, the church has a role as the guardian of the transcendent dignity of human beings—a role which leads to working for justice as a constitutive dimension of the preaching of the gospel[21]—and in academic matters, the Catholic intellectual has the role of calling her colleagues to the truth as she sees it; thus, the rejection of arguments which diminish or disrespect the insights of religion.

Tilley's last principle is Hellwig's first: faith and reason both seek understanding. This imparts a confidence to the tradition and it is this confidence that most worries the post-modern mind not informed by this tradition. "In present terms," Tilley writes, "what people come to understand by the practices of knowing and living in and out of faith cannot ultimately be incompatible. In a sacramental universe 'truth is one,' and God has given humanity the ability to come to understand that truth" (148–149). Here, more than any other place, we find the divide between the Catholic intellectual tradition and the rest of the American mind.

Experience with no song. Were Greeley's characters only drawn from the very best of the Catholic tradition, his work would be without depth or texture, and Kundera's dictum that every character deserves to be heard would have no import in his work. Yet it is precisely because Greeley's characters are very real types from the world we experience, that they live and have their being in the reader's imagination. Thus, many of his best characters are the characters most of us meet every day. None of these is outside the realm of our experience; and all of them are flawed and imperfect, just like us. Besides the best of the Catholic tradition the worst in human behavior, those vices associated with the seven deadly sins, often motivates Greeley's characters. Of these, envy most often moves their imaginative reality, and it is particularly important to understand this vice if we are to find coherence in Greeley's fiction. How might we begin?

---

[21] "Justice in the World," 1971 in Gremillion: "The uncertainty of history and the convergences in the ascending path of the human community direct us to sacred history: there God has revealed Himself to us, and made known to us, as it is brought progressively to realization, His plan of liberation and salvation which is once and for all fulfilled in the Paschal Mystery of Christ. Action on behalf of justice and participation in the transformation of the world fully appear to us a constitutive dimension of the preaching of the Gospel, or, in other words, of the Church's mission for the redemption of the human race and its liberation from every oppressive situation."

It is usually sound to begin at the beginning, and in moral arguments, this means giving the devil his due. Perhaps Mary Shelley's story may help illustrate the point. When Dr. Frankenstein "created" life, he thought that he had discovered Prometheus' secret: the gods no longer had a monopoly on life—human beings might be immortal! Yet the "Thing" was too ugly to bear, and Frankenstein found his "child" repulsive. Fleeing from his maker, the unnamed Thing learned how to survive and how to hate, first, himself then others. Thing became monster. Frankenstein could not respect his own creation because the Thing did not fit a presumed aesthetic-moral norm. Frankenstein's ecology of mind could find no place for the Thing, so rather than befriend it, he drove it from his presence.

After much experimentation, the Thing learned to read, and by negotiating a series of texts, he became the monster—graduated so to speak. In our version of Mary Shelley's story, we can say that it was because of his failed education that the Thing was unable to imagine a world wherein he had a place and in which he could discern his own beauty. Because he could not imagine such a world, he became resentful of those who possessed such. He lived only to revenge himself on his maker and his world. The Thing was made the monster by envy; his crimes resulted from his envy. And this moral vice destroyed him, his maker, and their common world—finally the ship on which they both depended.

Hatred, Aquinas tells us, is the "last step in the path of sin" because it opposes the natural love we ought to have for others. Hatred arises from sorrow, just as love arises from pleasure. We hate what displeases us, what we feel or think is evil. Envy "is sorrow for our neighbor's good" and is penultimate to hatred: out of envy comes hatred (*ST* II II q 34 a 6). The genesis of envy, other than hatred, involve tale bearing, detraction, joy at our neighbor's misfortunes, and grief over his prosperity (St. Gregory the Great in Aquinas, *ST*, II-II q 36 a.3).

Two illustrations: In Botticelli's "Calumny of Apelles" (Uffizi, Florence), Calumny drags Innocence to judgment before a stupid judge, who sits enthroned, counseled by Ignorance and Suspicion. Helping Calumny are Deceit and Fraud, parodies of the three graces. To the left is Repentance looking toward naked and ashamed Truth.

All stand amid the skeleton of a basilica decorated with medieval and classical allegories signifying the lesson of Botticelli's didactic interpretation of the theme.[22]

What is this vice which leads others to destroy innocence by corrupting judgment? As a vice, envy is distinct from fear, zeal, and indignation. Properly understood envy is sorrow over another's good because it surpasses ours, but not merely because it surpasses ours; the viciousness of this sorrow inheres in a grief over what should make us rejoice, that is, another's good (*ST* II II q 36 a 2). The vice is against love itself inasmuch as it is detraction from someone else's good; it is also a blow against self-respect because through envy we think ourselves lessened. (See *ST* II II q 36 a 1.) More formally, we might consider envy to be the result of unregulated self-love; it opposes a natural benevolence, which should bring us to love others; and it involves us in the depreciation of ourselves; it derives from a humiliation at who we are. This is a question very important to understanding contemporary political culture.

To fear another's good because that good might really harm us marks a prudential awareness that others are not always perfectly disposed toward us, i.e., we are not always loved. Thus, the good of the master instills fear in the slave. The slave's sorrow over the prosperity of his master is the natural result of understanding the evil in which all slaves find themselves placed. Yet envy is not the cautious awareness that we sometimes require defense against others. It is not the imprudent acceptance of any good as our own. So, too, it is not the same as admiration or zeal. Often we express admiration of another's good through our sorrow that we do not evince that which we admire. Our sorrow is not that others have a good thing, but that, as yet we do not have it, too. This is zeal and it springs from our natural hope that there be enough good for everyone, and that real merit is possible. Zeal is the expression of these hopes. As such, what we admire becomes the object of our joy and another's possession of it, a motivation, and example for us. We rejoice in the other while we grieve that we have yet to achieve what the other possesses. Likewise, envy is not the

---

[22] See David Cast. *The Calumny of Apelles* 29 and *ff.*

same as indignation. Indignation, the awareness that someone does not deserve the good he or she has, involves us in a judgment, which perhaps, positions us precariously close to real envy. Indignation, "the handsome brother of anger and hatred,"[23] may be just or unjust on our part. The trick is to know what others deserve and what we have coming to us. The trick is to be just.

Indignation, however, may involve us in the antithesis of that equality which is the beginning of justice and in the vice which can destroy our hope. Indignation leads to envy when our outrage over what others do not deserve directs our energies toward avoiding our own sorrow over an injustice, or when our energies are directed to satisfying our demand for what we think is ours by right. Indignation destroys zeal when we forget that justice is more than arithmetical or commutative. It is in light of this that we understand why we should not be judges in our own cases even though we may be the best judges of our own actions.

Envy, then, and its related vices, result from a sorrow that others have something good, which we do not have, and in our failure to rejoice in their good, we make their good an occasion for our own diminution. This selfishness makes possession deadly. To envy is not to love; what should make us rejoice, instead, makes us unhappy. We might ask about the cultural conditions that reduce joy to such sorrow. Envy really is more the product of a social configuration of values than of personal defect in character. Often envy is a cultural phenomenon resulting from an organization of values that places selfishness above respect and ego beyond community. The politics of envy are secret and deadly. Found wherever equality is perverted, envy ripens in societies where standards are eschewed and values disordered. Envy is the crime of mobacracy, something the ancients feared as the disease of democracies.

Essentially, envy is a torment which changes us. Henry Fairlie equates the torment of envy with its essential quality, mortification. He says, "[...] there is no gratification for Envy, nothing it can ever enjoy. Its appetite never ceases, yet its only satisfaction is endless

---

[23] Coleridge in *The Oxford Authors* 612.

self-torment [...]. One thinks of Envy as being a drag on someone, holding him back, with no reward or pleasure or help to him. The endless self-torment is an endless self mortification" (Fairlie 61).

Like Dickens' Uriah Heep, the envious continually worry about what is superior to them because it threatens their own sense of self. The envious are self-abasing and servile (62). Their cultures are such, and so are they. "Envy is not merely a grieving on account of another's good, which has the element of Pride in it," Fairlie writes, "but a grieving because one regards that good as diminishing one's own or even as reflecting disgrace on oneself" (64). This vice has its social effect in a destructive vengefulness which informs the attitudes of the envious. Nothing is ever good enough, even for others. Fairlie locates this attitude in a culture which assumes that every person can experience and enjoy every kind of good. When this assumption proves false, as it necessarily must, those who are the creatures of envy move to depreciate that which they cannot enjoy. Envy is a form of deconstruction. The diminution of canons of style, rules of behavior, and standards of discipline are all cultural signs of envy. Such a culture is one that cannot comprehend failure. It is the culture of optimism made real through redefining talent so that it may be possessed by everyone, but in fact, by no one. Such a culture is based on a distortion of equality. This is what Aristotle means when he notes that envy is the result of equality. As Fairlie puts it, "The idea that we are equal has been perverted into the idea that we are identical; and when we then find that we cannot all do and experience and enjoy the things that others do and experience and enjoy, we take our revenge and deny that they were worth doing and experiencing and enjoying in the first place. What we are unable to achieve, we will bring low"! (63–64).

Bringing low what we cannot achieve—the politics of envy. The great evil of envy is what it does to the human spirit. Fairlie argues, to be unable to find the unique in others, not to appreciate what is rare and inimitable in the world, not to be able to admire or to respect others, indeed, not to recognize what is noble and lovely, all diminish what is truly human in us, the tendency toward the exceptional (64). In place of gratitude, envy puts dejection, a narrowness of vision and a regretful bitterness that we are who we are. Self-hatred rather than self-respect marks the heart touched by envy. Such a heart lacks self-esteem and is inordinately in love with itself. Through a course of demolition, the envious heart attempts to structure a world wherein it might escape the disparagement it hurls against others. In this sense, envy marks a failure to live; it is a truly deadly sin (67): "Envy has no song. It does not sing," Fairlie writes, "it cannot bear to look, except through its slit eyes; it is unable to love because it is riddled with fear" (68). It is, he says, "a form of self-meaning turned against others [...]" (70). But because it has no song of its own, envy steals those of others. This is why envy is so difficult to combat, it is why good things can so easily disguise envious attitudes, and cultures can thrive on this deadly sin. It is why, in fact, democratic and egalitarian cultures can be destroyed by envy.

One of the things Greeley's fiction presents us is the culture of the US, and in some of his works, the subculture of its academy. Both are predicated on a kind of egalitarianism; both suggest that equality is an instrumental means to some end or purpose. Yet, today neither US culture nor its mirror, the academy, can unambiguously define the goal to which equality tends.[24] The reason for this may be plumbed in the economic system which underpins both. Here, the ecology of egoism sustains the drive to have more, even when having more may mean being less by an older standard of human activity. Fairlie puts it well. Our economic system is opposed to equality even though our political system essentially depends on it. "It is," Fairlie writes,

> because it is philosophically opposed to equality—or says that it is—that our economic system has been unable to provide its own one-sided egalitarianism—the equality of the consumer—with any moral or philosophical foundation. Its primary achievement—and perhaps even its primary object—has therefore been to turn the discontented citizen into a contented consumer; and it then turns round in surprise when it finds that, although the consumer may indeed be satisfied, as a citizen he is still dissatisfied, (72)

---

[24] See Bellah *et al.Habits of the Heart....*

In the human personality, the contented consumer and discontented citizen indicate two contrary drives in need of reconciliation: necessity and freedom. Yet in US culture, the first obscures the second. In such a climate, envy ripens. As Fairlie understands the problem, what we mean by equality is fair consideration. But, because our consumer society by its very definition neglects individual citizens in favor of differentials in wealth and power, equality of consideration is never afforded individuals *as* citizens (73). If we are wealthy or have the patronage of the powerful, we will be heard, but lacking economic connections, we are ignored. Envy works itself into such a system precisely because as citizens we have no way to defend or to protect the putative equality of our political culture. Yet it is precisely this principle of fair consideration that makes societies of human beings possible. Because we are discontented and powerless as citizens, Fairlie argues, we run the risk of becoming envious consumers given to incitement by any advertisement suggesting that we may no longer be equal to other consumers. We remain consumers because we have yet to become citizens.

This is especially acute in academic and ecclesiastical communities, which have transformed themselves into mirrors of the consumer society, i.e., into societies where equality is often misconstrued. Both claim to be meritocracies. A meritocracy is supposed to be the most rational and fairest in its means to the distributions of goods and services. Meritorious activity should confer rewards and should serve as the only basis for distinction and advancement. The best should emerge naturally through the test of experience. Meritocracies are, however, fatally flawed, or as Fairlie imagines it, each has "a worm at its core" (74). The twin assumptions upon which all merit depends are the equal chance to merit and the fair application of the rules governing the test of experience. But nobody starts from the same starting line, and experience, like wealth, more often than not teaches ways to evade fair rules.

Moreover, where everyone is considered equally worthy of being first without any standard or measure, envy justifies those who do not finish first. Thinking that what cannot be should be produces envy. It is the curse of any meritocracy designed to produce an elite that ignors the reality that not everyone is in fact qualified to be a part of that elite. In the end, envy is a self-justification of a meritocracy without merit: a justification that those committed to merit have no sense that they may not deserve. Envy is the child of unfulfilled desire. Its evil is in its thwarting of that desire. Here the dichotomy between consumer and citizen informs us. The notion of "consumer" necessarily leads us to the proposition that as consuming persons we ought to have all we desire, provided we can pay for it. So, the only distinction among consumers is economic resource, a cause for envy in itself. On the other hand, the idea of citizenship grows from the conviction that even though we do not possess the same talents, powers, or resources, we deserve and desire equal consideration by virtue of who we are, not in consideration of what we have. Citizenship is political evidence of a certain ontology of person. The office of citizenship appears in societies which seek to substantiate persons because they are worth more than things, because they take delight in things. Contrarily, the role of consumer depends on utilitarian considerations about what is useful in the satisfaction of desires. To confuse citizenship with consuming is to obscure ends and means. This confusion is a source of envy.

Virtue and experience. How does this confusion arise? In a sense, it comes from a view of living that conceives worth only in terms of achievement, a conception of individualism deadly to the human spirit. In an article entitled "Modern Dying," Michael Ignatieff suggests that today's commitment to an immunology that puts the burden of cure on the patient is an effect of America's credo that the individual is the master of his or her destiny. This is the credo of Prometheus: "man's will, will make him master of his fate" (Ignatieff 29). Such a credo belies the irony that life teaches us: that we cannot do everything nor be as all others, that we need others and stand as individuals only in solidarity (33). The credo of US equality suffers from this lack of irony. Considered only as an instrumental virtue, equality makes meritocracy into a rat race. According to Fairlie, this is because the consumer meritocracy cannot justify itself in terms of its basic assumptions, and because it hides a confusion about the nature of equality and its good in a society (Fairlie 75). Indeed, equality is instrumental, but instrumental of many things. If it exists to facilitate a just distribution of goods and services, then it depends on citizenship and on an understanding of the philosophical goal it tends to achieve. If, however, equality exists to justify an inequitable distribution of goods and services (equality=inequality Orwell would say), then the only way to secure this goal is to make equality an equal obligation to pay.

Ours is an equality based on such an ethic. Might it be otherwise? In a book entitled *Duty or Pleasure?* Albert Ple argues that an ethic is the result of lived experience "historically and geographically situated" (viii). As such, since the Middle Ages, Western ethics have been rooted in a neurotic attempt to secure order and stability. He uses the label neurotic because such ethics evince a divided personality in which good and bad, right and wrong, stand in Manichaean contrast to each other.[25] Their contrast is the result of failed affectivity, and consequently, of over rationalized intellect. Because security is paramount in an age of turmoil, men and women labor to construct a world in which their moral judgments "stand outside of time and the human milieu" (xiv), beyond irony as Ignatieff would say. Our individualism and our morality go hand in hand: if the person will pay by obedience, devotion, and service, he or she will be saved. The price is personal pleasure and happiness; the price is duty.

Stoicism, the acceptance of "the slings and arrows of outrageous fortune" over and against *eudemonia*—well being—is the dominant theme of ethical systems based on duty. Noting that the West has lost the sense of Augustine's great insight into ethics, that order is never static, but the dynamic harmony of human appetites (20), Ple suggests that we have become prisoners of duty at the expense of affectivity and happiness. Where, prior to the fourteenth century, ethical life had consisted in actions which embraced "the order of love" (Augustine), after about 1450 ethical systems were developed which smothered the spirit (27) while adorning the persons with heroic character and concealing the very self (27). Distortions of the idea of God, a redefinition of original sin, misplaced faith in patriarchy, and the fusion of political and religious authority, spread, along with the "contagion of Stoicism," to produce ethical systems that put faith in "a

---

[25] Recall Greeley's worry about his teacher's commitment to such Manichaeanism.

directing power" (Marcus Aurelius in Ple 42) external to the personal lives of those who were subjects to it.

Citing Ockham as exemplar of this newly emerging worldview, Ple summarizes as follows,

> [H]uman perfection consists in submitting blindly, but also freely, to the law imposed by God. Such a morality was seen as the best possible "tranquillizer." It enabled people to "get right" with God and their conscience and thereby find (illusory) peace. During this lengthy period of political and religious anarchy, it enabled people to rely wholly on divine and ecclesiastical authority, which by determining what was allowed and forbidden (under pain of serious sin), spared them all the risks of personal responsibility, since they now had only to obey. (55)

Such was the beginning of modern, Western ethical systems which culminate in Kant's categorical imperative. The Christian imperative to love was transformed: "If you love me, you will keep my commandments" (John 14:15) became "if you keep my commandments I will love you." Morality came to promote an infantilism and a rebellion which have marked the course of European culture. Legalism and casuistry sapped the energy of the affective life thereby diminishing human creativity and potential (72*ff.*), while Western intellectualism disguised the narcissism of children (75). Pleasure in doing good and in being the best, along with instinct, departed the academies and cultural centers of human activity. Happiness became a matter of conformism and rule following.

This analysis leads Ple to a consideration of the basis of moral happiness, which he locates in the pleasure instinctual to human beings. He says, "The human fabric, both in the material that makes it up and in its empty spaces, is woven of the search for happiness and pleasure. To experience and desire these is to be alive. We must not reject them or alienate ourselves from them. The whole problem of morality is to experience pleasure in the right way" (101). To do this, Ple argues, we should become persons of taste[26] who know how to

---

[26] See Hannah Arendt, *The Promise of Politics*, for a theory of judgment that makes sense of Ple's notion of taste.

experience the world so that pleasure and reality coincide to make us happy: "To act with moral rightness is to love rightly; to act wrongly is to love wrongly" (143). The trick is in the knowing the difference.[27] Greeley's anthropology of human sexuality as revealed in the healthy sexuality of many of his characters makes this very point. God as a character in Greeley's novels often is found in such relationships. Likewise, the misuse of human sexuality by his characters makes the point negatively.

Envy and the flattering illusion. George Eliot's *Middlemarch* contains a wonderful metaphor that captures the reason behind our tentativeness about knowing and loving rightly. She writes,

> Your pier-glass or extensive surface of polished steel made to be rubbed by a housemaid, will be minutely and multitudinously scratched in all directions; but place now against it a lighted candle as a center of illumination, and lo! the scratches will seem to arrange themselves in a fine series of concentric circles round that little sun. It is demonstrable that the scratches are going everywhere impartially, and it is only your candle, which produces the flattering illusion of a concentric arrangement, its light falling with an exclusive optical selection. These things are a parable. The scratches are events, and the candle is the egoism of any person now absent [...] . (297)

We are all egoist in the beginning. Our wisdom comes when we realize that events are not necessarily of our own making, and that we stand with others not impartially but as participants with them. Eliot's metaphor is that of the continuity of persons in community.

Ple says that the "task of morality is to humanize affectivity [...] to elevate what is 'animal' and infantile in it [...] to the level of rational intelligence [...]" (142), and quoting Aristotle, "[a] person is not a good person unless he finds his joy in doing beautiful actions." To be so is to be just, "as a person is, so does the end appear to him" (in Ple

---

[27] Hence St. Francis' warning that not knowing the value of things leads us to a false estimation of worth that destroys happiness.

143). What pleasure does is reward virtue. The two are requisite of each other. This is what ethics of duty cannot account for.[28]

The envy in our culture, stemming as it does from a misconstrued notion of equality, is symptomatic of a culture that denies the possibility of "living happily and nobly" as Aristotle would have it.[29] Rather, we have become a nation of consumers who ignore the office of citizenship. And there should be little wonder that envy is the standard attitude of such a society. We are taught to recognize that the world is a pay-as-you-can contract, while insisting that in the end the best of us rise to the top and are chosen and entrusted with the burdens of leadership. We learn to be content with the consumer society, which supports us, while we ignore in many real ways the inequities our measured equality covers over. Little wonder then that we become envious and disenchanted persons. How could it not be so? If others have more or stand higher, it must be because these others in having more, or by being better, have diminished those who are without. Our entire vocabulary of empowerment has brought us to this conclusion. Liberty for most consists of being able to make others do what they do not wish to do: making someone else pay because we have paid enough. This is a liberty that requires a reversal in positions of dominance and servitude; it is not, however, a liberation from the relationship of dominance itself.

This is so, in large part, because our economic system is predicated on inequality while our political system thrives only on true equality of persons. The contradiction requires either correction or disguise. Yet, we have disguised it with a rhetoric of false equality, by blaming victims, and by educating consumers rather than citizens. In fact, the economic system thrives precisely as the political system based on equality declines. Just citizens endanger unjust economic arrangements.

---

[28] Thus, education has as it moral warrant, the leading of individuals from childhood to the place where joy and pain are "rightly to be found" (172). We do this by "learning to taste the quality of pleasures, so that 'good things will be sought with greater eagerness'" (178). And wisdom is morality known for its savor. This is the sense of hope that human moral behavior bestows: "living happily and nobly" (Aristotle in Ple).

[29] See Sheldon Wolin on liberalism as a form of worry and loss in *Politics and Vision*.

The envy we experience, and which Greeley is so unrelentingly true in pointing out, results from covering up this contradiction. Until this is discovered, envy will occasion the bitter heart that seeks revenge and finds solace only in alienation.

Chapter 3: Greeley's Theology

Religious imagery and the inherent goodness of all that is. It may be argued, as Greeley suggests in *The Great Mysteries: Experiencing Catholic Faith from the Inside Out*, that religion stands at the midpoint between ethics and philosophy (145); it may also be argued that religion stands at the interstice between the private world of the family and the public world of the polity. Religion involves the experiential world of practice, which provides meaning to a life (145); it involves an orientation toward this world and is "a way of doing everything" (145). If, then, as Greeley suggests, it is the midpoint and interstice between such human activity, it follows that religion involves politics—indeed it may be the highest expression of that reality—anciently seen as the application of ethics and philosophy to public life. Religion, then, is an important aspect of politics, even when politics seeks to keep separate the realms of public life and religious expression.

We know religion not in terms of specific propositions, which are the result of attempts to articulate the "content" of a religion; rather, we know religion from its imagery. Images constitute the ideas we have about ourselves, our lives with others, and with that which we presume to be most significant to us. One of Andrew Greeley's great contributions to Catholic sociology has been his insistence that religion is best understood through its imaginative stories rather than according to propositional theology. Theology is not religion even though religion may involve theological reflection and its articulation.

The Catholic religion in its stories and its art, sustains the following images. The first is that all things are essentially good in and of themselves, and that any evil or corruption of this essential goodness does not destroy the goodness of the thing itself. Certain kinds of things, persons, have purpose; life is not random unless we make it so even when the power that sustains life may use random events to accomplish its purpose.[30] Thus, death is not an ending but a changing. Human nature is good though flawed by its very finitude. Society supports human nature and reflects that nature. While nature itself is perfected by grace, as such, it is in all of its manifestations sacramental, i.e., a symbol of God's love. We have been delivered from evil and death by God's life and love and are always to live as though we really believe in the truth behind this imagery. Because we trust that we have been given all that we need, we live in intimacy and have a love affair[31] with all that is. All that is (Being itself and God as the source of Being itself) passionately pursues each of us because he loves us. Because God loves us, we are able to love others. This means that God's love and our best selves are correlated: grace (God's life in us) corresponds to what is "most generous and most creative in our personalities" (146).[32] It follows that our response to God's passion for us involves not the selfish autonomy of a selfish individualism, but membership in communion with others (the Catholic imagination's idea of community and the common good as embodied in the Eucharist). Nothing human can be alien to someone who responds to God's passion. Thus, it follows that evil, the absence or misuse of good things, never triumphs over the inherent goodness of these things. Moreover, our vocation is to use our gifts to help grace perfect the world (the Catholic notion of personal and social responsibility), because in each calling we reflect God's giving of himself to us.[33]

---

[30] One of Greeley's continuous themes is that God writes straight with crooked lines.

[31] All of Greeley's fiction expresses this notion of God's love affair with the world at its heart.

[32] These images are my attempt to summarize for the reader Greeley's understanding of grace and of the goodness of creation. For a better explanation, see pp. 145–146 of *The Mysteries of Grace.*

[33] It is here that language limits what is intended. God as that than which nothing is greater cannot have gender, although gender involves dimensions of God's creative love. God's self revelation—the idea of the Trinity—is central to Catholic Christianity. My use of the male pronoun is therefore problematic.

This imagery constitutes a coherent view of existence (146) for Greeley, and at its heart requires a generosity that pervades all we do. The principles derived from such imagery are not provable, nor are they self-evident (147). They constitute a theory that when applied to the world of human experience seems to make sense. In this way, then, the Catholic theory of life is true only conditionally, and those who suspect that it works accept it as true. This is the Catholic "leap of faith" as opposed to Kierkegaard's. Greeley writes, "The theory may [...] seem too good to be true, but as we live it, we may come to see its truth" (147).

Thus it is that the Catholic faith can be made to fit certain intellectual propositions, but this is not what makes the theory true. Rather, the intelligibility of its propositions—that they make sense and drive human actions—is key. Catholic faith is to be lived, and thus, it impinges on every aspect of life. It cannot be privatized or individualized, nor may it be dogmatically politicized as ideology. Hence, the political dimensions of this theory are part of the theory's importance. How the Catholic practices the theory involves him or her in personal, social, economic, and political questions. My attempt in this work is to help explicate how we can say that faith should not be "ideological" even as it must be practiced and applied. This work is an attempt to tease from Greeley's novels, most often from of his characters, some of the political theory involved in the grand theory itself.

To help do this several matters require brief consideration. The first pertains to the imagination as the source of God's revelation to us. Early in Bernard Shaw's "Saint Joan,"[34] Captain Robert de Baudricourt learns that St. Joan hears voices that tell her what God wants of her: "'They come from your imagination,'" he affirms, to which Joan replies, "'Of course, that is how the messages of God come to us'" (Scene 1 59). This simple insight helps to explain how Greeley's fiction serves as a means by which he serves the People of God as a priest. This is why there is no contradiction between his work as a priest and as a novelist. Milan Kundera helps us to see further.

---

[34] Bernard Shaw, "Saint Joan: A Chronicle Play in Six Scenes." New York: Penguin Books, 1951: 59.

In his acceptance of the Jerusalem Prize for Literature on the Freedom of Man in Society,[35] Kundera uses the Jewish proverb, "man thinks, God laughs," to maintain that the novel has saved European individualism from the forces of humorless certainty, from the "nonthought of received ideas," and from the mass media's empowering of these. It has done so by insisting that great novels are those in which all characters "have a right" to be heard. Humorless certainty, the uncritical acceptance of received ideas, and the empowerment of both are, he says, "the same three-headed enemy of that born as the echo of God's laughter, the art that has managed to create the entrancing imaginative realm where no one is the possessor of the truth and where everyone has the right to be understood" (12).

The world of Greeley's imagination, where God uses imagination to reveal his great love for the world, is indeed, a world where everyone has the right to be heard. Only then does everyone have a chance to be understood. Greeley's characters—the good and the bad—possess and bestow a truth that can only be found in fiction, only in an imaginative world. The relationships these characters create, playing on our experiences of the world akin to them, mark a dimension of the truth embodied in Kundera's Jewish proverb:

> But why does God laugh at the sight of man thinking? Because man thinks and the truth escapes him. Because the more men think, the more one man's thought diverges from another's. And finally, because man is never what he thinks he is. The dawn of modern times revealed this fundamental situation of man as he emerged from the Middle Ages: Don Quixote thinks, Sancho thinks, and not only the world's truth but also the truth of their own selves slips from their hands. (11)

Greeley's use of the imaginative world of fiction to preach the Gospel, in part, comes from both Shaw's and Kundera's insights.

The Great Mysteries is Greeley's articulation of the key Catholic ideas at work in the real world, which is not necessarily the same as the "Real" world. But it is the world he refers to as God's world. This world

---

[35] "Man Thinks, God Laughs," Milan Kundera. *New York Review of Books.* June 13, 1985: 11–12.

is to be distinguished from Greeley's fictional world. The book's twelve chapters might be viewed as twelve topics that continually appear in his work. That his work is fiction rather than a work about the empirical, material world is an important point to underscore. His world of fiction is not a world of make-believe. Rather, it is a world of human experience born of the imagination that uses symbol and myth as the currency of meaning. Fiction rather than empirical fact is employed because it more completely reproduces the world of our experiences. The efficacy of fiction depends upon its verisimilitude to the readers' worlds, while the use of empirical fact requires methodologies, assumptions, and presuppositions that often are not available to those who do not pursue a particular range of study. Greeley, a master of empirical sociology, uses fiction as a means of opening his world of empirical study to those who do not have the scholastic or educational background necessary to an understanding of his sociological work. As any good teacher, he understands that the best way to teach or to raise questions is to appeal to an understanding that is common to both the students and the teacher. Since the beginning of humanity, the storyteller has been the primary teacher of experience.

Dimensions of mystery. In *The Great Mysteries: Experiencing the Catholic Faith from the Inside Out,* the first mystery, perhaps the first dimension of The Mystery would be a better way to put it, is that upon which all the others depend—the mystery of God. The sign of this mystery is found in two human questions: Is there purpose to my life? And why did God make me? (1). Bound to how we answer these is the supposition we bring to them about the goodness or lack of goodness of all that is. The Catholic imagination begins with the supposition that all being, and hence by implication, Being itself is essentially good. This value of all that is confronts us with the question of how we arrange the priorities of the values we find in all that is. This is the question of culture. If we view life and existence as random contingencies, our priorities will be different from the priorities of someone who thinks that life has some permanent value, and that being alive constitutes a set of moral responsibilities. If life is random and subject to meaningless change, we and the culture that believes so with us, will assign higher value to immediate gratification and to the rule of the strongest than those who see life as involving a permanent and specific order of value. Indeed, our postulation about the goodness of this world means that we wonder about different things than those who do not so postulate. If the world is good, then we must confront, at the very least, a suspicion of grace, for what is good is also gracious. Now grace is a word possessed of a complex intellectual, philosophical, and theological genealogy. In spite of this genealogy, the word signifies the possibility that there is something outside of ourselves that gives us insight into being more than our mere selves are. Grace represents the possibility of God intimately working in our lives, helping us do, say, and become what we otherwise could not. In Catholic terms, grace signifies God's life in us, hence, the complexity of the genealogy. Indeed, all attempts at human meaning—art, literature, science, philosophy, politics to name only a few—might be said to be our comments on grace. Greeley says this:

> God is humankind's attempt to explain experiences of wonder and the awe that results from them. Since the wonder experiences hint that whatever is at work in the universe is both purposeful and gracious, God, we assume, is the purposeful and gracious one who is responsible for the universe and for our life. There are many possible different interpretations of who God is; for humans must wrestle with the paradox of the graciousness and purpose they occasionally experience and the evil and absurdity that seem so typical of life. Fundamentally, religion is an attempt to harmonize graciousness and evil. God is the center of religion, and our image of God summarizes our response to the puzzle of absurdity and graciousness, of chance and awe. (4–5)

The question of purpose at least suggests its reality. Whether or not we reject this as a reality depends on many variables, perhaps the most important of which is the culture into which we were born or find ourselves immersed. Purpose might be possible even as grace may be. The political reality here involves the images that have become predominant in our lives. Do good and evil exist? How evenly are they matched? Which will triumph? Optimism or pessimism determines our answers to these, and these "answers" inform our political creeds.

If human nature is perceived as essentially an agency of evil, those who perceive it as so will have a view of government and of society that differs radically from those who are more optimistic about human behavior. If greed is perceived of as the controlling human motivation, then the economics of these perceptions will be essentially opposite those who see human nature as more benign. So it goes with almost every idea: justice as revenge *versus* justice as mercy, human degeneracy *versus* human progress, and hate *versus* love.

Greeley's point is that our ability to imagine the world affects how we live in it. Art and literature especially help us to see how cultures imagine themselves. In the Catholic world, art and literature have held essential places in education precisely because our ability to imagine constitutes part of our power to act. Indeed our images of God inform our art and literature. Greeley writes,

> Some versions [of religion] see God as benign but forgetful; humans must remind God of his promises and sometimes wake him up from his sleep (Egyptian). Others see God as crotchety and difficult, easily offended by those who violate his plan, and quick to take salutary vengeance; humans must constantly placate and calm him (Babylonian). Still others think that God is fundamentally uninterested in the universe he has created, leaving its governance to irrational, or at least nonrational, forces he has set in motion (Greek and modern deism). And still others find substitute gods in the pursuit of freedom or social justice or a better life for all here on hearth—a pursuit that is usually seen as part of some inevitable forward movement of humanity and acts as a substitute for a divine plan (Marxism, scientism). (5)

The God of Israel, the God who Jesus reveals to us, is the God who loves, who promises, who creates, who graces us whether or not we wish, or hope, or know him to do so. Greeley names this God "A Gracious Purpose" (6), the experience that marks what he calls the Catholic imagination.

In a very important article,[36] the noted sociologist Robert N. Bellah poses a question about American culture: why is it so difficult for Americans to understand the idea of the common good? To address this question, he asks about the Catholic contribution to "a revitalized commitment to the common good" (9). Citing Pope John Paul II's definition of solidarity[37] and David Hollenbach's paper "Is Tolerance Enough?", Bellah raises an issue that, for him, goes to the very core of what he calls the American cultural code. This code is historically the product of a Protestant theological understanding of the world, one that for purposes of analysis is committed to a specific definition of human nature and of the created world. Bellah suggests that this kind of analysis would be helpfully balanced by Greeley's notion of the sacramental or Catholic imagination.

Noting that he is not addressing confessional or theological doctrine in using the distinction between Protestant and Catholic, Bellah argues that this distinction is cultural.[38] The distinction involves the principles from which our US cultural code derives. Quoting Greeley,

> The Catholic tends to see society as a "sacrament" of God, a set of ordered relationships, governed by both justice and love that reveal, however imperfectly, the presence of God. Society is "natural" and "good," therefore, for humans and their "natural" response to God is social. The Protestant tends to see society as "god-forsaken" and therefore unnatural and oppressive. The individual stands over against society and not integrated into it. The human becomes fully human only when he is able to break away from social oppression and relate to the absent God as a completely free individual. (in Bellah 10)[39]

---

[36] "Religion and the Shape of National Culture." Bellah, Robert N. *America.* July 31, 1999: 9–14.

[37] The pope says that solidarity is "a firm and persevering determination to commit oneself to the common good, that is to say, to the good of all and of each individual [...]" (In Bellah 9).

[38] As he says, citing G. K. Chesterton, "In American even the Catholics are Protestant" (10).

[39] See Greeley. *The Catholic Myth.* Bellah notes here, "This is not entirely fair, as it overlooks the community-forming capacity of Protestantism so evident earlier in our history, but it does help us understand Margaret Thatcher's otherwise nearly unintelligible remark, 'There is no such thing as society,' a quintessentially Protestant thing to say" (10).

What Bellah exposes is what he calls the flaw in America's cultural code. Using his work in *Habits of the Heart* and *The Good Society*, he argues that the first language of Americans is utilitarian and expressive individualism, which asks, is it useful to me and does it express who I am? Our second language is biblical and civic republicanism, which asks, what are my responsibilities to others and what are my duties as a citizen?[40] All these cultural languages are the result of our history and the fact that our political history grows out of our Puritan heritage. He makes clear that the core of the American cultural code is the religious ideal of radical individualism. He uses Roger Williams as the archetype of this core. In search of an absolute freedom of conscience, something key to US culture, Williams moved from conscience as the core of the self to conscience as a means of isolating the self from community. Bellah writes, "Roger William was a moral genius, but he was a sociological catastrophe. After he founded the First Baptist Church, he left it for a smaller and purer one. That, too, he found inadequate, so he founded a church that consisted only of himself, his wife, and one other person. One wonders how he stood even those two" (11).

As important as freedom of conscience and the tolerance it requires are, there is a shadow side to such an emphasis. This shadow may be found, Bellah suggests, in the Protestant understanding of predestination and its consequences for the American cultural code. The Reformation's opposition to Catholic doctrines such as transubstantiation and to forms of Catholic piety led to an emphasis on the transcendence of God over his immanence. This had the effect of pushing God out of the social picture. The notion that predestination meant that everything had been preordained since the beginning of time became, without God, a form of determinism. Either the self was left alone in the solitude of the created world, or was left alone to face an atheistic determinism, or with the help of preordained grace, the lonely quest for personal meaning. In either case, the American cultural code is one of radical individualism; in each case the individual is divinized either as the master of his own fate or as the lone saint awaiting God's help; and in such a code the notions of solidarity and community prove to be problematical (11–12).

---

[40] For an extended discussion of these cultural languages, see *Habits of the Heart*.

"The flaw in our cultural code," Bellah writes, "becomes most evident when the radical religious individualism [...] is joined with a notion of economic freedom that holds that the unrestrained free market can solve all problems" (12). The result, he says, are "loose connections" and "porous institutions" (12–13). "Loose connections" are ties to others that do not demand loyalty over a long time. "Porous institutions" are those that do not hold the individual too closely together—marriage, for example. The result is the kind of social problem we currently face. The solution, Bellah suggests, is to be found in the Catholic religious tradition, specifically in those modes of living that treat the world as the sacrament it is. "I believe," he writes, "we need at this moment to reconstitute our cultural code by giving much greater salience to the sacramental life, and in particular, to the Eucharist" (13). Noting that the Catholic and Protestant religions both profess that worship is evidence of a community, he says, "the sacraments pull us into an embodied world of relationships and connections, a world in which, to quote Greeley, 'humans [are] integrated into networks, networks that reveal God rather than a world in which individuals attempt to escape from society'" (in "Religion and the Shape of National Culture" 13). If we want a society that is strong in its expression of solidarity, we require a cultural code that sees such networks as are everywhere needed for well-integrated persons to thrive as natural and gracious.[41]

At the core of the Catholic imagination is the postulate that all that is created, because it is a manifestation of divine love, is good no matter how implicated it might be in the evil so everywhere around us. Humanity fell from grace and has been wondering why ever since. But in this fall, goodness was never lost. Translating this into political ideas involves us in rejecting images of the world that exclude the possibilities of human goodness: the denial of freedom by oppression, the denial of human responsibility through the works of human agency, the denial of humanity, as the Stoics would have it, as a moral estate.

---

[41] I write here about the American need for solidarity in the months after the social disaster of hurricane Katrina. The people abandoned to their own devices, predominantly African-American in culture, were not merely overlooked by the government agencies that failed them; they were, rather, forgotten by these agencies. Americans found out about this forgetfulness only because it made good copy in the media.

If, then, the Catholic imagination is one that posits the possibility of human well-being and of a human kind of freedom, then a politics of hope makes sense of our experience. Here the Thomistic/Aristotelian view of politics has merit. Aristotle posited the human community as the place in which human agency—the ability to act—has maximum support. The individual person is the result of a complex set of interconnecting networks of relationship that we name society, and human beings depend upon society for all their needs. This is why the family is seen as the essential beginning of society in Catholic social thought. Yet, because human beings are individuals, i.e., because they are free, they are capable of informing through culture, law, and tradition, the kind of society upon which they depend. Thus, for Aristotle, a person is free to the extent that he holds a responsible place in the order of things. Centuries later, Thomas Aquinas would baptize Aristotle's notions of person and of society by insisting that human beings are made in God's image, and therefore, are of transcendent value in and of themselves. Hence, human being is not a function of one's place in society so much as it is a gift of God's love. That gift is imaged in the life of virtue, which is possible because of the human ability to choose.

The Western notion of political life more or less has been carried in this form, and much of human political history has involved contending over its meanings. At its root, however, has been the image that this life counts for something, that it has value in and of itself, and that human beings must learn how to live in light of this image. Such an image of human politics does not lightly dismiss the potential for or the actuality of evil in the world. In fact, it is very "realistic" in this regard. It places evil in the context of a world that is good, a world where persons count and can influence the world into which they are born. In the Catholic imagination, goodness is ordinary, evil is extraordinary. In terms of God and his graciousness to creation, this means that grace is everywhere and in all things—sometimes even in spite of us. The world is flooded with grace and our role is to have eyes to see it as so. "Yet in our experience of graciousness," Greeley writes, "we do get the hint that whatever it is that is stirring up our awe and wonder, it is, overwhelming in its graciousness. We are afraid to trust our intuition that whatever or who ever is out there beyond the limits could be so gracious. Life couldn't possibly have that glorious a purpose. Could it?" (9)

That it not only can be so, but also actually is so, constitutes the good news of Jesus, Greeley tells us:

> Christians are quite simply those who believe that Jesus was right, and that we are right when we are willing to push our intuition of graciousness to its farthest limit and even beyond. But such belief is not merely the dull assent to an abstract proposition. To believe that Jesus was right means I share in his experience of a God madly in love with me, and then live as one must who is caught up in such a love affair. (9)

For Greeley as for all who believe, that we are loved is proof that God is.

Does this mean that God as religious experience and politics are one and the same? In spite of a history of attempts to make Christianity into theocracy, there is evidence that the confusion of these two realities constitutes a great error. This said, it is also the case that religious people have a place in the public realm along with other citizens. It is perhaps the religious person's duty to know how to keep the two separate without destroying the integrity of either or both. Greeley's novels are a resource for those who grapple with this distinction. The point here is that religion as a theory of life can and does offer an important postulate to political thought. This is that our religious attitude toward human potential informs our political expectations about human reality. Too much or too little faith in that potential creates very inhuman political realities.

The second dimension of Greeley's mystery is revealed in the person of Jesus of Nazareth, for it is upon this person that the grounds for hope depend. Humanity in the first mystery serves as the agency of hope (14); Jesus is about trusting in that hope (15); and in this trust there is a promise, a promise that our wildest hope is only a shadow of what is in store for those who love.[42] In Catholic thought, Jesus

---

[42] It should be noted here that Hannah Arendt's idea that human hope is rooted in our natality—the fact that we are born—comes from her consideration of St. Augustine's work. More will be said on this in subsequent chapters.

is the sacrament of God (16);[43] Jesus' life is the life that reveals how hope joins faith to love; Jesus saw the Kingdom as already present (17), while we see it as not yet here. Faith involves us in seeing and being like Jesus. He went to his death because he hoped (18). In this hope, he taught us our humanity. His hope was in the power of God, not in the power of the world, and it was this hope that proved true in his Resurrection. That Jesus hoped is the point of his life. This point, Greeley writes, implies that because he is truly human, as God is truly divine, we can live

> a life of courage, vigor, confidence, commitment, and generosity. One never stops trying, never gives up, never sinks into a rut, never turns back, never refuses an opportunity to help, never rejects the possibility of reconciliation, never thinks that it is too late to begin again. For the follower of Jesus who hopes in the kingdom of God, tomorrow is not merely the first day of the rest of his life; tomorrow will also be different even when today is the last of his life. (21)

This hope implies a paradox, an apparent contradiction. Ours is to understand true paradox and real contradiction. We have minds that help in our hope, and it is here that the Catholic mind relies on politics as applied hope. We work with minds and hearts either to save something of value or to change to something more valuable. Thus, the commitment to Jesus as the hope of all is also a commitment to live in the world, not of it, but in it, in order to participate in its renewal.

From hope, the Catholic imagination moves to trust and to its prior question: do we have reason to trust, is it safe? This translates into the theology of the Holy Spirit. Is she God? (*The Great Mysteries* 25). The conservative philosopher Michael Novak postulates the ethical question presented by the very human awareness of death's inevitability: "Granted that I must die, how shall I live?" (Novak 48). This existential question raises the religious question that Andrew Greeley spends much effort to get us to see. Is it nothing or is it grace that lurks in the darkness of our lives? Understanding the existential

---

[43] See, for example, *Christ, the Sacrament of the Encounter with God*, by E. Schillebeeckx. Translation by Paul Barrett. English text rev. by Mark Schoolf and Laurence Bright. New York, Sheed & Ward, 1963.

meaning of both these questions implies, for Greeley, becoming vulnerable—at least as vulnerable as we really are. When we do, he suggests, we are "called forth" to live (27). He writes,

> We are made with the capacity to challenge and to be challenged by others, to be stirred up, "turned on." The attractiveness of other humans, as well as their tenderness, opens up to us the possibility of intimacy with them. We quickly learn that intimacy can only succeed if one is willing to give death to shame, and let the other one see us as we really are, taking the risk that he might laugh at us, ridicule us, break our heart. Intimacy can be achieved only if we are willing to be defenseless, vulnerable; it can survive only if we are willing to give to the other such untrammeled power over us that he can break our heart. In an intimate relationship, we must remain vulnerable; we must knock down defenses every day of our lives. (27)

In Catholic theology, marriage is the formal sacrament of intimacy whereby the secret of intimacy is revealed, where more than in any other kind of friendship we discover the Holy Spirit, the intimacy of God. (See 28.)

One of the major, perhaps the dominant, themes of Greeley's novels is the role human sexuality plays in humanizing or dehumanizing our lives. As a writer of fiction, he takes this human reality—contemporary culture might call it the only reality—and places it in its context as a theological reflection of God's interior life. His characters come to God, and they are able to trust because the Holy Spirit teaches them how. This is revealed in one of Greeley's archetypical symbols, the dance (29). Not to understand this dancing God is to miss the importance of Greeley as a storyteller, as it is to miss the point of his fiction. He is not the author of "steamy potboilers" or "dirty novels," as some believe, who often have an opinion of his work without having read it. Rather, he tells the ancient story of God's passion for the world, and especially, for human beings. Here he speaks for himself.

> Jesus told his apostles that they need not be afraid when he left them to return to the Father, because the Spirit would come to

them. The Spirit is light, fire, and wind. [The Spirit's] light is truth, [the Spirit's] fire is passionate commitment, [the Spirit's] wind is enthusiasm. The great wind and the tongues of flame at Pentecost showed the Spirit "turning on" the apostles, filling them with a confidence and an enthusiasm that sent them out to convert the world.

The Spirit is the Paraclete, the helper, the advocate, the comforter. [The Spirit] calls us forth with his dazzling fire and his howling wind, but he also encourages us and reassures us when we are discouraged and frightened. The Spirit calls us forth out of our narrow fears and our timid anxieties by stirring us up, by attracting us, and then by reassuring us when the fears and timidities reappear. And thus, it is with any lover whose beloved is fearful and hesitant.

The Father is the God who creates, the Son is the God who speaks, the Spirit is the God who calls.

The mystery of the Holy Spirit does not tell us that life is completely safe. It does not tell us that despite all evidence to the contrary we can trust everyone and take every risk. It does not assure us that we will not get hurt. It does not hide from us the evil of death. It does not claim to protect us from all pain that vulnerability entails. The mystery of the Holy Spirit merely tells us that there are grounds for trust, that it is all right to take risks, and that being vulnerable to others is a better way to live. (29)

By connecting human development to the intimacy of sexuality and identifying these with the Holy Spirit, Greeley confronts the fundamental question of why we should trust another. He writes, "The intimate vulnerability that is required for love is terrifying, but the mystery of the Holy Spirit tells us that with all the agonies and sorrows abroad in the world, it is a place where it is safe enough to love. The Holy Spirit guarantees it" (30). Not only does this mode of reflection raise uncomfortable issues in terms of the body's connection to the soul—sometimes too neatly separated in traditional Catholic thought—it also raises the problem of the self, another mystery.

The self—that core of who we are that remains the same even as it continually changes—has been a great source of reflection, at least, since

St. Augustine. His *Confessions* is one of the great works of Western thought precisely because it addresses the mystery of the self as it is connected to the mystery of God. Again Greeley,

> But the Spirit does not remake us. The apostles on Pentecost were not turned into men they never were before. Rather they became themselves for the first time. The Spirit called out of them that which was most creative, most courageous, most generous, most fully and completely human; and he does that to us, too. He broke through the barriers of the apostle's petty ambitions, their blind materialism, their cowardly fears; and he can do that for us, too. The Spirit did not transform Peter and James and John and the rest into totally new human beings. He liberated that which was best in each of them. He did not attempt to create a new kind of man. He spoke to those depths of the personality of each apostle who had already heard his call but feared to respond. Saint Paul tells us that the Spirit speaks to our spirit. The God who calls speaks to the spark of divinity that is in each one of us. The God without speaks to the hunger for God within. God's Spirit touches that finest, sharpest point in our personality, the very core of our identity, which tells us that we can be far more than we are. (30–31)

"Too late have I loved you, O Beauty so ancient and so new [...]"[44] Augustine writes, as he discovered that God and the self are intimately connected. The Catholic tradition discusses this connection in its speculation about the Holy Spirit. This third person of the Triune God[45] is the love

---

[44] Augustine's *Confessions.* Book 10, Chapter 27.

[45] The doctrine of the Trinity is central to Catholic thought, whether it be theological, philosophical, social, economic, or political. It, however, is also beyond the scope of this work even though it remains an essential idea that must be understood to interpret Greeley's fiction. This is what Greeley says in a "Theological Note" to Chapter Three of *The Great Mysteries:* "The doctrine of the Holy Trinity was not revealed to us to test our faith or to provide an abstruse puzzle for metaphysically inclined theologians. It was reveled to tell us something about God, and hence something about the purpose and meaning of human life. Briefly, the doctrine of the Trinity means that while God is one, he is not solitary. God is rational, God is interactive, God is a community, God is interpersonal life. The God who creates, the God who speaks, and the God who calls have been involved in an eternal love affair with one another and are now inviting us to join their dance of loving joy and joyous love. If the invitation is frightening, the reason is that we are being asked to join very fast company. But we are free to bring our friends" (35–36).

between the lover and the beloved—the call from the Word of the Creator. That sexual generativity is, for Greeley, a metaphor for this reality ought not to be surprising. Yet much of the negative criticism of Greeley fictions hovers around the misunderstanding of this metaphor, a misunderstanding that has confused Catholicism with Puritanism and Manichaeism. Such criticism seems to involve a sexual immaturity especially in American Catholicism. Perhaps the criticism of Greeley's characters, their randiness, is indicative of a basic distaste for plurality and diversity. Greeley writes,

> The God who creates is the principle of unity in the universe; the God who calls is the principle of variety and diversity. The more special each one of us becomes when we respond to that which is most authentically us, the more different we become from others. And as more human beings respond to the Spirit that speaks to that which is most creative in themselves, the greater the variety and heterogeneity in the world. (32)

One of his characters remarks, "God is a pluralist" echoing Aquinas' insight the diversity of creation proclaims the greatness of the creator. In Catholic social thought, it is the notion of the universal good that supports the ideal of the common good. And it is this notion more than any other that distinguishes Catholic political thought from all others. Catholic social thought is countercultural, not in the sense of rejecting the goodness of this world, but in the sense that what is good cannot be relativised to fit convenience or ease. Greeley writes,

> The spirit of this world tells us not to be different, to stay in line, to go along, to avoid the deadly sanctions which envy can impose, to flee from the risks of self-revelation and the shame of having that, which is most secret in us seen by all. The spirit of this world wants to keep the world a neat, orderly, gray, dull place. (32) [46]

The Spirit's enthusiasm also requires some caution. "God's Spirit," Greeley writes,

---

[46] Any reader of Greeley's fiction should very early on pay attention to his use of weather, especially Chicago winters.

is not, however, a spirit of mindless irrationality. If he speaks to that which is best in us, he certainly speaks to our minds as well as to our emotions. Spontaneity and creativity are not the same thing as undisciplined frenzy. The Spirit liberates the authentic self, not the unrestrained libidinal *id*. The dance of the Spirit is not the dance of drunken revelers. False spirits, as well as the Holy Spirit, are abroad in the world. The voices we hear in the night may be voices of evil, irresponsibility, and destruction. The most destructive of undisciplined human enthusiasms both to the individual person and to the social order are those that confidently but naively claim to be inspired by the Holy Spirit, when in fact they are the possession of the spirits of madness, of this world, and of all those little hurts, angers, and resentments that have been turned in on the self for so long. (33)

This caution is borne out in Greeley's fiction through a profound respect for the science of psychology and for empirically based therapy. Because we are gifted with intelligence and reason, as well as with faith and love, we have the capacity to discern what is good, and therefore, good in all cases, from what is only apparently so. The human capacity to name what is good is the precondition (a grace) of our openness to the dance of the Spirit. In this sense social and political thought are essential to religious and theological reflection.

This caution is found over and over again in Greeley's fiction especially in its protagonists' rejection of ideology in favor of critical thought and real intelligence.[47]

If it is God's Spirit, there is no nervousness; no frantic, fierce, anxious tensions; no desperate need to convince or to convert others; no compulsion to force others to share in our joy. God's Spirit brings peace, patience, kindness, tolerance, generosity, gentleness, tenderness, perseverance, serenity, openness, and respect for the freedom of others. If our new beginning, our rebirth, our new enthusiasm, and our sudden discovery of self are not marked by those characteristics, then they are the

---

[47] See, for example, *Virgin and Martyr*.

work of a false spirit, a spirit of hatred, punishment, and self-deception. (34)

In his discussion of the fourth mystery or sign of God, Greeley raises the question of evil, or in Catholic parlance, the question of why Christ died on the cross. This discussion revels another theme found in his fiction, that of the pathology of sin and of how it may be addressed. How can a world created by an all-loving and all-powerful God seem so dominated by natural, social, and moral evil? That we are able to ask this unanswerable question reveals to us the problem of our consciousness. Human beings are the only animals who trouble themselves with unanswerable questions like this one. Does this capacity indicate the meanness of fate—as the Greeks once maintained—or does it lead us into mystery, to the place where God may be found? Birth and death comprise the cycle of life. The *philosophical* question is, "why?"—a question beyond our abilities to answer. The *religious* question, however, the question that reveals the rumor of grace, is, "with which reality, birth or death, do we align ourselves?" For Greeley, this religious question, the question of human experience is about both evidence and imagination.

Greeley says that the problem of evil is not in accounting for it in a God-filled world, but in accounting for what is good in a world without God. Logic will tell us that the problem of evil cannot be solved and that it may even be "rational" to reject God in the face of the overwhelming evidence of evil in the world[48]; yet, even when we do this, we are left with explaining the existence of the good in a Godless world (43).

---

[48] "Attempts to free God from the charge of being the 'cause' of evil is the work of what are termed 'process' theologians and philosophers. They think of God as the 'great Improviser' who respects completely the freedom of his creatures (even the freedom of the forces of nature to create its own disasters), and then subtly adjusts his plans and goals so that their fulfillment will come despite and through the exercise of creaturely freedom. The approach is interesting and persuasive, especially because it permits us to say that God suffered and died for us in and through Jesus, (a traditional Christian conviction based on the custom of attributing to the divine 'person' the actions of the human Jesus). The main weakness of this approach is that it seems to assume that God grows and even changes—an idea, which is not false

What Christ reveals in his life, death, and resurrection, Greeley tells us, is that we can imagine that life trumps death and that love is more powerful than death: "The Christ event reveals to us merely that evil is not ultimate and good is; death does not have the final word, life does. And hence we live, not dominated by the fear of death but filled with the expectation of life" (43). This is for Christians the scandal of the cross. Jesus

> taught the fulfillment of the promise Yahweh made to the Hebrews, yet the leaders of the people feared and envied him. He came to bring life, indeed "life more abundant," yet he spent the last year of his life "one the run" to escape those who would kill him. Finally, he bravely went up to Jerusalem to confront those who wanted to destroy him, won all the points in direct argument, was betrayed by a friend, treacherously arrested in the dark of night, deserted by his friends, convicted on trumped-up charges, tortured and beaten, and then executed by a cruel death reserved for rebels and slaves. (43–44)

Yet, out of this envy, malice, misunderstanding, betrayal, and despair, something new arose: the possibility of eternal life. The question of faith is whether we might live according to this possibility: "The resurrection of Jesus," Greeley writes,

> is a "sacrament," a dazzling burst of illumination that brings light to the darkness in which we live. It does not solve the problem of evil; rather it tells us that in the end the greatest evil of all will lose. Life conquers death. My life will conquer my death. All of our lives will conquer all of our deaths. The hints we have that death is not final, the suspicions we experience that the resurrection experiences of our ordinary life are

to the scriptural data, but which certainly goes against much of the philosophical and theological premises of the Christian tradition. However, the process scholars argue that growth is a perfection and hence ought to be found supremely in God (at least in what they call the 'consequent nature of God'). Whether this subtle and attractive, but disconcerting approach, can be reconciled with the Catholic tradition is a question that will have to be answered in the future. A number of very respectable Catholic philosophical theologians have argued that the rapprochement between Thomistic theology and process theology is not only possible but absolutely necessary" Greeley notes (49).

revelatory, the ineradicable hunch from which we cannot escape that life is stronger than death—these are confirmed, validated, ratified, and reinforced by the resurrection of Jesus [...] .(45)

That death terrifies us is the prerequisite of our faith. The eyes of faith see beyond this terror or its inevitability. We who are of the kingdom are called to live as though it has already come. What sustains us in the face of the proposition that eternal life "is too good to be true," and therefore, might not be true are the ordinary and extraordinary moments of grace that help us to ask, "what if that good really is true?" And even if we do not fully believe in the possibilities of eternal life, when we free ourselves from the fear of death, we are free to live (47).

Greeley's consideration of original sin, his fifth sign of the mystery of God, reveals something essential to understanding his characters. If creation originally had an integrity of its own, if it were really good, what happened to that integrity after the fall? What, if any, of this integrity remains, and how does this question reveal something about the Creator?

The disorder in this world and especially in ourselves cannot be denied. Likewise our involvement in what is good, or true, or beautiful, however rare, leaves us with a sense that the world's disorder is not complete or final. Like the apostles, we, too, know the possibility of salvation (51–55). The major paradox of Christianity is that death reveals life, suffering reveals integrity, and the empty tomb signifies eternal purpose. According to Greeley, Jesus' followers

> experienced his death and resurrection as the cause of their liberation and reconciliation. They were free and they were one because Jesus had suffered and died. He had given them an example of how to live, he had revealed to them the love of the Father; he had shown them that evil could not conquer good, that hatred was weaker than love, that death would have to yield to life. He had shown them the "secret hidden from the ages," that God has a saving and loving plan at work in the world, that God intends that there be reconciliation and love,

and that nothing would prevent the ultimate realization of this plan—not even the terrible death of the man who was most intimate with him. (56)

When we distrust the world, Greeley writes, we commit the sin of "refusing to believe that this universe [...] is trustworthy and therefore the sin of refusing to believe that the power that produced the universe and placed us in it is trustworthy" (58). We fall from grace rather than into it, as we should. This distrust informs all our relationships. It is what Greeley understands by hate (58). Yet, we nonetheless know that trust is a possibility and in realizing this possibility, we participate in the grace that was once original to creation; we participate in creation as evidence of God's life.

Here is an important distinction between the Catholic imagination and other religious images of the created order:

> The Catholic Christian believes that there is more good than evil in human nature, more cooperation than selfishness, more trust than distrust, more love than hatred—though sometimes just barely. He believes that in the human personality there is the capacity for reconciliation, reconstruction, and restoration. Because of personal and hereditary limitations, we can exercise this capacity only imperfectly, but such an exercise is by no means impossible. (58–59)

Recognition of this possibility sometimes produces the attitudes found in Catholic thought[49] that we can walk to heaven on our own or

---

[49] Greeley writes, "Catholic social theory does not think you can remake human nature by changing its social and economic environment. Yet it is committed to such change because a more open and just human society frees the individual to make more of his own personal decisions about liberation and reconciliation. In particular, it does not believe that an all-powerful state can produce a new kind of human within a generation. Neither does it believe, as does the old liberal rationalism that society is made up of struggling, antagonistic, isolated individuals. Human nature, in the view of Catholic social theory, is not nearly as pliable as the Marxists believe, and not nearly as individualistic and selfish as the rationalists and some Protestants seem to believe. Humans are fundamentally good and fair and cooperative unless they are afraid. Salvation is God's revelation that there is nothing of which we ultimately need be afraid. Catholic social commitment means working for a social and political and economic order where the causes of fear are steadily diminished" (64).

make heaven be here below through social engineering, but these errors are not the ideas of the Catholic imagination. All is grace. This truth begins both the Catholic wonder at the world and the critical reflection on how we have made the world as it is. This reflection does not deny the fall from grace so much as it affirms that God's creation cannot be destroyed by human hatred. This is the mystery of God's great love for the world. This love is always the main character in Greeley's novels even as this character is always born of the interrelationships between and among his characters. He writes,

> Love for the Catholic Christian is not so much the desire to possess someone else as the desire to be possessed by the other. Love is the passionate and devout commitment of one person to the welfare and happiness of another. In such a commitment, the personal identity of the first person is not lost but enhanced because the most noble and most generous aspects of his personality are called forth. To possess another in love does not mean to be possessive of him. It means rather to graciously accept his passionate and devout commitment to my welfare and happiness, to assume that there is a tendency toward permanence in that commitment and at the same time, to respect the radical freedom of the other. (59)

This kind of love is the motive and the goal of all Greeley's characters, even those who fail to know or to accept this kind of love: "[Human nature's] self-defending hatred conflicts with its self-giving love" (60). Revealed in this idea of the flaw—creation's finitude (58)— is the idea of a God who is greater than anything we can conceive. God gets us all back from the very beginning. God trusts us to be free and we are called to return the favor (62). Such is the promise of Jesus.

The conjunction of human freedom and responsibility—sometimes expressed as guilt—leads to a deeper question, one that Greeley addresses under the rubric of grace. Can we be forgiven? Are there ways we might overcome our lesser natures? The answer Greeley gives is that, of course, we are forgiven. That is what love means; with a wave of the hand we forgive those we love. With love, forgiveness is automatic. And if God is love in the absolute sense, then God forgives us. This is the mystery of sanctifying grace (65). This is the truth behind the parables of the prodigal son, the good shepherd, the woman taken in adultery (68). This is what grace is and does: "God acts with grace; he gives himself to us with unrestrained and sovereign generosity, asking only an equally unrestrained response from us. God intends that God and man shall meet in a communion of mutual giving and receiving. Grace, then, is God's gift of himself to us; it is God giving himself to us" (69).

If God freely shares divine life with us, then we must be capable of that sharing. How can this be so since we are finite and limited while God transcends these limitations? The answer seems to be that God makes it so and tells us this through the everyday moments of grace that are everywhere around us. God pursues us like a great hound[50]; we find God in our best moments and especially in the miracle of forgiveness[51] (77*ff.*). As we are able to forgive so are we forgiven (72). This truth presents the issue of human integrity: what kind of person must we be in order to be able to forgive? This is the challenge of love. This challenge is everywhere found in Greeley's fiction.

The question of love's challenge to us to be fully human, occasions a related question: how do we discover this humanity in ourselves and in others? The answer, Greeley suggests, is found in the Catholic notion of the Eucharist. The Eucharist as understood in Catholic thought—that Jesus is truly present in bread and wine—reveals to us the concept of friendship, a concept that tells us something about what God might be like. The Eucharist is an insistence that true friendship, and the reconciliation always necessary for its continuance, is possible. Through it, we discover ourselves. For Greeley, the best examples of this are marriage and ecstasy.

> In the highest moments of human friendship, we forget about ourselves and we leave behind our fears, our inhibitions, our restraints; we remain fully who we are. Indeed, we are more fully ourselves at those times than at most other times, and

---

[50] See "The Hound of Heaven" by Francis Thompson. Nicholson and Lee, Eds. *The Oxford Book of English Mystical Verse*, 1917.

[51] See Arendt's discussion of this miracle in the context of human action in *The Human Condition: A Study of the Central Dilemmas Facing Modern Man*. New York: Doubleday, 1959: 212–223.

yet we exist for and through and in the other person. We are concerned about them in a way that we normally reserve for ourselves, and we are able to be ourselves for them in a way that is impossible in other circumstances. Despites the emotional intensity of such friendship, we do not grow weary from it. (76)

The Eucharist is founded upon the idea that our friendship with God derives from our friendship with other men and women. Thus, Holy Thursday and its *mandatum* is "I do not call you servants, I call you friends." At Emmaus, this is recognized (*77ff.*). Greeley says of this event's importance to the apostles,

> Their hearts burned within them, as the two disciples who met Jesus on the road to Emmaus said. When they were with Jesus, the apostles found that they were freer to be themselves than in any other circumstances. In the warmth of the attractiveness that flowed from Jesus, it was not necessary—and was a waste of time—to pretend, to defend, to hide. Jesus seemed capable of complete dedication to them, and in their own narrow and unperceptive fashion, they responded with dedication of their own. (77)[52]

Friendship liberates us from our narrow selves. Thus, Christians take the Passover meal as emblematic of the sign of the Eucharist. As God led Israel out of bondage to freedom, so too, Jesus leads us from our selfishness to others, and thus, to our real selves. This communion is witnessed in the meal that is the Mass. It is rooted in our need for nourishment and the gift that food represents. The thanksgiving that the hungry feel when they are fed tells us something about God as complete love, as do the celebration rituals of nature found in almost all religions. "The God who had produced life was present again in such rituals, continuing his work for people. And thus, his people ordered the life of the fields and the cooperation with him in bringing forth the rich and fertile abundance of the harvest" (78–79).[53] God's

---

[52] Note how this is very like what Greeley attributes to the gifts of the true Spirit. See page 69.

[53] One of Greeley's recurring emblems is that of the Feast of the Assumption of Mary, August 15, which is in older parlance the Feast of Mary in Harvest.

generosity, as seen in nature, and in Jesus' forgiveness constitutes the basis of the Eucharist. But there is more to it than this. The Eucharist is celebrated so we learn and continue to be generous and forgiving in our daily living. Without generosity and forgiveness, there is no chance for community. In fact, these are essential to it. The Mass, which is both the intimate meal we celebrate with those we love, and especially with Jesus, and the reenactment of the sacrifice of Christ on the cross, is the sign and the symbol of the Catholic community. Without it there is no community, there is no Easter.

Inhumanity and the absence of unity go hand in hand. Yet human beings also have the same hopes, share joys in the same ways, and seem to know, at least, that they ought to be connected to each other in some important ways (87–89). At the heart of our humanity is a desire to be at one and at peace with others. Because we are social by nature, this desire for unity seems to be something primal that we need. Yet the more complex our societies become and the more advanced they are in technologies, the further removed we seem to be from others and from ourselves. Unity, that ever-elusive reality that sits in the heart of every human being, is possible. The question is, how so? History seems to suggest that the greater the desire for unity among human beings, the more destructive it becomes when it is achieved. We have only to review the history of the twentieth century's nationalism, racism, and imperialism to see this fact. Unity can be a dangerous thing if it is done incorrectly.

The mystery of the church is the sign of a nondestructive unity appropriate for human beings. What is "catholic" about the Catholic Church is the good news of Jesus—his revelation of God's love in the Easter event. The power of the mystery of the church has been its ability to adapt cultures and norms to this Good News. Speaking of the writers of the second century, Greeley writes, "Anything that was good, anything that was true, anything that was beautiful was welcome in the Christian community no matter what the cultural source. In the exuberance of the still fresh Christ experience, they were hardly ready to draw narrow and tight boundaries, and were completely unthreatened by fears of losing the uniqueness of their message" (90).

The genius of unity has been the church's openness to the diversity of ways human beings live and have their being.

> Humankind responded to God in the same way it lived, not as isolated atoms, or as a massive collectivity but rather as a collection of small local communities, united in a common faith and a common goal. Global in its aims and vision, local in its daily life, federal in its organizational structure, the assembly (*ecclesia*) offered the model by which human unity would eventually be restructured; that is, universal world vision, local autonomy, and organic structure linking the various local communities in a variegated but integrated unity. (91)

One need only look at the history of the church to find that at its greatest it has embodied this model; its failures are marked when and to the extent that it deviated from it (91).

The church's perfection is Christ; all else remains imperfect until the end of time. The mystery of the church—the possibility of a human unity that respects diversity of individuals, of cultures, of histories—is the mystery of Christ in the world, remaining with us, speaking to us, waiting for us, as the truth behind both community and person. "We have a Church," Greeley writes, "because we need help to respond to God's gifts of himself, to the Good News that even our wildest dreams fall short of the truth. The Good News is too startling, too staggering, too demanding for us to be able to do anything about it by ourselves. We need the help of others" (93). Thus, it might be said that there is no one who is not in some miraculous way beyond the embrace of God's Church, which surely must be the same as God's love (94*ff*.).

This does not mean, however, that the historical structures and the hierarchical order of authority as established are identical with this mystery of unity. In light of the mystery of the church—both its reality and the human failures to achieve this reality—Catholic social theory evinces certain key characteristics. Greeley notes,

> Catholic social theory, reflecting on Catholic understanding of the revelations about the nature of human nature in the

Christ event, takes a more benign view of human society than do many others social theories. It does not think of society as an oppressive agency that forces cooperation on uncooperative and aggressive individuals. Instead, it believes that society is the actual result of the social nature of humankind, and that the dense and intimate network of social relationships of each human exists, not to oppress the individual but to facilitate his or her growth. When oppression does occur (which is not infrequently), Catholic Christianity believes that it is the result of an abuse of social power and not its natural exercise. Because of this respect for the web of human relationships, particularly the most intimate and local ones, Catholic social theory is skeptical of attempts to change society through drastic, once-and-for-all techniques; and it is generally committed to organic growth that, instead of wiping the social slate clean, moves individuals and communities forward from where they are. Furthermore, its realization of the crucial importance of the local church community leads Catholic social theory to insist on the principle of subsidiarity, the idea that nothing should be done by larger and more centralized agencies that can be done equally well by smaller and more local groups. Needless to say, the Church has not always followed this principle itself in regulating and organizing its own life. Catholicism does not believe that specific solutions to concrete social and economic problems can be derived from the Gospel. Individual Christians and groups of Christians can and must take stands on specific issues in light of how they see the Gospel applying to specific situations, but they must not claim unique validity for their application of principles to practice [...]. What makes Christian social action unique is not so much the specific solutions it offers (though it will incline toward maximizing personal freedom and local initiative when it is being true to its own best insights) but the style with which it is exercised. The Christian acts with patience, serenity, flexibility, refusal to hate, eagerness to reconcile, and implacable perseverance no matter how many defeats and frustrations he suffers. (100–101)

This translates into several important claims: (1) Contrary, then, to much modern social theory, Catholic social thought maintains that society is not a war of all against all; society is (or should be) a positive reality in our lives. (2) It involves a union of good women and men who are capable of realizing the common good of all. Society mirrors human nature and reflects its social dimensions. (3) When society is oppressive, it is because of the misuse of power, the misuse of something that is good. Human relationships are to be valued and protected. Hence, (4) social change is best achieved as the result of a growth in time and in history, that is, gradually, rather than as the product of radical revolutions. Thus, (5) solidarity—our connection to everyone and to each one—is balanced by subsidiarity—our respect for doing things at the individual and local level rather than at some higher or more centralized level. (6) The Gospel is not a rulebook that covers every human contingency. Rather each person and each group must apply the principles of the Gospel to the contingencies of contemporary life. No person or group has a monopoly on the Gospel in this regard. (7) Social action defends the transcendent value of each person while being a witness to God's love in the world.

Can we live without or beyond our nature? Raising the question of baptism in this way reveals something original in Greeley's thinking. Our intellect confers the important responsibility of stewarding creation. Not to be stewards of nature is to risk nature's vengeance. Immersed in matter, we can choose to live in resentment of this fact, or we can see in this immersion a sign of God's life. Water is the sign of this seeing. Water is essential to all living things. Greeley writes, "As the primal element in our world, the primary matrix of our life, water participates in the fundamental ambiguity of life. It brings both life and death. Which part of its revelation is most essential? Which is a better hint of an explanation of the meaning of our existence? (105)." Christians choose living waters, the sign of God's life in the natural order.

> God gave his supreme gift of himself, his ultimate revelation of himself, not in the form of a Gnostic angel but in the form of a man who eats, drinks, grows weary, and falls asleep like all other men. God had entered the cosmos, not as pure spirit but

as very much part of the material world. Therefore, that world was holy. The body of Jesus shared in the resurrection, and that settled the matter once and for all. The world was good. It was both the object and the means of salvation. It was the recipient of grace. It revealed God's gift to us. Indeed, it was part of the gift. The world is grace. (106)

In the waters of baptism, we receive the "fellowship of grace" (107); in baptism, we are reconciled to our immersion in matter. The material world becomes for us grace-giving (107). The material order, when seen this way, is restored and made holy; it is evidence of God's life. Hence, the rich material symbolism of the sacraments. Hence, Greeley's originality.

> In the Christian view of things the natural powers—water, fire, air, fertility—are not sacred in themselves but rather in what they reveal. The Christian might more appropriately speak of them as gracious instead of sacred. They reveal goodness because they participate in goodness, or, to become metaphysical for a moment, they reveal being because they share in Being. Grace, then, lurks everywhere [...]. The environment is a sacrament, and to ruthlessly exploit it is a sacrilege [...]. The world is grace, and not to appreciate it is ingratitude. And grace is not merely lurking around the corner waiting for us; it is chasing us madly down the street. (109–110)

Whither, then, sexuality? This is another dimension of Greeley's originality. Sex, he argues, reveals God's intimacy. The commitment between a man and a woman signifies God's commitment to the world. Both are covenants, each is the same. If we truly believed this, we would never be afraid. Yet sex scares us (113). Why? Because it is the most basic, the most intimate confrontation with the other, with someone who is not like us. And because it takes us as close as we ever get to our animal nature—sex makes of us natural things (114). This is why we are so afraid of it yet continually chase after it. As such, it is a powerful sign of God—the one who chases after us, the one who is the fullest expression of desire.

In Mary, the feminine aspects of God find a place in Western religion. Greeley writes,

> If there were truth and goodness and beauty in the notion of a feminine deity, Christianity would take over the idea and integrate it into its own world view. If sexual union was revelatory, then feminine humanity, as well as masculine humanity, could reveal God to us; and Mary was God's self-revelation through femininity in its perfection. And thus, there came to the Western world what may well be the most powerful cultural symbol it has known for the last two thousand years. (118)

> That symbol, of course, is Mary as mother, as virgin, as spouse, and as *pieta* (118).

The last two basic mysteries, heaven and Christ's return, are connected to the reality of life's unfairness and to how the Christian ought to address that reality. To hearken to the world's diversity and to recognize the fundamental differences embedded therein is to confront, as Greeley puts it, the unfairness of things. We are not the same; some are better, there is an inherent unfairness to life (126). How we deal with this inequality is what makes the difference. One of Greeley's consistent literary themes is of envy and the damage it does to all who are touched by it. Envy may be an answer to life's inequalities, but it need not be. Those who envy fail to make an important human distinction between unfairness and injustice. These are not the same. Human beings can confront life's unfairness without envy. They can seek amid the differences some modicum of human justice.

For Greeley, the mystery of heaven is the sign that the quest for *human* justice may be evidence of a *higher* justice. "Most of us," he writes, "don't think about such elaborate ideas as 'universal ethical imperatives,' but we do perceive a demand for judgment and justice to be in the very nature of things, and hence we feel that whoever or whatever is 'out there' must also be a judge" (128). Job confronts his innocence and discovers that he must let God be God. Christians see in the Easter event this very discovery and they are comforted by it. Those who were first to experience Easter experienced the judging God as a God of grace who revealed himself in Jesus. In the resurrection of Jesus, the forces of evil were put to flight, and by God's grace, we were united with Jesus.

> The judging God was the one who leaned over backward to forgive even before forgiveness was asked. Mercy and judgment were not in conflict; mercy had been extended to humankind, the forces of evil were being dispersed. Unfairness was driven from the earth, and with the coming of grace, we were awarded fairness in superabundance. We were no longer in the position of Job who could complain about what was taken away from him; God had given us something so beyond our wildest fantasies that we had no complaints at all. We had already won everything. (130)

Christians discovered that justice is mercy. They have had trouble with the world's justice ever since. Heaven is our imagination's attempt to probe the truth of God's mercy. This attempt is vouchsafed in the mystery of Jesus' return. This return is tied to the promise of God's love as revealed in Jesus' resurrection. The meaning of this return is not contained in any special knowledge of when, where, and how it will come to be, but in the fact that we believe we shall see Jesus again as he promised. Because we believe in his return, our task as Christians becomes living our lives *as though we really believe that fact.* This compunction determines not what we do in our lives, but *how* we do what our gifts enable us to do. We are known as Christians by how we love.

Chapter 4: The Character of Authority and Freedom

The mid-twentieth century political philosopher Hannah Arendt affirms that authority has vanished from this world.[54] In fact, she argues, the whole history of the politics of the twentieth century might be seen as the result of a crisis of authority. Authority's failure is nowhere more evident than in child rearing and in education, both pre-political areas in which young strangers, children, are made ready for life in the polity (92). Her essay, "What is Authority?" (*Between Past and Future)* asks what this concept once was and was not.

Arendt first claims that authority is neither power nor violence, or any kind of physical coercion; nor is it the result of argument or persuasion (93).[55] Where authority holds sway, neither persuasion nor coercion is required. Tradition and religion are its sisters: tradition being that "thread" that connects us to how we read the past, and

---

[54] "Since we can no longer fall back upon authentic and undisputable experiences common to all, the very term has become clouded by controversy and confusion. Little about its nature appears self-evident or even comprehensible to everybody, except that the political scientist may still remember that this concept was once fundament to political theory [...]." (in *Between Past and Future: Eight Exercises in Political Thought.* New York: Penguin Books, 1968: 91.)

[55] "The authoritarian relation between the one who commands and the one who obeys rests neither on common reason nor on the power of the one who commands; what they have in common is the hierarchy itself, whose rightness and legitimacy both recognize and where both have their predetermined stable place" (93).

religion being the institutional safeguard of the faith that emerges from that tradition (94). Authority serves as the "ground" for human action and constitutes the hierarchy on which we rely in the world, *as it has been* in order to live in it (95). Any rule of authority is one that sees its source as being outside itself. Thus, for Arendt, authoritarian government—authoritative would be perhaps a better word—is neither totalitarian, which is always self-referential and based on terror, nor tyrannical, which always involves the rule for a particular person's or class' private interest (96–98); rather rule by authority is pyramidal in form, where all commands have their legitimacy in reference to a source external to government itself. This source might be the past, either the foundation myth or mythic ancestors as in Roman culture, or the Godhead as in Judeo-Christian religions. But what is distinct to authority's rule is its reliance on inequality as the result of the hierarchical arrangement of society. Each has his or her place and is bound to it as part of the very structure of social life.[56]

What is essential to an understanding of authority, however, is that it is more than the diastolic argument between liberalism and conservatism, between the claims to freedom and to obedience (*Between Past and Future* 94ff.). To miss this point, Arendt tells us, is to fall victim to the notion that anything may be named anything as long as these serve the same function.[57] Such a mistake involves a failure to distinguish between phenomena and to lose the capacity to name realities. Where concepts have no solid meaning, they cannot be debated; nor can they be understood. Her endeavor is to understand

---

[56] Cf. 98–99. Although not directly related to this work, it should be pointed out that Arendt sees the form of totalitarianism as like the onion, concentric rings "in whose center, in a kind of empty space, the leader is located; whatever he does—whether he integrates the body politics as in an authoritarian hierarchy, or oppresses his subject like a tyrant—he does it from within, and not from without or above. All the extraordinarily manifold parts of the movement; the front organizations, the various professional societies, the party membership, the party bureaucracy, the elite formations and police groups, are related in such a way that each forms the façade in one direction and the center in the other, that is, plays the role of normal outside world for one layer and the role of radical extremism for another" (99).

[57] Both liberals and conservatives make the same mistake of thinking that "authority is whatever makes people obey. All those who call modern dictatorships 'authoritarian,' or mistake totalitarianism for an authoritarian structure, have implicitly equated violence with authority [...]" (103).

85

the world that has been lost to us, i.e., the world where authority served as a pre-condition for political life (104).

To understand this world, we must rely on Arendt's distinction between the public and the private realms. The Greek polity, in Arendt's mind, involved the public world where equals came together as equals and debated the nature and role of the public good. The family, on the other hand, stood for the private realm in which all relationships were relationships of subordination. In the world of the household, of master and slave, husband and wife, father and child, there was no freedom, nor choice. Even the master, who was always "vested with the power to coerce," was not free within this realm (105). He had to leave the private world and enter the public realm in order to be free. Thus, his coercive power, that of all parents as parents, was inappropriate to the public realm (105).

Authority, on the contrary, involves an obedience that is political in nature and public in fact (106). Thus, as Arendt says, Plato finally vested the laws with authority over the public realm. But these functioned as despotic rather than authoritative, hence ending the public realm, as it had existed before Plato and Aristotle.[58] Both philosophers are famous for their attempts to introduce reason—the supreme philosophical concept for both—into the realm of the political, where each citizen as equal held his own opinion as true. Thus, each was confounded by the antithesis between rule by philosophical reason and rule by discussion and common opinion. The polity had killed Socrates, an act that compelled Plato to search for some way to rule other than

---

[58] Arendt writes, "In Plato, the despotism originating in the household, and its concomitant destruction of the political realm as antiquity understood it, remained utopian. But it is interesting to note that when the destruction became a reality in the last centuries of the Roman Empire, the change was introduced by the application to public rule of the term *dominus,* which in Rome [...] had the same meaning as the Greek 'despot.' Caligula was the first Roman emperor who consented to be called *dominus* [...]" (106).

reason (107) and which caused Aristotle to abandon Athens to prevent it from sinning against philosophy twice by killing him.[59]

Yet, for Arendt, political life takes place within the Cave of Plato's allegory. It involves the world of images and opinions, where each has an equal claim to consent and to consensus (109). Plato's problem was integrating the beautiful and the good into a form of political wisdom (112), a problem he never completely solved: for Plato and the Western tradition philosophy remains at odds with politics. Nor does Aristotle, his famous student, solve the problem. For Aristotle there are two realms, the household, which is ruled as a monarchy, and the polity, where there are many who rule and are ruled; in the former necessity is ameliorated and in the latter, a second kind of life, the "good life," is made possible (117). Aristotle is certainly correct to say that until necessities are met there can be no good life. But, like Plato, he never solves his dilemma. His explanation of those who rule and those who are ruled depends, according to Arendt, upon examples taken from the realm of the household, and thus, involves him in a contradiction like that of Plato (118): where necessity rules there is no freedom, and where inequality is the model of rule, there can be no equality, except as a presupposition for meritocracy.

What Arendt sees as contradictions may be only a recognition that the private and the public realms are intimately and intricately related to each other. They are as circles superimposed upon each other. Where they interlock seems to be the world of humankind, creatures subject to the necessities of material and physical life who are capable of both wonder and reason. Arendt seems to admit as much in her discussion

---

[59]"Very early in his search he must have discovered that truth, namely, the truths we call self-evident, compels the mind, and that this coercion, though it needs no violence to be effective, is stronger than persuasion and argument. The trouble with coercion through reason, however, is that only the few are subject to it, so that the problem arises of how to assure that the many, the people who in their very multitude compose the body politics, can be submitted to the same truth. Here, to be sure, other means of coercion must be found, and here again coercion through violence must be avoided if political life as the Greeks understood it is not to be destroyed. This is the central predicament of Plato's political philosophy and has remained a predicament of all attempts to establish a tyranny of reason" (108).

of education, where the young are introduced to the affairs of the old in anticipation of their taking on the role of mature adults (119).

It is to the Roman experience that she turns in order to explain authority, for it was the Romans, unlike the Greeks, who were unafraid of authority and tradition as "decisive" in their political thought.[60] The Roman concept of authority comes from the Roman concept of religion.[61] The *augere* (to augment) root of the word *auctoritas* has to do with augmenting the foundation of the Roman state (121), she tells us, not as artifact, but as source. The Roman founders (the *Patres*) constituted the Senate—the authority but not the power of the state. Roman religion and Roman politics were, thus, intricately connected (123). The "child was father to the man" in the Roman mind because the ancestor always directed moral and political action.[62] Arendt writes,

> [t]radition preserved the past by handing down from one generation to the next the testimony of the ancestors, who first had witnessed and created the sacred founding and then augmented it by their authority throughout the centuries. As long as this tradition was uninterrupted, authority was inviolate; and to act without authority and tradition, without accepted, time-honored standards and models, without the help of the wisdom of the founding father, was inconceivable. (124)

---

[60] See 120*ff.*

[61] Arendt writes, "In contrast to Greece, where piety depended upon the immediate revealed presence of the gods, here religion literally meant *re-ligare* [from Cicero]: to be tied back, obligated, to the enormous, almost superhuman and hence always legendary effort to lay the foundations, to build the cornerstone, to found for eternity. [See Cicero, *De Re Publica*, III, 23.] To be religious meant to be tied to the past [...]"(121).

[62] "Contrary to our concept of growth, where one grows into the future, the Romans felt that growth was directed toward the past. If one wants to relate this attitude to the hierarchical order established by authority and to visualize this hierarchy in the familiar image of the pyramid, it is as though the peak of the pyramid did not reach into the height of the sky above (or, as in Christianity, beyond) the earth, but into the depth of an earthly past" (123–124).

For Rome, then, authority was the pre-political source of the public realm, a realm that could not exist without the ground of the family and its values. The church (in the West) would be the continuation of this authority, using Christ as the "cornerstone" of the new foundation (125).[63] In doing so, Arendt argues, the church amalgamated the "transcending measurements and rules" of Greek philosophy with the Roman idea of authority (127) as a beginning and a foundation. Thus, Christian political thought would combine the idea of the foundation as a beginning (Rome) with a notion of "transcending measurements and rules" (Greece). The Christian foundation married reason (127–128). The church, then, in Arendt's argument, adopted the Roman trinity of religion, authority, and tradition (126), an adoption that kept the Roman distinction between authority (the Senate, now the church) and power (the People, now in the hand of the emperors) (126).[64] The church would develop the doctrine of hell as a means of influencing those who did not see her rule as authoritative, much as Plato developed the myth of Er for the same reason in the *Republic*.[65] This would be, she suggests, an introduction of violence into the church's political system and would constitute one of the major reasons

---

[63] Arendt writes, "The Roman spirit could survive the catastrophe of the Roman Empire because its most powerful enemies—those who had laid, as it were, a curse on the whole realm of worldly public affairs and sworn to live in hiding—discovered in their own faith something which could be understood as a worldly event [the coming of Christ] as well and could be transformed into a new mundane beginning to which the world was bound back once more (*religare*) in a curious mixture of new and old religious awe. This transformation was to a large extent accomplished by Augustine, the only great philosopher the Romans ever had. For the mainstay of his philosophy, *Sedis animi est in memoria* ('The seat of the mind is in memory'), is precisely that conceptual articulation of the specifically Roman experience which the Romans themselves, overwhelmed as they were by Greek philosophy and concepts, never achieved" (126).

[64] "Since then it has turned out, and this fact speaks for the stability of the amalgamation, that wherever one of the elements of the Roman trinity, religion or authority or tradition, was doubted or eliminated, the remaining two were no longer secure. Thus, it was Luther's error to think that his challenge of the temporal authority of the Church and his appeal to unguided individual judgment would leave tradition and religion intact. So it was the error of Hobbes and the political theorists of the seventeenth century to hope that authority and religion could be saved without tradition. So, too, was it finally the error of the humanists to think it would be possible to remain an unbroken tradition of Western civilization without religion and without authority" (128).

for the modern abandonment of the Catholic religion. It would also involve new forms of foundation that rely upon violence, and thus, upon those who possess the superiority of arms, not as outside the polity, but within it.[66]

Be this as it may, what has been lost by ignoring the Roman idea of authority, according to Ardent, is a common experience of the politics of beginning, of action itself. She writes,

> [f]or to live in a political realm with neither authority nor the concomitant awareness that the source of authority transcends power and those who are in power, means to be confronted anew, without the religious trust in a sacred beginning and without the protection of traditional and therefore self-evident standards of behavior, by the elementary problems of human living-together. (141)

This idea that "authority transcends power" is key to understanding the character of authority in Greeley's fiction. That Catholicism carries this "religious trust" means that authority, in Greeley's novels, ought always to respect the "self-evident standards of that trust."

Arendt begins her discussion of freedom[67] with an aphorism: Our consciousness tells us we are free; the world tells us we are not free but subject to causality. Yet without freedom, there can be no accountability or judgment in this world. Yet when we study the world, we seem to be fated not be responsible. Arendt writes,

> [f]or the moment we reflect upon an act, which was undertaken under the assumption of our being a free agent, it seems to come under the sway of two kinds of causality, of the causality of inner motivation on one hand and of the causal principle which rules the outer world on the other. (144)

Thus, it may be argued, as indeed Arendt does, that freedom in the political sense is never "in the mind" or "in the will" but must be found in human experience (145). And for Arendt, this human experience is of a particular kind. To be able to act, a person must be

---

[65] See 128–135.

free from the claims of necessity and must be in the company of equals in a common public space (148).

It is because of her understanding of equality and public space as necessary for action that Arendt says freedom does not begin where politics ends (149); freedom is, rather, the ability "to call something into being which did not exist before, which was not given, not even as an object of cognition or imagination, and which, therefore, strictly speaking, could not be known" (151). For Arendt, to be free is to act; to act is to recognize principle; and to be an actor is to demonstrate virtuosity in action (152–153). In this sense politics is the place of action where men[68] perform according to those principles that they enact (154). And they cannot enact principles without freedom. Thus, freedom is the first principle of the polity. She writes, "[i]f, then, we understand the political in the sense of the polis, its end or *raison d'être* would be to establish and keep in existence a space where freedom and virtuosity can appear" (154). She writes, "[…] in politics not life but the world is at stake" (156).

This idea is foreign to us, Arendt explains, because the Western philosophical tradition has held, almost from its beginning, that freedom comes when we leave the community of others or when we discourse within ourselves, between me and myself (in thought), or when we question what we should or should not do (in ethics).[69] Finally, the question hinges on the distinction between what I want or will and what I have the capacity to do. Political freedom, for Arendt,

---

[66] See 136–140.

[67] "What is Freedom?" in *Between Past and Future: Eight Exercises in Political Thought.* New York: Penguin Books, 1968:143–171.

[68] The gender-specific reference is due to Arendt's own language and her understanding that the Greek polity was the place where freedom was discovered in its and her political understanding. Such is an irony immediately appreciated by Arendt, herself a woman.

[69] "Our philosophical tradition is almost unanimous in holding that freedom begins where men have left the realm of political life inhabited by the many, and that it is not experienced in association with others but in intercourse with one's self—whether in the form of an inner dialogue which, since Socrates, we call thinking, or in a conflict within myself, the inner strife between what I would and what I do, whose murderous dialectics disclosed first to Paul and then to Augustine the equivocalities and impotence of the human heart."

involves the conjunction of "I will" with "I can" (160): on *may* versus *can*. Hence, the nature of power and of power's role in freedom. The move to make virtuosity a matter of willing, i.e., "I will" and "the will to power," is modernity's idea of freedom. It involves a radical move away from politics as the Greeks understood it, to sovereignty, i.e., to the ability to command and to dominate others: the "I" as all powerful; *l'etate c'moi,* of political absolutism.

Against this modern version of freedom, Arendt posits freedom as a form of beginning, of creating something new. She writes,

> [m]an does not possess freedom so much as he, or better his coming into the world, is equated with the appearance of freedom in the universe; man is free because he is a beginning and was so created after the universe had already come into existence *[Initium] ut esset, creatus est homo, ante quem nemo fuit.* In the birth of each man, this initial beginning is reaffirmed, because in each instance something new comes into an already existing world which will continue to exist after each individual's death [...]. God created man in order to introduce into the world the faculty of beginning: freedom. (167)

This view of freedom makes sense only against biological necessity and historical recurrence of events (168), and it marks a kind of miracle. Arendt continues,

> Every act, seen from the perspective not of the agent but of the process in whose framework it occurs and whose automatism it interrupts, is a "miracle"—that is, something which could not be expected. If it is true that action and beginning are essentially the same, it follows that a capacity for performing miracles must likewise be within the range of human faculties. This sounds stranger than it actually is. It is in the very nature of every new beginning that it breaks into the world as an "infinite improbability," and yet it is precisely this infinitely

improbable which actually constitutes the very texture of everything we call real. (169)[70]

Leo Kelly, a character in Greeley's *Summer at the Lake*, enacts this kind of miracle when he insists that the truth of the past will make him and everyone involved in it, free. It is also how Herman Hugo Hoffmann connects authority and freedom in *The Priestly Sins*.

Arendt's view of political freedom, the priority of freedom and its relationship to authority, makes the concept of freedom central to her thinking. She seems to mean that it is as though the moment between past and future presents us with the potential to act to avoid the evils that define our own time. Arendt's notion of freedom as beginning informs that moment, according to Jerome Kohn.[71] Arendt writes, "The miracle that saves the world, the realm of human affairs, from its normal 'natural' ruin is [...] the birth of new men and the new beginning, the action they are capable of by virtue of being born" (*The Human Condition* in Kohn 127). Her idea of freedom is identical to this "realm of human affairs" and the very ability to act is what is at stake today. The destruction of freedom is the destruction of that which makes us human. This, too, is central to Greeley's characters.

Arendt's work on totalitarianism reveals its elements: anti-Semitism, nationalism, imperialism. What she discovered was that these diseases did not go away when their carriers were defeated, i.e., Hitler and Stalin, but that beneath them lay a nihilism: "the possibility and necessity of its will to annihilate every aspect of human freedom" and that this nihilism was "unlimited" (Kohn 118). Totalitarianism, the use of terror as a form of rule, depends on this annihilation of human

---

[70] Arendt goes on to write, "Our whole existence rests, after all on a chain of miracles, as it were—the coming into being of the earth, the development of organic life on it, the evolution of mankind out of the animal species. For from the viewpoint of the processes in the universe and in nature, and their statistically overwhelming probabilities, the coming into being of the earth out of cosmic processes, the formation of organic life out of inorganic processes, the evolution of man, finally, out of the processes of organic life are all "infinite improbabilities," they are "miracles" in everyday language" (169–170).

[71] See Kohn, Jerome. "Freedom: the priority of the political" in *The Cambridge Companion to Hannah Arendt*. Cambridge University Press: Cambridge, 2000, 113–114.

freedom. Human freedom depends on plurality, and plurality depends on "individuality," and individuality depends on the space that language creates and which actions define (cf.118). Freedom as action defines individuality. This claim is what makes the political paradoxical for Arendt: without the public space that politics creates and which speech protects—for our speech both unites us and distinguishes us each from the other—there is no individuality, and without individuality we are reduced to being instances of a mass. This paradox reveals that no individual can act alone or beyond community (123).

Thus, throughout her philosophical work, and especially in *The Human Condition*, Arendt distinguishes the realm of labor, which human beings share with all other animals, as the realm of necessity; the realm of work, in which men and women fabricate things and processes that enable them to escape the most rigorous requirements of the realm of labor and which initiate the possibility of art, as the realm of utility; and the realm of action, which belongs only to human beings, as the realm of freedom.

What makes us human, i.e., distinct from other animals, is our capacity for action. In addition to labor and to work, human beings initiate—they freely act. In acting, human beings create a human *world*, i.e., they organize what is necessary (labor) and what is useful (work) such that individuals can be free of these necessities. The human world, in which the individual as individual survives as person, depends on the presence of and the cooperation with others (see 243-244 of *The Human Condition* in Kohn 124). This is the essential social nature of human beings. Without each other, we are nobody. Without a stage (a public space), there are no actors. Without this "space of appearance and without trusting in action and speech as a mode of being together, neither the reality of one's self, of one's own identity, nor the reality of the surrounding world can be established beyond doubt" (*The Human Condition* 208 in Kohn 125).

Another scholar of Arendt's thought, George Kateb, describing the nature and advantages of political action,[72] suggests that the reality of

---

[72] See George Kateb. "Political Action: Its Nature and Advantage" in *The Cambridge Companion to Hannah Arendt*: 130–148.

political evil confronted by Arendt forced her into a lifelong analysis of it. Perhaps her consideration of the excellence of political life is the other side to this confrontation (Kateb 130). Like Niccolo Machiavelli, she labors to restore the ancient prestige politics once had (131).[73] Two questions emerge for Kateb: what is "the authentically political," and what advantages are unique to it (132)? Consideration of these entails inquiry into what appears to be political but is in reality inauthentic. Authentic politics is neither ruling nor using violence (132—133). Authentic politics is action in communion with others and its primary mode is speech.[74] Kateb writes, "The heart of Arendt's account of action in her writings is that authentic political action is speech—not necessarily formal speeches, but talk, exchanges of views—in the manner of persuasion and dissuasion. Political speech is deliberation or discussion as part of the process of deciding some issue pertaining to the public good" (133). Such deliberation involves the faculty of judgment.

For Arendt these deliberations and judgments make up the authentically political, according to Kateb, and their primary importance lies in their being preconditions for political action (133). Political action revealed as speech become memorable—a key element in Arendt's definition of political action—when men and women "think of something other than their interest" (134).[75] Thus, the proper content of politics is not economic policy nor social interests

---

[73] Kateb writes, "Her premise is that if the authentically political can be conceptualized properly, it will present itself as something so attractive, as well as so advantageous, that in the minds of her readers, and of others by a radiating influence, the dignity of politics will be on the way to being restored. The irony is that for Arendt the dignity of politics has nothing to do with using government as a weapon or instrument of social reform or even adaptation of social change" (131).

[74] "What, then, is Arendt's definition of politics? Scattered throughout her work is the idea that politics is action and that action is speech in public about public affairs" (132). See also *The Human Condition* 180.

[75] See also *The Human Condition* 215–216 and *On Revolution* 258–266.

but the precondition of political life itself.[76] It exists for its own sake (134) and is like any "beautiful thing" (134).[77] Authentic politics is most closely related to "natality," i.e., "the newness of every human being" (135).

To be authentically political is to possess courage, to seek public happiness, to value public freedom, and to praise excellence in all things for its own sake (136 and 137). But these virtues are not necessarily moral in character, nor is Arendt's notion of authentic politics necessarily moral.[78] The great deeds and the great words of authentic politics are not necessarily morally good, even as there are limits of a moral kind.[79] It seems as if the best we can expect is a possibility of morality co-existing with authentic politics.

---

[76] Kateb writes, "The content of authentic politics is therefore deliberation and dispute about what policies are needed to preserve and keep in good repair a political body, a form of government that has been designed to carry on its business by free deliberation, discussion, and dispute; or in an insurgent situation about the creation of a government that institutionalizes the spontaneous deliberation and discussion that are now trying to bring it into being (*The Human Condition* 8; "What is Freedom?" 153). Constitutional questions, questions concerning the spirit of the laws or the interpretation of the laws or (especially in modern times) changes in the political ground rules—all these are the stuff of authentic politics" (134).

[77] Kateb again, "That means in part that authentic politics cannot be contaminated by the necessary or the useful, but rather has an affinity to all beautiful things, to the realm of the aesthetic. Arendt characteristically accords as much dignity to great art as to authentic politics. Granted, the deeds of politics are not objective as works of art (including literary ones) are. Political speech can be worthy of memorialization, but as spoken it lives in the moment of its performance. At the same time, engaging in authentic politics is not like playing a game. Politics is deeply serious; it can be mortally serious, depending as it does on the actor's willingness to risk his life" (134).

[78] Kateb writes, "Arendt's views on morality in authentic politics have perplexed some of her readers. She seems to countenance indifference to morality, and even immorality. She contrasts what she calls "human behavior" and political action. Only the former is judgeable by "moral standards" (the quotation marks are hers) that take into account motives and intentions, and aims and consequences. But the only criterion of authentic politics, she says, is greatness, because it is the nature of action "to break through the commonly accepted and reach into the extraordinary" (*The Human Condition* 205).

[79] Kateb again, "Authentic politics cannot be great, however, if it is too cruel: the reason is that too much cruelty or wickedness of any kind tarnishes glory. Ruthless short cuts violate the spirit of the activity; they are inelegant. Hence we could say that Arendt, like [Niccolo] Machiavelli, tends to substitute aesthetics for morality as a restraint on political action. Nothing too awful can be great, but nothing great can be innocent" (139).

This is an important element in her theory of authentic politics especially when we realize, as Kateb suggests Arendt realized, the moral dangers involved in any politics committed to moral reform. Certainly, this was Machiavelli's animus to Savonarola as a false prophet. The greatest mistake the leaders of the French revolution made, according to Kenneth Clark, was to believe themselves virtuous.[80] Greeley makes this same point in his fiction when he criticizes the moral arrogance behind the social activism of the politics of the sixties. As an example, see *Virgin and Martyr*.

Moral revolutions always seem to produce more evils than they alleviate and usually end in inauthentic politics. This may tell us something about the limits of politics in Arendt's thought,[81] just as it

---

[80] See Clark 300. Kateb writes, "The charge that Arendt excludes morality from authentic politics is reinforced when we consider her analysis of the failure of the French Revolution. In a harrowing account, she attributes the destruction of incipient authentic politics—the face-to-face politics of municipalities, clubs, and other small political association—to the effort to solve the urgent question of starvation. The revolutionaries were overcome by keenly observed and intensely felt compassion for misery, the misery of hordes of people. The compassion transformed itself [...]into immitigable anger that brooked no opposition and established a despotism that was meant to be radically remedial. Arendt laments the demise of authentic politics at the hands of powerful moral passions and their derivative sentiments. Boundlessness enters the fragile political realm and ruins it. The necessities of sheer life overwhelm the experience of freedom. Thus, Arendt suggests that the great threat to authentic politics comes not from wickedness or even from apathy, but from the profoundly misguided attempt to act from intense moral distress" (140).

[81] Here I disagree with Kateb's conclusions. He writes, "It is very hard to avoid the sense that Arendt has produced a utopian picture of authentic politics, a picture cut off too drastically from the very reality of those infrequent episodes of actual authentic politics" (141). "Her goal is not so much to show that authentic politics has actually been guided by her own view as to infer a moral view that authentic politics can be said to engender on its own and from its very nature. Her moral precepts are 'the only ones that are not applied to action from the outside, from some supposedly higher faculty or from experience outside action's own reach' (*The Human Condition* 246 in Kateb). Just as every game has its own set of rules that creates, shapes, and confines the play, so authentic politics must have its own morality to inhibit and even inspire action. The only alternative to a morality that is internal to authentic politics is, oddly, not the doctrine of the lesser and necessary wrong, but the 'moral' standards inherent in the Platonic notion of rule." These standards turn out to be based on "a relationship established between me and myself, so that the right and wrong of relationships, with others are determined by attitudes toward oneself" (*The Human Condition* 237–238). But, Arendt insists, "proper self-rule is no model for interaction with others" (141). My reasoning is above.

does about the same limits in Machiavelli's thought. Catholic political thought leaves to prudence the character of morality in political action. Perhaps this is something of what Kateb means. It may be, too, that just as in Catholic political thought, for Arendt politics has its limits. This would certainly be implied in Arendt's insistence that the great evil of totalitarianism inheres in its control of all areas and aspects of human life. Her distinction between the private and the public realms also seems to imply a limit to authentic politics. Moreover, that Arendt sees moral principles, like philosophy itself, as excluding freedom might argue that morality is pre-political or post-political, but not properly the stuff of authentic politics.[82] This leaves the political realm open to evil men and women, but it also leaves it open to just and moral persons.

Of its advantages, authentic politics constitutes a space where equality allows us to disclose ourselves to others. Equality allows us to determine our full identity (Kateb 143). Equality confers freedom, another advantage. Equality and freedom make life meaningful because they allow us to be who and what we are, both positively and negatively. This allowance presents us with choices. We may chose to live as other animals bound by necessity and dependent on the technologies we produce to supply what we need for survival, and we shall live in the despair of our natural progression toward death that is part of our biological existence. Alternatively, we may affirm our stature as human beings capable of a destiny different from other animals. This affirmation is done through action, a capacity for grandeur, as Kateb writes. In this sense, we might see equality as the presumption we make about others as capable of our friendship and freedom as the risk we take in order to make beginnings. (See Greeley's discussion of trust in *The Great Mysteries* and mine on Greeley's idea of original sin above, 72*ff.*)

In summary, we might say that Arendt maintains the following about political authority and freedom: first is that authority is neither power nor violence; the second is that freedom is not an individual attribute but the ability of persons to act in concert with others;

---

[82] We should also remember that Arendt died while in the middle of her considerations on judgment and may have hoped to solve this problem in her thought through aesthetic considerations.

third is that authority is the ground of freedom in that through a tradition authority serves to organize our relationships according to the overarching good of being able to initiate our own lives.

From this, it is not false to infer that for Christians, God is authority, pure and simple, and as such, is the precondition for living as the People of God, i.e., the church properly construed. This inference, moreover, is supported by the Catholic tradition's conception of authority and its limits. In Catholic thought, all authority is properly a function of service. From at least the thirteenth century, the idea of office has supported the ideal that those who hold positions of authority are accountable to those they serve. Thus, limit has always been understood as part of offices of authority. Because authority exists to serve in some way, limits to its use and jurisdiction have accompanied the kindred idea of office. Aquinas, for example, argues that authority may be defective in two ways, either through its origin or in its command. The first is constitutional and involves how those who will weild and be subject to authority create and sustain it, i.e., how it is constituted. Authority's political constitution serves as foundational to it in Arendt's sense, and only those who meet such formal requirements and who follow the established procedures for appointment to and holding of office may be said to possess real authority. To cheat or to defraud in obtaining a position of authority makes that authority null and void.

More to the point, however, is the second limit to authority, the terms of its command or use. In this sense, authority may be defective in two ways: either its commands may be beyond the authority's competence or jurisdiction, or its commands may be immoral. In the first case, obedience to an incompetent command would depend on the prudential judgment of that authority's subject. In matters of morality, however, the subject is not free to decide whether to obey. An immoral command does not have the authority of law and must be resisted or disobeyed. In fact, the subjects to such commands are morally compelled to rebel against such commands because they lack the power of the law, which must be reasonable, given by competent authority for the common good and be part of the public domain.[83]

---

[83] See Aquinas On Law, *ST* I II, q. 90–96.

The third insight of Arendt, that authority is the ground of freedom and that through a tradition, it serves to organize our relationships according to the overarching good of being able to initiate our own lives, is especially important to understanding Greeley's characters. It is our ability to act as unique and individual beings—our natality according to Arendt—that makes us free. In the Catholic tradition, we are not free to be anything we will; rather, our freedom is determined both by our nature and by our humanity. Precisely because we are subject to nature and its necessities, human freedom in the Catholic sense stands as one of the greatest of God's gifts. In Greeley, this freedom is often a disguise for grace. The virtuosity of a character's actions, as in the case of Father Herman Hoffman,[84] stands as a sign of God's great love for human beings. To repeat Arendt,

> [m]an does not possess freedom so much as he, or better his coming into the world, is equated with the appearance of freedom in the universe; man is free because he is a beginning and was so created after the universe had already come into existence *[Initium] ut esset, creatus est homo, ante quem nemo fuit.* In the birth of each man, this initial beginning is reaffirmed, because in each instance something new comes into an already existing world, which will continue to exist after each individual's death [...]. God created man in order to introduce into the world the faculty of beginning: freedom. ("What is Freedom?"167.)

In the character of Father Hoffman (Greeley's *The Priestly Sins*) we meet someone who constitutes his freedom by acting in a world already defined by authority as well as by its abuse, and in doing so, he begins something new: he becomes the agent of God's grace in the world, and hence, his own perfection. How so?

One meaning of "politics" involves the connotation that the political is a realm of deceit and the manipulation of means to ends, of power and of violence. This connation in the history of political philosophy usually implicates the great (and the first) modern political theorist, Niccolo Machiavelli (1469–1527). Often considered the

---

[84] See *The Priestly Sins.*

founder of *modern* political science, his name has become synonymous with the politics of violence and the ethical school of "Might makes Right." This "Machiavellian" notion finds its development in European political history in the radical ideological divide between Protestant northern countries and those Mediterranean countries that remained Catholic. (Shakespeare is one of the first to identify Machiavelli with the devil—Old Nick.) Machiavellianism would bring with it the idea that political life, indeed, the existence of the nation-state itself, justifies any means to that end. This "Realist" theory of international political relationships—relationships that are ultimately mediated by the institution and law of war—survived into the twentieth century and explains much of the violence of the last four hundred years.

The argument is quite simple—and therefore suspect—and is at least as old as Plato, whose character, Thrasymachus, disturbs the dialogue of Socrates in the *Republic* by his ill-mannered, indeed violent, interjection that what is right is what the strongest says is right, i.e., the rule of the strongest interest.[85] Because the city is essential to the well-being of its citizens, given their social natures and natural dependence on each other for the necessities of life, those who rule the city are given permission to break the basic rules of ethical behavior, e.g., "Thou shalt not kill," in the pursuance of the security and well being of the collective good or interest. The philosophical problem behind this "Realism" involves the difficulty of determining what the collective good or interest may be. In Catholic social teaching, collective good is known as the common good, or that set of conditions and resources without which there can be no individual or social good. This tradition maintains that the good remains the good no matter at what level it may be realized. Thus, in Catholic thought, Machiavellian realism involves the ruler in activities that endanger, not only his or her soul, but also the very well-being of society. There are, in other words, moral limits to what is allowed in war and in diplomacy.

It is therefore ironic, if not merely scandalous, that the Catholic Church, through its official hierarchy, is often identified with deceit and manipulation of means to an end, especially in the administration

---

[85] See Book I of *The Republic*.

of temporal matters. This is especially so in light of the reforms of the Second Vatican Council (1962–1965).[86] This irony is often evident in Greeley's fiction because it is so much a part of the modern world and of the Catholic imagination. His novels rely heavily upon it, and tell us something about the Catholic understanding of the political. Many are set in the context of the institutional church and deal specifically with how Machiavellian realism destroys or obliterates the true understanding of political authority.

Although much of Greeley's fiction can be said to raise the issue of Machiavellian politics, two novels, *The Priestly Sins* and *Summer at the Lake*, will illustrate how Greeley handles Machiavellian politics from the standpoint of the Catholic ideas of authority and freedom. Both novels elaborate the negative meaning of politics that is part of its reality and demonstrate how individuals subject to authority are able to be free in the sense Arendt uses the term.

The Priestly Sins (2004) is specifically about the pedophilia scandal in the American Catholic Church.[87] It centers on the sinful and criminal actions of the church's administrative hierarchy in their attempts to keep sexual abuse of children and adolescents secret. "Down Town" or the administrative center of a fictive Midwestern diocese is rendered in all its ignominy. The archbishop is both ambitious for higher ecclesiastical dignities and not all too bright. He has surrounded himself with men with second-rate minds and hired laymen and laywomen who tell him what he wants to hear. As in the real world—God's world according to Greeley—this fictional world reveals the real sinfulness of child abuse. Horrible as it is, it remains the result of imbalanced minds and immature personal development, while the real crime is the hierarchy's attempt to cover up these actions and reassign its culprits to positions involving the care of children.

The hardball tactics used by the legal arm of the diocese embody Machiavellian "Realism": not believing the victims, treating them as enemies of the church, secrecy in keeping records from those who have

---

[86] See "*Lumen Gentium*" and "*Gaudium et Spes*" in *The Documents of Vatican II*. Ed. Walter M. Abbott, SJ, New York: Guild Press, 1966.

[87] See "Ratzinger and New York Times Agree on Sex Abuse By Priests," Greeley Web page.

a right to see them, denial of the problem, failure to treat the abusing priests, the claim to false loyalty in the Presbyterate, and isolation of witnesses from the community of the church. All would make the devil proud.

Enter Father Herman Hugo Hoffman, a young priest who witnesses the rape of a boy by a fellow curate, Father Lyons, and reports it to his bishop. Hoffman is sedated and imprisoned for six months in a mental hospital as a delusional homosexual. The real culprit is reassigned to parish work, while Hoffman is vilified for casting dispersions on the name of a good priest who has been cleared of all charges. Although the institutional church escapes from its real responsibilities to the People of God for much of the narrative, what we learn about Hoffman sets the ultimate choice between Machiavellianism and the politics of the common good.

Greeley takes us into the life and development of an almost perfect human being. His power as a priest—and interestingly, his flaw—in large part, derives from his hard work at perfection. Again, we see in Greeley's characters the fundamental question of grace and its role in the world: "Grace does not force nature, but it perfects it." Thus, the imperfect is portrayed as the place where men and women find themselves, but they are not left to their own devices, although they are required to use those devices as grace affords them. Rather, their effort over the long haul is rewarded.

Herman is the son of the German-Russian immigrants who farmed the Midwest and made it abundant. He falls in love with his childhood friend, Kathleen, but gives up family life and sexual intimacy in order to serve, not the institutional church, but the People of God. He chooses the life of the celibate priesthood because he has experienced the love of his family and friends. He wants to help others come to that love. Thus, the play on his name, Herman, which derives from Hermes, the messenger of the divine. Herman Hoffman is God's messenger in this novel. As in all good comedies, the protagonist defeats Machiavellian distortion of the world by his honesty and good nature. We learn in the novel that Hoffman has visited and anointed the abuser priest in his death agony; no other priests were forthcoming. Herman forgives his enemy and in doing so triumphs.

As in all of Greeley's fiction, however, he does not achieve triumph by himself. He is aided by his one-time lover, now his supportive friend, Kathleen, and her husband, as well as his parish. Another childhood friend is his lawyer, and through his help, the legal system sustains Hoffman in giving witness to the truth. In the end, "Downtown" is brought before the bar and held accountable for its great crimes. In his After Note, Greeley holds those who knew of the abuse and did nothing, or who knowing, reassigned the abusers to be responsible for the real crime. The pedophiles were sick, the bishops, criminal.

This notion of politics as manipulation is countered by the development of the novel's main character. In *The Priestly Sins*, we can see the relation of Arendtian authority to freedom. The book begins in the form of a court transcript, a device used to convey the facts of the case. By using it, Greeley seems to be making a distinction that will have great import for the novel. The distinction is between *fact* and *truth*: facts are those things which cannot be denied; the truth involves how those facts are given meaning. Arendt makes a distinction like this in her essay "Truth and Politics."[88] The truth results from the interpretation of facts according to agreed upon criteria of evidence and interpretation. Precisely because facts are open to interpretation by those who experience them and discuss that experience with others, we need to find a consensus that will grant some credence to what facts may mean. Thus, the standards of scientific inquiry, the function of logic in philosophy, the importance of the definition of terms in all disciplines of knowledge, and the rules of evidence in law are the results of such consensus. Facts produce truth but not just in any way we wish. For understanding the idea of authority as freedom, this distinction is important.

Authority in the political sense depends on its purpose. In Catholic thought, this purpose is the common good. Thus, authority is limited in what it may and may not do in terms of that good. In Catholic thought, the human person is possessed of a special dignity that inheres in the person's ability (potentially or actually) to develop, and perhaps, to prosper. As the image of God in time and history, each person is to be afforded the freedom of his or her development and the

---

[88] *Between Past and Future*. New York: Penguin Books. Reissue 1993.

respect for his or her innermost conscience. The personal development of freedom properly construed is the special characteristic authority serves.

Thus, in the Catholic tradition, all authority is limited and proscribed by this understanding of the human person. It is for this reason that Catholic thought agrees with Arendt's notion that authority transcends power. Hence, we know in reading *The Priestly Sins* that "Downtown" and its hardball tactics in the matter of pedophilia by priests involves both a corruption of authority, and perhaps, grave sins by the bishop and his creatures. This corruption of reality and its sinfulness is what Catholic men and women are called to resist and to remedy. It involves both the work of social justice and the action of all persons of integrity. In this novel, that work and integrity belong primarily to Father Hoffman. Hoffman has been accused of lying about pedophilic rape, and we learn that he spends six months in a mental institution because of this accusation. He, however, knows the facts and the criteria for interpreting them.

The denial of Hoffman's truth by his society is informative. He first tells his pastor (15), who denies the possibility. But Hoffman has developed the habit of keeping a diary, of writing down his observations on a daily basis. His journal keeps the facts independent of his memory and safe from the drug therapy his doctors use to convince him that he is a repressed homosexual who has either made up his charge or projected it upon Father Lyons. The second denial of the facts comes from the father of the victim, Dr. Sweeny (15). Rather than believe that a priest had violated his son, he denies the facts, which Hoffman brings to him in his attempt to help the victim. Then, when Hoffman goes to the police, he is told that it is none of their business because the diocese is a powerful, social, and economic resource in the region. It is a matter of church, not state (16). Finally, he tries to go to the archbishop with his story, but the bureaucratic structure of the diocese is that of a corporation with all its faults and yes-men. The archbishop is protected from all bad news by his staff (17), and Hoffman's brother priests have warned him that he will receive no satisfaction. They, too, know that the culprit, Father Leonard Lyon, has a well-deserved reputation for pedophilia, but they advise Hoffman to do nothing that might bring scandal to the priesthood (16–17). The result of this corrupt structure of authority—with the addition of a good deal of incompetence—is the charge that Hoffman, himself, is a homosexual who has fantasized the whole matter.

This series of denials signifies the corruption of authority and the use of power to perpetuate violence against an innocent priest, who is only doing what he has been taught to do by the very authority itself. If, as Lord Acton proclaimed, power corrupts and absolute power corrupts absolutely, is there any redemption to be had in this world? Greeley's characters seem to think there is, and this redemption is found in the freedom that Hoffman has developed in himself through the communities in which he lives. Remarkably, this freedom constitutes the valid authority that has been his teacher all his life. We see this in how he responds to the situations in which he finds himself. After Hoffman is committed, he figures out that he ought not to take the narcotics prescribed for him, and he spends his time in the institution doing the work of a priest. He uses his knowledge of canon law to obtain an independent confessor, and he employs his knowledge of German to use his one phone call per week to ask help from his father in securing the safety of his journal. After his release, he uses the chance to pursue graduate studies (22) as a means of investigating his Volga Dutch immigrant history—knowledge, like his German language, which he will use to serve the People of God.

Herman Hugo Hoffman is the corrective of abusive authority; it has no moral effect upon him, and he knows how to defend himself from it. This is his freedom. We see how it has been developed out of the family and the community from which he comes. His development as a person has also been his development in freedom. We see this in the story of his life. As a freshman at a large state university, he is placed in a freshman dorm where he is forced to defend himself from violence (90) by going to the university president, who finds him an advisor who will work with him and who calls the police to clean out his dorm (91*ff*.). What had been an accepted norm of bad behavior is changed by his initiative. Later, he defends himself and his girlfriend from assault by using the martial arts he has studied (109). Hoffman is emblematic of the Catholic tradition's understanding that knowledge is found everywhere and in all places, and that its good use (wisdom) is the result of wedding faith to reason. This he has achieved through his hardworking farming family and from his Catholic grade school education. Hugo's ability to initiate action, his power to act in the world as he finds it, has been expected of him by his parents, his teachers, and his friends all his life. The source of this tradition, its authority, has been his Catholic faith with its rules of right action, and the family that has embodied it, tempered it, and passed it on to him. They have loved him enough to put into his hand the tools that would serve him well.

Later, when Hoffman successfully negotiates a parish from an unfriendly chancery, again because he knows canon law and what it requires of duly constituted authority, he comes to establish true authority with his people by knowing that its purpose is to serve them and the truth of the Gospel. We see this earlier in the novel in his advice to his friend Father Horvath, who assumes the pastorate of Hoffman's hometown parish immediately held by a very old and very beloved priest. To avert the parish's resentment as their new pastor, Hoffman advises Horvath to keep Monsignor O'Brien on as mentor and advisor (119). In this way, the old man's sense of himself is preserved, the new pastor has lost nothing but gained a friend, and the members of the parish have been consulted and heard. This act of charity strengthens rather than diminishes true authority.

The source of tradition for Catholics is the reality of God, especially the presence of the Holy Spirit. This is demonstrated in the love between Herman and Kathleen (83) and in the happy death of Hoffman's great grandfather (125), as well as in the guiding presence of the long dead Irene(125), his great grandmother. It is she who accompanies Hoffman throughout the novel and becomes visible to him at important moments in his life. These symbols of God— physical love, dying, and rising, and the Communion of Saints—are emblematic of the idea that the root of Catholic authority is love itself, another name for God. In doing the good because we want to do so, Catholics believe that we participate in the real presence of God in this world. This willing the good for the other person explains how

Hoffman can minister to the dying Lyons, the very person who is the cause of his plight, annoyance, and suffering (219).

Corruption of authority inheres in doing the right things for the wrong reasons: ambition, priestly solidarity, protecting the public image of the church at all costs. Corrupt authority is also anti-intellectual (147); it portrays truth telling as disloyalty to the faith (279); it is disrespectful and contemptuous of its subjects: and it presumes an asymmetrical relationship of power, which usually disguises incompetence (150). Doctor Straus, the psychologist for the diocese, and Monsignor Meaghan, the Vicar General, exemplify the mediocrity and mendacity that lie behind titles of authority (150*ff.*). Hoffman's freedom is his defense against corrupt authority. In his intellectual scope, he studies a dimension of history that seems to have no direct connection to his priestly life. In doing so he discovers the great tradition of the compatibility of faith and reason. And he learns that "Criticize [...] means merely to search for understanding" (167). Thus he uses what he learns to oppose the anti-intellectual reactionaries who serve as toadies to "Downtown." He does this because he has been raised differently (175). This difference is manifest in Hoffman restoring the position of the laity in the parish of Saint Cunegunda. As Pastor, Hoffman consults with the parish on all major decisions, giving them the authority to run the Catholic school (244), and later, in securing his medical records against the day of false witness (287). In all, Father Hoffman understands that human life is also a common life, "Humans, it turns out, are at their best when they're taking care of one another" (276). This is Aristotle baptized by the Holy Spirit.

Leo Kelly[89] also embodies Arendt's understanding of freedom. Although we might not see the "political" directly in Greeley's novels, it is implied in both their action and their characters. *Summer at the Lake* is the story of two generations from four families bound to each other by a terrible accident. As in real life, circumstance and seemingly random events affect the course of their lives. The cause of a car accident in 1948 is finally resolved in 1978. The Keenans, the Murrays, the Niclolas, and the Clares are all rich, well connected and established in their social rank and class. The Devlins are parvenus working to

---

[89] *Summer at the Lake.* New York: Tom Doherty Associates, 1997.

break into the upper middle class; Leo Kelly is the interloper, whose friendship with Patrick (Packy) Keenan gives him access to the rich and well-to-do.

The novel is layered with symbols, e.g., the fatal and fateful accident takes place on the vigil of the Feast of the Assumption of Mary—the ancient Irish Mary's Day in Harvest Time, when the fullness of the year comes due. Leo Kelly and Jane Devlin witness the car crash that kills James and Eileen Murray; Kelly is able to pull Phillip Clare free from the fire. Through the venality of the local police and the political connections of the Clares and the Murrays, there is no investigation into the deaths or into the large sum of money found in the wreckage. Kelly is suspected of being the driver, and it is this suspicion that drives him from this vacation society and from Chicago until his return in 1978. His untangling of the events of 1948 involves the revision of "history," and as a consequence, a reconstitution of the human relationships among the characters. As Leo says to Jane, by reinterpreting the past they may "'[e]liminate the evil that has imprisoned both of us for so long. Then the past will be transparent and we can take an honest look at the future'" (240). [90]

The action begins on Pentecost-Memorial Day, 1978. Pentecost is the feast celebrating the third of the great mysteries of the Catholic faith—the coming of the Holy Spirit. It follows the Feast of the Incarnation, when God became man in the person of Jesus, and the Resurrection, when Jesus Christ rose from the dead. Pentecost is called the birthday of the church—the mystery of Christ among the People of God. The Holy Spirit is the love between the Father and the Son, a love that vivifies this world and calls all creation to its completion in God.

Thus, the action of Leo Kelly in his determination to discover the truth about the accident that controlled his life and that of his love, Jane Devlin, might be seen as a form of the Holy Spirit's working in time and place through the agency of human beings. In this sense, Kelly's actions are works of freedom, as understood in Catholic theology. As such they are God's work, but work that depends on the

---

[90] See Arendt's notion of history and memory as political acts in "The Concept of History: Ancient and Modern" in *Between Past and Future*.

cooperation of human beings. This cooperation, in turn, depends on human agency as informed by knowledge as wisdom; it uses knowledge for good. Wisdom—one of the seven gifts of the Holy Spirit—helps Leo free Jane and himself so they might love each other fully. Leo says, "'I knew then I had to solve the mysteries if I was ever to have a happy life'" (37). The analogy, then, of Leo's actions to the initiation Arendt sees as the essence of freedom is not far fetched. Leo must figure out the truth about what happened on the fateful night of August14–15, 1948, if he is fully and truly to be free to disclose himself to Jane and have Jane disclose herself to him. Upon this freedom, their very world depends.

Jane, whose brothers will be central in the resolution of the puzzle, is the daughter of a mother driven by social ambition and drink. The mother's near pathological drive for social acceptance marks all of her children. Jane's psychological wholeness depends on resolving the violent treatment she receives at her mother's hand. Her freedom depends on a psychological insight—that her mother was the cause of her own self-hatred—an insight analogous to the tongues of fire that descend upon the Apostles at Pentecost and by which the Apostles were able to be understood by all.

The next division of the action is St. John's Night, midsummer's eve: quoting Theseus from Shakespeare, when "'Lovers and madmen have such seething brains, such shaping fantasies that apprehend more than cool reason ever comprehends. The lunatic, the lover, and the poet are of imagination all compact'" (65). Here Greeley, through his characters, reveals Catholicism's debt to ancient Celtic culture, a debt that too often is repressed by the Puritanical branch of the hierarchy. The ancient celebration of the body as good, and sex as life giving, stands in stark contrast to the repression of human sexuality so common in pre-Vatican Council Catholicism. Maggie Ward Keenan says, "'It [Catholicism] doesn't mind human love, Leo, as you very well know. And if passion leads people too far, it was always understood down in the villages and the parishes that the passion itself is not wrong. Rather it hints at how God feels'" (65). The analogy of human passion to God's love, especially the love of the Holy Spirit, is central to Greeley's fiction and imagination. Leo's summer of 1978 will be a "Catholic" summer.

Leo's equality, what makes him able to be political in Arendt's sense, is accomplished through his education and his service in the Korean War. Both are Catholic in Greeley's characterization. A poor kid from the West Side Irish neighborhood, Leo Kelly has become a highly regarded political scientist, who has served in several distinguished universities. His return to Chicago is as provost to "the" University of Chicago. His education and scholarship are what has earned him this position; his Irish political good sense and savvy enable him to succeed. As a marine and prisoner of war in Korea, he earned his patriotic warrant and is able to understand the changes that for immigrants have constituted a revolution in the American polity. His prisoner-of-war status also serves the Greeley theme of resurrection.

The question becomes, does Kelly's social-economic success mean that he is "political" in Arendt's meaning? Again, he should be understood as a fictional character. But it is not too far to suggest that the analogy still holds. This seems so when we discover Leo's take on the "revolutionary politics" of the late 1960s. Under the rubric of the Fourth of July,[91] we learn of Dickie Devlin's offer of a million dollars to establish a chair in honor of his family. Leo muses:

> I reflected on the half century of my life. When I was in grammar school, we all seemed poor, except the Devlins and the Claros. Then came the war and the years afterward and we spent our time catching up on all the things we missed in the Depression. When Kennedy was inaugurated, we were convinced that the American "know-how," which had won the war, would solve all the social problems in the country and the war. Then came Vietnam, the assassinations, the riots, anti-war demonstrations, Cambodia, Kent State, protest marches, Woodstock, the Days of Rage, Watergate, the Nixon pardon, the Arab oil embargo. All the institutions of our society seemed to disintegrate. There was no credibility left.

---

[91] It is also important to know that Arendt's theory of freedom's relation to "the political" is worked out in part in her book *On Revolution*. See Kateb.

> One of my younger colleagues, a self-proclaimed radical with a thousand dollar stereo system in his apartment told me five years ago that the revolution had already occurred and that in a few years the whole of American society would fall into the hands of his generation to remake. (142)

Leo, like many of Greeley's protagonists, is not convinced. The common sense of the American electorate in rejecting the utopia of the radicals along with the disgrace of radical politics in its agents' selfish pursuit of material goods, conspired to move the country to the right (142).

For Arendt being "political" is about not being centered on either economic or social matters. The "political," for Arendt, means the space in which equals contend with equals about the prerequisites essential to this public space. "Politics is about politics," Kateb writes, and if this is not to be a meaningless tautology, we need to be able to locate political action within the affairs of men and women. Leo Kelly seems to do this. He is a character who has overcome his social and economic subordination, and as the rest of the action will demonstrate, he enacts a radical initiative by recalling the past to it, i.e., he memorializes the past so that it might serve as the foundation for the future. Leo does for his world what the founders of great states did for their own.

The idea of initiation, of beginning, depends upon the virtue of hope. In Catholic thought, hope is the virtue that connects faith to love. Together these three virtues are called theological, i.e., they are evidence of divine life in us. They come as pure gifts, and cannot be earned because they represent God's very life—at least from the human vantage point. Hope comes to the relationship between Jane and Leo, which had been blighted by his reported death while in Korea. In the novel, Jane marries Phillip Clare, a good-for-nothing rich boy, to achieve social status for her family and because her hope—Leo—is apparently dead. The question then is, whether or not this "event," false though it proves to be, can be overcome. Can hope, once lost, be regained? Are there second chances? Is there resurrection?

Because Leo has achieved equality with his former friends and because he has rejected the subordination to which their social status once delegated him, Leo is able to act. He has left the realm of necessity, of family, and of social status. He fabricated a world where these necessities could be satisfied, and thus, proves capable for freedom. His action is embodied in his resolution of the mystery surrounding the fatal accident. Kelly discovers that someone wanted him dead. The car involved in the accident had been "his car" for that summer. Its brakes had been tampered with. He also discovers that his orders to Korea had been falsified. Originally, he was ordered to embassy duty in Paris because of his facility in languages. Another officer received his orders and he, his. He was supposed to die in the accident, and when he did not, he was sent to Korea in a unit where the survival rate of junior officers was very low.

The novel's denouement takes place under the rubric of Labor Day, at the celebration of the bequest of the million dollar academic chair in Irish Studies honoring the eldest Devlin son. Throughout this novel, the three Devlin brothers have been toughs in the service of their corrupt father and mother. Their wealth has disguised this fact. The chair in Irish Studies seems to be yet another bid for social respectability. What Leo Kelly discovers is the violence of the Devlin's mother. It is she who paid to have the breaks cut on Leo's car. The accident happened only because Phillip Clare had taken it, along with James and Eileen Murray, to deliver illegal money for his father. The accident had happened to the wrong people. It was also Ita Devlin who bribed the military personnel to switch the orders, sending Leo to Korea and a PWO camp. It was her violent attempt to keep her daughter, Jane, from marrying the wrong class of man—Leo Kelly— that caused the blight of hope and the disruption of the lives of so many. This initiation into the truth of the past is the action that frees not only Leo and Jane, but also the Devlin brothers. A new family is constituted, not by the realm of necessity—in which the Devlins were not able to escape their subordination to their mother—but through political action. The truth sets them free. The novel ends under the rubric for the Feast of St. Michael and all Archangels. This feast is celebrated at the end of September and was for centuries the feast that began the fall semester in academic life. Under the auspices of the angels, the characters begin their new lives.

Chapter 5: The O'Malley Saga: From Necessity to Freedom

If Herman Hoffman and Leo Kelly illustrate the kind of freedom that can be found in action, the authority that makes freedom possible is also found in the development of Greeley's characters, the O'Malleys. If politics is more than the machinations of interests, the pursuit of power, or the use of violence, then it must involve the intelligent and reasonable organization of the social world. That certainly is the meaning of the term for Arendt. Her key ideas in this regard are natality and freedom. Both involve the person in relationships of authority and power, but these relationships take place among equals and any subordination in them involves the reasoned choice of free individuals. We see both natality and politics throughout the development of these Greeley characters, especially Charles Cronin O'Malley. A *Midwinter's Tale*[92] is the story of his childhood told from his point of view as a nineteen-year-old sergeant in the US Army of Occupation. He has been assigned to Constabulary Headquarters in Bamberg, Germany, immediately after the defeat of Hitler.

In his refection on his youth, we learn that he is a child of the Depression, and thus, a driven young man who, he thinks, has his life planned. He shall earn his GI Bill benefits, attend Notre Dame, become an accountant, and marry a mild and well-ordered wife. He will always fear the return of the Great Depression. Four women have

[92] *A Midwinter's Tale*. New York: Tom Doherty Associates Book, 1998.

formed him: his mother, April; his older sister, Jane; his younger sister, Peg, and her best friend, Rosemarie Clancy. His younger brother, Michael, as well as his father, John the Evangelist O'Malley, architect and artist, have also been important in making him who he has become. O'Malley[93] maintains that of all the "Crazy O'Malleys," his father is the sanest of the lot.

That family has been primary in his young life is important to these characters inasmuch as family derives from what Arendt has determined the realm of the necessary, what is essential to human development and to human society. Without family, there is neither society, nor can there be any politics. From the point of view of Catholic social theory, this necessity sometimes becomes a surrogate model of organization that is applied improperly to free men and women. When the model is adapted for use as a means of organizing social reality, patriarchy results. Pushed too far, the family becomes the model of fascist social life wherein the person is subordinated in value and dignity to the group. Many of Greeley's characters are either victims of or culprits in this model, especially in the administrative dimension of the Catholic Church. In one sense, the novel is about Chucky's coming of age, something about which he is still unsure at the end of the story. His time in Bamberg is his time of personally coming to terms with who he is to be. It is not without some irony that O'Malley learns to be a human being while working as a Catholic in the defeated Nazi state. That his personal story takes place in a time between war and peace is also significant.

It might be argued that political authority involves the mediation of persuasion and force: that is to say, reasonable men and women are often initially persuaded to follow the rules that give good order to their lives and by which they take part in the common good. Over time, this persuasion forms a tradition in the sense of a political foundation, and subsequent generations obey, because of the tradition of obedience rather than as a reasoned outcome following from some principle. When they forget why the rules make sense and work to their benefit, an arm of society must then force them to comply.

---

[93] O'Malley will always be "Chucky" in his family, even after he has become its patriarch. Thus, does Greeley assure us that we can never escape, for good or ill, the effects of our families.

Thus, the police function in any society is a function that depends ultimately on a common agreement or covenant among the members. This social contract has been the stuff of modern political theory precisely because it is the element in public life that distinguishes free individuals from those who are mere factotums in a social complex. Without an understanding of the reason for legitimate force in society, the common good fails.

Thus, Charles' role as a member of the US Constabulary, not a police force so much as a mechanism of order in the defeated German state, becomes important. Likewise, the fact that the state of war is over and the peace yet to be organized places the characters in a primary state of nature: a hypothetical place in which persons are in the process of developing or losing political order. How Charles Cronin O'Malley behaves in this situation determines both his place in the order of equal men and women as well as the quality of the political state that is in the process of coming into being. In this sense, Greeley has written a novel about the perennial problems of political foundation.

Arendt uses the idea of natality as the notion through which she introduces and explains equality and freedom in the affairs of women and men. For Arendt, natality stands for the complex of talents and the uniqueness of each human being initiated by the very act of being born. Quoting St. Augustine she writes, "That a beginning be made, man was created." For her, natality is the instrumentality by which the cycle of nature and of biological life are invested with newness. Because each person is potentially unique and has never yet existed in time, each person brings to our common life the possibility of the future, i.e., the possibility of something becoming new.

Late adolescence is perhaps the time in a human development when natality is most obvious and most tentative. Charles Cronin O'Malley is at that place in his life. We learn that he is ambiguous about his own talents and his own "history." The record would indicate that he is both a great athlete—having made the winning touchdown in his senior school year, a win that would catapult Fenwick High School to a championship—and he is also a hero having saved his prom date from drowning. In both cases, Charles sees it differently. The touchdown resulted from a freak catch and from being slammed across the goal line by the opposition's tackle, and his date was very likely in shallow water and she would have saved herself. His ambiguity about his talents, about his natality, continues into his military career. He sees himself not so much as intelligent, as glibly Irish, he certainly does not possess the skills of a consummate politician, except perhaps as an Irishman from the Westside of Chicago. It is pure happenstance that he saves a German teenager from rape, and his skills as a sergeant are hardly merited, at least according to his own self-image.

We see, however, that there is more to this Irish young man than meets the eye. We see this in how he addresses three situations: the first involves his handling of the threat posed by Nazi guerrillas, the second in how he saves his German girlfriend and her family, and the third in his successful plan to capture military black marketers. In each of these situations he is called to intelligent, reasoned, and prudent action for which there are no models and no precedents. In each, he renders necessity into freedom by virtue of his political good sense.

General Radford Meade, his commander, sees him as a person of good judgment and flexibility. Together they see the absurdity of the existence of a Nazi resistance group known in the American press as Werewolves. Yet, for reasons of publicity, they must pretend to take the claim seriously, and O'Malley is ordered to take a *Life* photographer on a mission into the Bohemian Forest to find them. As all men in the state of nature, Chucky is in terror of the potential violence that might await him: "If the werewolves were good soldiers, they would hear us coming. If they had as many weapons as they were supposed to have, they could cut us down in about three seconds" (141). Preparing for the worst in spite of his reservations about the existence of this enemy, he makes an examination of conscience in anticipation of a perfect Act of Contrition. He really might be killed. At this point in the narrative, he thinks of his sometimes antagonist and often time friend, Rosemarie Clancy, and of his need for her forgiveness. He intends to write, "'Maybe I've grown up a little here in Germany, not much but perhaps just a little. So I want to apologize to you for all the times I was rude or sarcastic to you. Maybe you know that it was a silly little game that both of us played, but I was the one that kept the game going, and I'm sorry. I hope we can be friends when I return'" (141).

This allusion to friendship, i.e., to love, is central to the political. The purpose of political life is friendship, as Aristotle and Aquinas teach us, and friendship takes place only among equal and unique beings. That Charles O'Malley is debating whether to love Rosemarie goes to the heart of his coming to consciousness as a human being. That he has been loved by his family and Rosemarie, a foster child of that family, is what makes him capable of this deliberation. What makes love essential to the human endeavor is not just that it is the basis of good families, but at the intellectual level, it involves willing the good for others. This is the core of the common good, and thus, the core of political life. That God's covenant with his people has been the inspiration for the social covenant among men and women is no happenstance. Nor is Greeley's continual use of marital and sexual love as metaphors for God mere happenstance. They are, perhaps, dimensions of the same reality.

Upon O'Malley's conviction that he must be forgiven and he must forgive before he can love, the action ends in comedy. His unit breaks into the cottage putatively holding the Werewolves only to find an old German couple, their children and grandchildren huddling to keep warm. They do find a cellar containing old and useless Nazi arms that had been deposited years earlier, but alas, no Nazi guerrillas. *Life* gets its photos and story, and the comedy continues.

Charles has experienced something about his mature self: he requires love in order to love, and he understands that all love begins in forgiveness. This epiphany comes slowly, however. With his friend Jack Berman, a Jewish psychologist who believes that all Germans are guilty of the Holocaust, he argues philosophy in the darkroom they share. Yet the guilt of Germans is not of the same degree, and arguing about it, never obliterates their humanity. This becomes more than an academic point when O'Malley finds the German girl, Trudi, being raped by soldiers who are in the business of selling medicine on the black market. She has come forth in order to save her sister, who is dying of pneumonia. The Russians, who would summarily shoot the father and rape the women to death, seek her family as Nazi war criminals. Such is the legitimate law of war.

What is O'Malley's moral duty? He has been ordered to help the FBI find and arrest the Wolves. He learns that Trudi's father is dead and was never an important person in the Party. In fact, he and his family probably became Nazis because they had no other alternatives. Certainly, the children could hardly be guilty of war crimes deserving such a sentence. O'Malley does what any morally developed person would do; he shelters the women, procures false papers for them, and drives them to the French sector where they have friends and where they will be safe. He does this in contradiction of his office of authority as a member of the police and secreted from his commanding general.

O'Malley's crime is that he falls in love with Trudi, and together they engage in the sexual delights of young lovers. Though he is never sure after the fact that Trudi loved him for who he was, rather than for what he could do for her and her family, he understands that he is both right and wrong in the same moment. Certainly, his fornication is morally objectionable according to the rules of the Catholic Church, just as his delivering the women from harm goes against the rules he is sworn to uphold. Yet his love for her and her family must count for something: "'In truth I loved her then and love her now, but my love, like all love, is problematic and equivocal'" (169). Whether or not his love is ambiguous, O'Malley is still required to act, and he does—covertly and in secret. In fact, he gives up Trudi because he wants to be sure she and her family are safe. Thus, he deliberately does not learn the names of their friends in the French sector.

These first two examples of the political, one farce and one against the order of violence set the tone for O'Malley's third adventure. His success in arresting those involved in the black market indicates, perhaps, the most explicit example of the political defined as the intelligent and reasoned organization of social life. O'Malley knows that his arrest of black marketers will not, once and for all, solve the problem of social disorder. Another black market will take the place of the one arrested. The political world is never safe from the effects of the evil human beings are capable of. In this sense, the evil of the Holocaust hovers always in the background of this story. The point is, however, that human beings are capable of sustaining a human world only if they rely on their intelligence, reason, and prudence to create it. That a beginning be made, men and women are created.

In the end, the black marketers are arrested due to the intelligence and planning of Charles O'Malley and his band of soldiers. Many of those arrested receive just sentences; some of the leaders do not. Life goes on. But finally, it is the good we do that counts in the world of men and women, and this good is done not by heroes, though often some men and women are heroic, but because ordinary people put their minds and hearts at the service of others, and working with others, achieve the common good. The German state is reconstituted within a year of O'Malley's service in the US Constabulary. It is a divided state and will be so for nearly a half century. But democracy does emerge, just as the child O'Malley emerged into an adult. Not perfect, but real and powerful.

Younger Than Springtime (1999) provides a further way of seeing what Arendt means by the realm of necessity. It is part of the saga of the O'Malley family and involves a story within a story. The outer tale is about Charles Cronin O'Malley, who has just returned from military service in the US occupation army in Europe. The narrative tells the story of his pursuit of Rosemarie Helen Clancy, his sister's best friend and the honorary member of the O'Malley clan. She is a drunk and a victim of the abuse of her drunken mother and avaricious father. Chucky's story is about his unjust expulsion from Notre Dame and the trials and tribulations of a young man coming to maturity in 1949. Within the story, the tale of his father's courtship of his mother is revealed. It is the story of the family O'Malley, what Arendt might find as the quintessential place of necessity. Without family, there can be no individuals, and without families, there can be no public realm, no place for the political. The inner story is about John the Evangelist O'Malley's maturation and his development as a person appropriately on the verge of his public life during the 1920s.

His reading of his father's memoir convinces Charles that although the terms of the tale may be different, the same theme runs throughout his own life. Each person becomes a person through the relationships that are established in and by the private realm, most importantly the family, and then, secondarily, through the modes of education that are provided by the society of families. Rosemarie's life, for example, is blighted by her father and mother, both of whom are part of John O'Malley's earlier tale. Locating this story at the center of the story of the son's coming of age, Greeley helps us see the depth and necessity of the private realm. Without it, we are nothing. Because of it, we are directed and informed in ways we often cannot control. And it is only because we have endured, and to an extent mastered, the necessary that we can begin to be free. Thus, in this story and throughout the O'Malley saga, the Depression has a role almost of a character. The fear that it might return haunts Charles, and even though he is intellectually convinced that the Great Depression will not occur again, he lives his life as though it might.

Three scenes help illustrate the private realm of necessity. The first involves the description of the ambience of Notre Dame in the late 1940s. Almost all Catholic institutions of higher learning of the time might fit this description. Involved is what Greeley's characters know as "locker room Catholicism" (45).

> The assumptions of the system were simple enough: if you gathered together a group of young men, kept them under strict disciplinary supervision, constrained them to sit through sixteen required philosophy and theology courses, pressured them to receive Communion every day and go to confession often ("hit the rail," "hit the Box"), minimized as best you could their contacts with young women, warned them against the dangers of reading forbidden books, and imposed on them strict habits of study and memorization, then you would produce devout Catholic laymen who would be successful in the world of business and profession. (44)[94]

This kind of education violated everything in the intellectual tradition of Catholicism. It might be argued that this kind of education was the result of a confusion of categories. While early education is part of the realm of the private (part of what families are expected to provide their offspring) and is based on discipline and authority, higher education involves the introduction of the young

---

[94] That the education for women followed the same system seems also to be the case, even though without a "manly" component.

mind into the public world, into the realm of freedom. Such education involves authority but ought not to make authority its end. Rather, authority leads the mind to freedom such that this mind becomes its own authority, especially in matters of conscience. Father Pius (most inappropriately named) framed Charles O'Malley and summarily expelled him from Notre Dame. This blessing in disguise occurs on his twenty-first birthday, the day of his majority. To keep adults locked in the realm of necessity is to keep them perpetually childish.

The second scene that helps illuminate what Arendt means by the realm of necessity is the hilarious portrayal of Monsignor David Redmond's dinner party. At this ordeal, Charles is first introduced to his date's pretentious family in the context of the even more pretentious household of a member of the Catholic hierarchy—"the son of a hod carrier from Bridgeport who didn't have a pot to piss in" (99). During the evening, the party listens to a summary by an English Jesuit[95] of *The Mind and Heart of Love*. Charles reflects during this conversation,

> "One form of love, I could not determine which, was called 'agape' the other 'eros.'
>
> "Love, it seemed to me then, was obviously love; debate about such ethereal questions was ridiculous. If you had ever been in love, you know what love is, right?
>
> "Wrong, Chucky Ducky, dead wrong, but you were too young then to be expected to know any better.
>
> "Perhaps also too much 'in love.'"

The Jesuit replies to his host's question about which form of love is the higher of the two:

> "'I don't know that I have a solution [...] it may be one of those ultimately insoluble puzzles, a maze from which there is no escape, if you take my meaning. Still, I wonder sometimes whether one might not come moderately close to an answer—

---

[95] See footnote 193.

know the direction of it, you see—if one says that love, of God or of another human, is not so much the desire to possess the other totally as the desire to be possessed totally by the other [...].'" (106)

This distinction will be what Charles, and later Rosemarie, will discover throughout the reminder of their lives. It is in learning this that Greeley's characters come to understand the way from necessity to freedom. Those characters who do not learn it are destined to egotistical, and sometimes, violent lives of unhappiness.

Another scene illustrating the private realm of necessity involves Charles self-reflection during his "melancholy ride" home on his twenty-first birthday, having just been expelled from Notre Dame:

"I was shattered, ashamed, guilty. I had done nothing wrong, I had been framed, yet still I felt guilty.

"How can you be ashamed when you're innocent?

"Authority, I would later learn, has the power to make you ashamed when it decides, however unjustly, that you are guilty.

"If enough people tell you that you are a criminal, then you begin to think and act like a criminal." (140)

The narration continues into the future where Charles learns that Father Pius had framed many young men. Then there is this. "Religious orders ought not to permit themselves to be suckered into the position where they are trying to regulate the lives of laity the way they regulate the lives of their own members. They can't do it effectively. Moreover, they turn people away from the church when they try" (140). At the heart of this *obiter dictum* is the realization that adults ought not to be imprisoned in the realm of the family. In fact, the process of maturation must involve the freeing of persons from the discipline and authorizations of the family. This is why the family ought not to be the model of either the polity or the church. The authority of the father and the mother ought not to be the model of either.

The novel ends with the O'Malley family's discontent during the Christmas of 1949: Charles has not become Rosemarie's lover; his sister Peg has not achieved the love of her Italian-American suitor; their married sister, Jane, and her husband, Ted, have not liberated themselves from his family of the "Doctor." Yet, the power of Christmas is upon them. The final scene intuits the solution of how the transition from the realm of necessity to the realm of freedom might be accomplished; how "one might not come moderately close to an answer—know the direction of it, you see—if one says that love, of God or of another human, is not so much the desire to possess the other totally as the desire to be possessed totally by the other [...]" (106).

Charles reestablishes "diplomatic relations with God" (342) through his imagination. "In previous conversations," Charles reveals, "the Deity had not bothered to reply to me. On that particular night, He seemed ready to engage in a long conversation, though it was merely my imagination making up the responses. Maybe" (342).

"It's nice to see you back."

"You noticed?"

"Oh yes ... I notice everything, as you well know."

"I know."

"Rosie was right, you know."

[....]

"What was Rosie right about?" (342)

[The validity of Rosie's advice about Charles' talent as a photographer is revealed here and might mean that he would be unhappy as the accountant he intends to become.]

"Was she right about breaking up?"

"It's about time you got to that."

"Well, was she?"

"Nope."

"Nope?"

"Nope ... I want Rosie."

"Should God want a woman?"

"God wants everyone. I need help usually. It's your help I need with Rosie. We both love her desperately, I more than you."

"Ah."

"She's the best hint of what I'm like you'll ever encounter. You must not let her get away."

[....]

"Why do you sound so much like me?"

"Because I have to work with your imagination."

"You also sound a lot like Rosie."

"That because she's always in your imagination."

Then He signed off. (343–344)

The notion that it is through the imagination that we escape the solipsism of consciousness hits Charles as a revelation. Imagination is the faculty by which the human person relates to others and to the world. Greeley's characters suggest that these relationships are also relationships with the wholly other, i.e., with God. The world of the necessary, the world of matter and time, gives way through imagination to the world of freedom. This means that freedom involves the person in something like the divine.

By 2004, the O'Malley family has had adventures in six fictional tales: *A Midwinter's Tale, Younger Than Springtime, A Christmas Wedding, September Song, Second Spring,* and *The Golden Years.* From the adventures of John Evangelist and April O'Malley and their children, especially Charles Cronin and Rosemarie O'Malley, we might continue to trace in their lives the process of augmentation that lies at the heart of Arendt's ideas of authority and freedom. Could it be that contrary to her erudite claim that this ancient notion is no more,[96] we might have rediscovered it in the fictional world of the "O'Malleys?" Perhaps it is better to say, using Greeley's distinction, that in God's world the idea has been lost as Arendt contends, but in the fictional world of the Catholic novel, it lives on with much to teach us.

A Christmas Wedding is the story of the marriage of Chucky and Rosemarie O'Malley, covering the period from 1950 to 1961. It involves the mystery of the deaths of Rosemarie Clancy's mother and father, as well as the reconstitution of Rosemarie—the grace of this novel—in light of her brutalization by her alcoholic mother and her rape by her vicious father. Both of these are unknown to the O'Malleys at the time of the wedding, but they serve as the obstacles to its success. In short, Rosemarie serves both as the muse for Charles' art and the foundation of his family. As such, she is the embodiment of the motherly role essential to the family. As such, too, she is subordinate to the father as the children are subordinate to the parents, just as Charles and Rosemarie are to their grandparents, benignly in the O'Malley's case, and maliciously in the case of the Clancy's. Embodied in the family model of the O'Malleys is the realm of the household. The question of the novel is whether that realm can be transcended such that the principals become truly equal, and thus, capable of truly loving each other.

Like all of Greeley's novels, this one is about second chances; about the renewal of love and the power such renewal can have in the lives of the characters. Those who learn how to renew their love become well-integrated personalities, while those who reject this renewal or who, for some extraneous reason, are kept from such renewal, remain underdeveloped and unhappy. Such are the roles of Rosemarie's parents, Jim and Clarice Clancy. Jim was an underdeveloped child, spoiled by his mother and his wealth. His rape of his daughter is a terrible misperceived attempt to love her, indicating how far removed from the world of human beings he really is. His wife's beauty and his own wealth do not save her from her alcoholism and this, in turn, has

---

[96] See "What is Authority?" in *Between Past and Future: Eight Exercises in Political Thought.* New York: Penguin Books, 1968: 91–141.

driven their daughter, Rosemarie, into the O'Malley family—a family that she realized at age ten was different from her own and which she saw as her means to redemption.

The book begins in the subzero cold—a Dantean reference to the absence of love—with doubts by both Charles and Rosemarie about their suitability for marriage. Complicating this cold doubt is the social and religious history of the 1950s: a time when the Korean War would disillusion the generation that had defeated Germany and Japan, when prosperity would be disrupted and dreams deferred, and a time in the Catholic Church when the faint voices of renewal were condemned.[97] This history makes the development of these characters all the more extraordinary. That both Charles and Rosemarie are educated outside of Catholic colleges suggests the obstacles overcome by those who want to remain sons and daughters of the church. Both are educated at the University of Chicago, and both have vocations that their own worlds would not expect or predict. He thinks he should be an accountant—in fact, his fear of the Depression will persist until his fiftieth year—and she knows that to be a mother is not to abandon the talents she possesses in considerable number. If together they are not to become stereotypes of the conforming 1950s,[98] they must, on their own, constitute a new beginning—a foundation—for a new kind of life. Together they must learn how to be actors on their own merits and through the grace of each other's love.

As in most of his fiction, Greeley begins with an assumption of economic sufficiency. His characters almost always have enough money and resources to live in relative economic freedom.[99] Charles is able to earn sufficient money at the Board of Trade, even in spite of the machinations of his father-in-law, and Rosemarie has inherited wealth to be able to support the new family. This reversal of roles, again, is evidence that this novel is about more than material success. Educated and successful from the beginning, the more important question may

---

[97] See 38 and 21.

[98] A stereotype that these characters themselves recognize as false even as they are subject to the same forces that constitute this stereotype.

[99] In fact, if Greeley's characters have an economic ideology, it is that of Chicago Democrats.

be asked: what makes us happy? Both Charles and Rosemarie are successful, he as father and artist, she as mother and helpmate.

Here is the rub of the novel. Again, in Arendt's terms, we might see it as the question of human freedom. Can we be more than our families make of us and more than the material necessities which compel life? In Catholic thought, the same question involves whether or not there is more to the human calling than this world would suggest. We know, for example, from the reviews of Charles' photography that he does not see his wife or women as objects. As a reviewer writes, he is "a photographer of sacraments" (187). "His work is a hymn to life, but it is a hymn that ends with a question mark. No one can deny the beauty of his Rosemarie or his April, but he knows, even more surely than we who walk hypnotized through the gallery, that such beauty is transient. It will not last forever" (187).

The novel's central question is what will last forever? The answer is embedded in the physical love that, for Greeley, is always the sign of God's love for his creation. Sexual love becomes the metaphor of God's action in our lives. As such, we might say that the physical love between Rosemarie and Charles represents the authority of God's action in time: God's foundation in time. As that love waxes and wanes in their marriage, their coming to their own completion likewise fluctuates. This comes to issue at the center of the novel when Rosemarie discovers that Charles has an illegitimate son from a liaison prior to their marriage and before he, himself, knew who he was.[100] This discovery plunges Rosemarie into a drunken stupor, not unlike the behavior that had occurred throughout their courtship and marriage, and it is the reason Charles sets a stark choice before her. Either she gets psychological help for her drinking, and more problematically, for her abuse by her father, or he will divorce her and take the children.

This is, for Rosemarie, a moment of foundation; either she establishes herself as herself, or she loses all. It is through her actions, a new beginning for herself and her family, that she constitutes herself as a full-fledged person in her own right. What she must learn is that

---

[100] See *A Midwinter's Tale.*

not only have the O'Malleys been her lifeboat and salvation, but also she has been grace to each of the relationships that make up that family and its immediate circle of friends. As Charles puts it at the end of the novel, "I wouldn't be a photographer if she had not edged me into it. Both my sisters' marriages would have fallen apart if she hadn't intervened, rather dramatically in fact. My brother wouldn't be a priest, much less the effective priest he is, if Rosemarie had not installed herself as his confidante. My parents would not be as happy as they are today if Rosemarie hadn't mandated that they be happy. God only knows how much she has helped our nieces and nephews and our friends" (333).

Rosemarie's authority as a person, however, is not the work of the lone individual, even as she must individually come to terms with her past. Rather, her authority as a person is the result of grace that is always reciprocal. It was Charles' sister, Peg, her best friend from first grade, who saved her from her mother's insane wrath—Peg pushed Mrs. Clancy to her death in an attempt to wrestle an iron poker from her as she used it to beat Rosemarie. Charles discovered the cruel joke her father hoped to play after his death—Mr. Clancy had left two letters accusing Rosemarie of murdering her mother—and destroyed the false evidence. Thus, her being grace for the O'Malleys involves their being grace to her. And she cannot come to know this, just as Charles cannot come to know it, until she becomes her own person. It might be said that the authority that gives rise to the space of freedom, where each person becomes who he or she is supposed to be, is located in the initial act of deciding either to remain in the realm of the household—a subordinate by definition—or, though a personal act of foundation, establishing oneself as an actor within the confines of human community.

September Song (2001) is a story about the marriage of Charles Cronin O'Malley and Rosemarie Clancy O'Malley and the period between 1965 and 1974, years of great trauma in the political system of the United States. As Greeley revives these years through the characters of this novel, he confronts us with politics at its most pragmatic, at the level of the prudential as St. Thomas Aquinas and his mentor, Aristotle, would have it. In it we are asked to recall, or perhaps learn for the first time, the events of 1965—Martin Luther King's march from Selma to Montgomery, demanding voting rights for the disenfranchised—and 1968, that tumultuous year of Johnson's lies about Vietnam and the political damage such lies did to the Democratic Party; the murders of Martin Luther King and Robert Kennedy and the disillusionment these effected; the disastrous papal encyclical, *Humanae Vitae*, and its condemnation of artificial birth control, and the failed revolution of the young at the Democratic Party's 1968 convention. Chucky, Rosemarie and their five children take us through these events and the consequent failure of politics in the early 1970s.

On one level, Chucky and Rosemarie live their married lives, raise their children, and directly participate in the major political events of their adulthood. Returning from a term as Ambassador to West Germany where he had served as a staff sergeant after World War II, O'Malley refuses to support LBJ in his policy of expanding the US role in Vietnam. The O'Malleys marched with Martin Luther King at Selma, and together they served on the commission established during the Second Vatican Council to study and make recommendations on changes in the recent teachings of the church on birth control. They witnessed the debacle in Chicago when the Democratic Party self-destructed on live TV, both being beaten by out-of-control police. They lose two children to the war: their oldest daughter, April Rosemary, who severs herself from her family while at Harvard, by retreating into the world of drugs, sex, and revolutionary violence, and their oldest son, Kevin, listed as killed in Vietnam, while in fact, being only wounded. And Charles O'Malley is, himself, lost in Vietnam while on a photographic tour. Each of these events places these characters directly into the historical events themselves. Thus, they are witnesses to and judges of what occurred, and hence, called upon to make practical political judgments about how to behave and to act in these events.

Within this action, Rosemarie goes through a process of self-discovery, helped by therapy and the grounding of her Catholic religion. She experiences the claims and culture of the early days of feminism as she comes to discover her own self worth—she is a reformed alcoholic and the daughter of an abusive, alcoholic mother whose violent death saved Rosemarie's life. Throughout this process, Chucky is the loving and understanding friend.

The role of Charles O'Malley is interesting in light of Rosemarie's self-discovery and the larger historical events within which it takes place. Having gone to Vietnam to assess the reality of the war—the US press having sided with the ideologues for peace and the US government continuing its dishonest policy of disengagement at the cost of thousands of American lives and millions of Vietnamese—he finds himself bobbing in the North China Sea, nearly murdered by North Vietnamese fishermen but saved by the marines, who happen to be working covertly in the area. In his communication home, he notes that although the US military and the government found him missing, he knew where he was all the time (166). These words epitomize the sense of many individuals who lived through these trying times. Certainly in the novel, the O'Malleys stand for the citizens who, to the best of their ability, informed themselves about the political situations in which they found themselves—although, in this novel, the politicalization of the press (253) (through the character of Walter Cronkite) makes that very difficult—and who acted pragmatically to effect as much good as they could given these circumstances. They know where they are at all times.

This plays itself out in O'Malley's relationship to Rosemarie. This relationship is itself an emblem of how God acts in this world, and thus, tells us something about who God is. O'Malley's relationship with Rosemarie is that of a friend, a passionate friend, indeed, but nonetheless, truly a friend. O'Malley somehow knows that to love Rosemarie is to allow her to be herself in her best sense. He is, in this way, subordinate to Rosemarie, always understanding her moods and manner, always supporting her search of self-discovery, always advising, but never insisting on his point of view—even when he is proven to be right. He lets Rosemarie be who she is. Doing so sometimes means that his considerable intellect must not always shine, that his knowledge and view of the world—he is after all a world renowned photographer—might have to be obstructed because he knows that these cannot be for Rosemarie what they are from him. This role is like the role of God as friend, as one who waits, often silently, for the beloved to come to him. This is the God who respects human freedom, especially regarding the human person's pilgrimage to herself.

Chucky's subordinate role gives Rosemarie the support she needs to enact the freedom required of her own self-discovery. Maggie Ward, her psychiatrist, helps her to this self-discovery, but only because Rosemarie is both loved and free to love in return. Rosemarie has been writing all through her marriage, but she would never reveal her stories to anyone. When she does reveal them to her therapist, we discover that her modesty is really not modesty at all. Modesty is the virtue that recognizes things for what they are. It is immodest for a gifted artist to decline the gratitude and praise of her audience; it is immodest to use the body as a thing, just as it is immodest for married people to be ashamed of their love for each other. Maggie Ward helps Rosemarie admit that her reticence in revealing her talent is really her attempt to hang on to her own lack of self-worth, a disguised form of dishonesty. When she realizes this, she begins to see who she is and what she can accomplish as herself.

Chucky's subordination and Rosemarie's self-discovery may seem unrelated to the pragmatic politics implied by the events of this novel, but they are not. Rather, without the subordinating role of support that others play in our lives, there is no real politics, because without this essentially human quality, there can be no political freedom. And authentic politics, especially the low-down, everyday practical politics whereby men and women determine how they will enact their solidarity and subsidiarity, cannot be had without free individuals who chose for the right reasons to give way to others.

We witness this integral freedom in the apparently contradictory ways the O'Malleys respond to Martin Luther King: once at Selma and once in Chicago's ethnic neighborhoods. In Alabama, non-violent protest and civil disobedience proved to be successful because as an instrumental form of political action, it had a clearly defined purpose. The point of non-violent civil disobedience was to protest an immoral law by refusing to obey it and taking the consequences for that disobedience. Non-violent protest against the denial of the vote to black Americans had as its purpose the demonstration of the unfairness of such a legal denial. It was in the political forum an appeal to the conscience of the American polity. Its effectiveness depended on the violent response of white racists. It involved the courage of putting one's body on the line to make a moral point such that a majority of people might see that moral point as deserving legal protection. Thus, the O'Malleys happily marched from Selma to Montgomery in support of what would become the Voting Rights Act of 1965.

When Martin Luther King brought his campaign against racial discrimination to the North, where its conditions were not legal but social in character, the effect of non-violent political protest proved to be very different. The racism of the North called for a different political response. By marching in Chicago's ethnic neighborhoods rather than in its rich suburbs where "white flight" and economic advantage came together to protect racism from public view, King alienated the very political base of his movement. By treating Richard Daley's City Hall as the enemy, while ignoring the political process of the City of Chicago, King was forced to abandon Chicago achieving nothing but bad feelings from those who previously had supported him.

This same failure to appreciate pragmatic politics explains, in part, how the war in Vietnam continued long after it ought to have ended. The claim here is essentially that the peace movement, by ignoring the electoral political realities of 1968, helped elect Richard Nixon, whose administration and policies continued the war until 1975. The Tet offensive of early 1968 had proved a Pyrrhic victory for the North Vietnamese. O'Malley's presence in the US embassy during the Tet assault on it convinces him that he had been correct all along in his analysis of the situation: the war was un-winnable not because US military might proved lacking, but because the strategy of the US military ignored the realities of guerrilla warfare. The defeat of South Vietnam was not due to American failure in war, but because South Vietnam lacked the political will to survive, even with the backing of the military power of the United States. Those who fought and died did not do so without valor, honor, and courage; they were betrayed by a policy that found that valor, honor, and courage expendable.

In electing Richard Nixon and not Hubert Humphrey, who would have ended the war because it was un-winnable and was a war that the American people saw as such, the peace movement enabled and abetted the backlash upon which Nixon's election and policies depended. History would vindicate those who saw those policies as self-destructive. It is within this context that the O'Malleys confront the peace movement and their daughter's participation in it. When April Rosemary asks why her parents do not support the peace movement, her father responds,

> "There are different ways of opposing the war, darling. You have to persuade the American people that we should withdraw. We're not there yet. A lot of our people still think that we're doing God's will by resisting godless Communism. They need convincing. I'm afraid that protest marches by those they consider spoiled rich kids will delay their change of mind." (197)

He goes on to point out the contradiction of the peace movement's claim to the moral right to force peace on the country. Such moral blindness would move April Rosemary to cut herself off from her family for a time. Greeley writes in his Author's Note,

> What happened to all the young radicals of those years? Most of the young people of that era were not all that radical. They couldn't sell out because they had never really bought in. For some of those who did buy in, sex, drugs, and rock and roll were the outer limits of their radicalism—combined with an occasional protest march. Most of them returned to the upper-middle-class fold from which they came. Some would say they "sold out" and permitted themselves to feel fashionably guilty about that while they enjoy the good life with some superficial and self-indulgent modifications of life style [...]. Others repudiated their radical experimentation and became at least as conservative as their parents. Others abandoned more or less the trappings of radicalism but continued their intense political commitment [...] . (371–372)

We can see the problem of practical politics in the confrontation of the peace movement with the Chicago police during the Democratic Convention of 1968. Again, the O'Malleys are *there*, not merely indirect observers, but with their cameras—the recorder of facts. We find through Rosemarie O'Malley why things went so terribly wrong. Both the Yippies and the press came for the purpose of making trouble in Chicago (252).

> Whence, the paradigm? I think some of them, like that faker Walter Cronkite, really hated the city, for no other reason than, like the man said about Mount Everest, it was there. In the WASP (and Jewish) minds Irish Catholic politicians like the Mayor were an inherently evil people as were the 'white ethnic hard hats' who voted for him. They were the people who the media blamed for the war. Hence, they must be punished. So the media made common cause with the crazies and the kids and in favor of the disruption of the convention
>
> [...].
>
> They ignored the fact that the Mayor was antiwar as were the "white ethnics" whose sons were fighting it. Such facts never bothered people like Cronkite when they made up their minds. (252–253)

The O'Malleys, therefore, remained committed to pragmatic politics and were beaten by cops run wild.

Their two oldest children will take two different roads in their attempts to live politically in this world. April Rosemary will go to Harvard, fall under the influence of one of the many charlatan academics of the time and drop out, cutting herself off from her family, which she now views as the cause of the suffering and death in Vietnam. They are the enemy in the simplified quasi-Marxism of the time inasmuch as they enjoy the benefits of their hard work and enterprise. Her brother Kevin drops out of college too, but to serve as an officer in Vietnam. Two forms of political action, one a failure the other a success.

The novel ends, as all Greeley novels do, in resurrection. Kevin is listed as killed in action, only to be discovered wounded and alive. He has lost a foot in an action that saved his men from destruction. Kevin's version, however, is less dignified. Finding himself caught in a firefight because his commanding officer was using his authority to make a name for himself (347), Kevin leads his men in a rear guard action, running "away quicker and slicker than anyone else" (348). The daughter returns in September, bringing with her a Harvard educated Boston doctor who plans to be her husband. Shorn of her college past, she comes home as though she as been gone only a short while. She has returned to her roots, the implication being that the passion for politics that drove her to her folly has been amended to be more practical in the future.

At the level of the family, we witness through Greeley's characters the machinations of church politics in its conclaves of 1978, the year of the three popes. *Second Spring: A Love Story*[101] continues through the history of the second half of the twentieth century. In this novel, the fire of political activity and the fire of love both diminish. O'Malley's midlife crisis is ameliorated through the loyalty and the love of his wife, Rosemarie. Although this novel is not about the papal elections of 1978, they serve as part of the novel's structure. As such, these elections afford viewpoints of committed Catholics on how their church is governed, and give another angle of vision on politics. The O'Malley eyes, Chucky's and Rosmarie's, are embodied in a photographical enterprise dependent on Chucky's talent for catching his subjects "at their best" and a literary enterprise found in Rosemarie's ability to observe and to record the way things are. Together they observe the politics of papal government.

The election of John Paul I, we are informed, was an attempt to moderate the liberal and the conservative forces in the Curia—the bureaucratic center of the Vatican state—which had been spawned by the historical confrontation between them during the Second Vatican Council (1962–65). This Council, the highest expression of church authority, was an attempt to open the church to the twentieth century, to read the signs of the times so as to bring the truth of the faith into effective action in the world. In its most simplistic form, the Council pitted Tridentine ideologues, who believed the church to be changeless, against those who sought to bring the theology of the church into dialogue with the modern world. The death of John

---

[101] See *A Midwinter's Tale, Younger Than Springtime, A Christmas Wedding, and September Song.*

XXIII and the elevation of Paul VI mark that divide. Paul VI would anguish over how to put the reforms of the Council into effect, while more conservative forces warned him that papal authority was at stake if these reforms were effected. Nineteen sixty-eight was the year of the papal birth control encyclical, which disregarded the theological and scientific advice made by the papal commission on birth control, and this ecyclical decreed, in the face of contrary evidence, that every act of sexual intercourse must be open to life if it were not to be sinful.

The birth control encyclical caused a firestorm which is still damaging the magisterium of the hierarchy on the matter of sexual ethics. It may be argued that the wisdom of the church's teaching on sexual ethics has been buried beneath the rubble caused by this encyclical.[102] It also may be argued that the damage done by this encyclical—the laity simply ignored and continues to ignore the hierarchy on the matter—was done for the wrong reason. The advice given to Paul VI was that his teaching authority, and thus, the prestige of the papacy, was at stake. To admit that the teaching of the church on birth control might develop and change according to the best knowledge of human and sacred sciences was, he was told, to threaten the constant teaching of the Truth. In affirming his authority to define the matter, although he removed the line that said the teaching was infallible, Paul VI reduced that authority to ridicule. His means were not appropriate to his end, no matter how noble that end might have been. And the encyclical in its ignorance of the reasons to change and its contempt for the commission invoked to inform the pope on the matter, smacked of authoritarianism, which, in Catholic teaching, is always contrary to true authority.

In taking the name "John Paul," the man elected to the Sea of Peter attempted to bring the liberal and conservative forces together. This was not to be. Albino Luciani was the compromise that did not live. Elected in August of 1978, he died in late September. The circumstances of his death are clouded by the evasions and lies of the papal household such that the charge he was murdered may seem

---

[102] See *Humanae Vitae* and its background in Robert McClory, *Turning Point: The Inside Story of the Papal Birth Control Commission*. New York: Crossroad Publishing, 1995.

credible. Again, to avoid controversy, here about the matter of how the health of John Paul I was cared for, Vatican officials lied and tired to cover up. Only the truth suffered; most probably, he died as a result of medical incompetence (166).

John Paul II, Karol Wojtyla of Poland, the fifty-eight year old pope-elect, would rule for over twenty years, and his reign would mark the church for weal and for woe. The novel fictionally illustrates the talk and the politics that may have led to his election. (See 186*ff.*) Through it, we see the venality of men who should know better and a process of politics that is less than edifying. Yet, the family O'Malley is not to be the victim of such political machinations. Although they have no way to change the politics of papal elections and must deal with the world as we have made it, they are not without their own means of saving themselves from the effect of Machiavellian politics.

As a successful photographer, O'Malley is asked to exhibit at the Chicago Art Institute. Controversy about this exhibition and its later, contracted venue in New York, will demonstrate that Chicago politics can outdo the devil. Early in the narrative, Chucky receives the following note,

> O'Malley,
>
> I am writing to you to inform you that I shall come to Chicago in November to learn your tricks with the camera. I propose to devote my life to honest photography, especially photography which tells the truth about patriarchal discrimination against women, the young, nonwhites, the gays, and lesbians. I believe you have a serious moral obligation to share your secrets with me as I can present an alternative to your racist, sexist, ageist, homophobic vision of the human species. In studying with you, I will engage in honest dialogue about the meaning of photography as art. I will not become a wage slave or an assistant to you as that would reveal false consciousness. However, I expect to be paid a wage commensurate with my talent and experience.
>
> Ms. Diana Robbins

Recall that the 1970s were a time of "consciousness raising" and produced as the effect of the late 1960s radicalization of politics, the politics of violence. As a sane human being, O'Malley disregards the note as some aberration of such politics. We do not hear of Robbins again until her review of O'Malley's photography at the Chicago Art Institute. In that review, she maligns O'Malley as a fraud and his work as "vomit," mentioning five portraits as being in the same room. One of these is especially repugnant to the radical feminist, that of his wife, which Robbins calls "a quest for sexual titillation ..." (283). The review is notable for its moral rectitude and its social relevance. According to it, no moral, self-understanding person with any humanity could possibly appreciate O'Malley's "fuzzy eye of a box camera." Such is the rhetoric of the self-righteous. In fact, this review sounds very much like the output of the Vatican News Office, though from a very different political stance.

Again, the law comes into play. Using his lawyers, O'Malley threatens to sue for defamation, while quietly keeping his analysis of Robbins' syntax to himself. When the venue in New York reneges on his contract for the show, O'Malley reveals that the review could not have been written by someone who had, in fact, come to Chicago and seen it. The five portraits mentioned as being in the same room, were, in fact, not in the same room. When confronted with this reality, the publisher and Ms. Robbins argue that one need not see a show to know that it is morally and socially objectionable. In fact, a group of feminists of this mind has promised to boycott any New York venue for the show. Not only are the publisher and Robbins required to retract and apologize for their false statements, the publicity for the show comes as free. This difference, however, makes the case. Where Robbins employed the lie, and the Vatican the venality of the men seeking high office, to fail, the O'Malleys used the truth and the sagacity of their wits to succeed.

The idea of authority as foundation is likewise evident in the sixth chronicle of the O'Malley family. It is the story of the changes in the family as its members move into and out of their role as *Patres*. The deaths of the patriarch, John Evangelist O'Malley, and his wife,

April Mae Cronin, move Charles and Rosemarie into a new position of authority. This change is important to this installment of the story both in terms of the chronicles of the family and in terms of the sacramentality of its symbolism about a second death. John Evangelist O'Malley had "died" of influenza in 1918 while he was in service. He had been delivered from another death—this one most surely as a middle-aged soldier in action during the early days of World War II in the Pacific—by the initiative of his teenage son, Charles. These "deaths" stand emblematically for physical dying as prelude to the resurrection, which the family O'Malley celebrates for their parents and grandparents. After his first death, we learn, John O'Malley worried about nothing (59). Surely, this is the attitude of one who truly believes in the Resurrection of Jesus Christ.

Not only do Charles and Rosemarie—it would seem untoward now to refer to the paterfamilias as "Chucky"—have to contend with the responsibilities of burying their dead, which means dealing with their psychologically disturbed sister, Jane, they must also solve the riddle of the disappearance of Joe Raftery's wife and daughter.

That Charles is now the authority in the family and community of the O'Malleys is, from the beginning, ironic because he considers his authority as assumed only. He never believes his own publicists: neither his reputation because of his performance in his senior year during a close game of football, nor his heroism in the military constabulary, nor his courage in Vietnam. Yet the irony is especially rich because he possesses real authority, not because of what he believes did or did not happen in that game, nor when he was in the army, nor during his service to the nation as ambassador; rather he possesses it because of what he *can* do. He has the authority of the author—one who knows what to write—not the authority of an audience—those who merely perceive.

This genealogy of authority is reveled in the homily Father John Raven gives at the first funeral. In it he points out,

> all the instances of resurrection in our lives—the baby must die to become an infant, the child must die to be reborn in high school, the teenager must die to rise as a young adult,

the young adult must die to become a spouse, and the spouse must rise to become a parent. Life and death are patterns of life. John O'Malley was now experiencing another death and rebirth, one in which we all would eventually join him. (100)

He ends with lines from Francis Thompson's "Ode to the Setting Sun": "Are Birth and Death inseparable on earth; /For they are twain yet one, and Death is Birth."

Yet authority is more than the result of life and death, even though these are the same sacrament. Authority is also the result of reason and experience. Charles O'Malley is authorized to act as he does because of his art. He is a famous photographer who knows how to capture the essence of a person's character (155). This ability to read people is a characteristic of all true authority, at least in the tradition of Catholic thought. We are the authors of our own agency to the extent that we can know the substance of the agent we authorize. This is reveled throughout in this protagonist's actions. How does Charles know that Raftery's wife and child are alive? It would seem the CIA killed both in order to protect a rouge agent. How does he know that the Soviet empire will implode when Reagan's policy experts cannot see it (194)? How does he know about the mistaken identities of Bride O'Brien and Raftery's wife? How does he know enough to find evidence that the CIA is behind these mistaken identities?

The answer to all of these questions is that Charles O'Malley is both intelligent—he knows how to use the data of this world in light of his experiences to figure things out, and he exists within a specific community—he has connecting networks of relationships that empower him to find things out and do things about what he discovers. Simply, he is a creature of both reason and faith. He can know some things correctly, and he trusts that where he does not know, he may find those who do know. Thus, the Raftery mystery is solved when O'Malley reveals Bride O'Brien to be a great United States patriot and uses his intellectual and social connections to help her start over in a new life. His sister Jane, the oldest of the O'Malley children, on the other hand, tries to displace Charles as the head of the family but fails because she understands authority only as power derived from the perceptions of others.[103] The book ends with the mysteries solved and the O'Malleys tentatively trying out their new roles as authors of their own lives.

---

[103] Her suicide results from her mental disease, which itself is connected to defective modes of perception.

Chapter 6: The Wisdom of the Sacramental Imagination

The essential components of the Catholic intellectual tradition[104] serve as a way to locate multivalent dimensions of Greeley's characters. The first is Greeley's insistence on the compatibility of faith and reason, producing what Greeley calls the sacramental imagination, while the second involves the inference from this view that the world is a source of an extraordinary array of wisdom from all times, places, and cultures.

Greeley's fiction is rich in what he names the epiphany of Being in being; the world always is more than it seems. This world is always a sacrament. God lurks in it, throwing out countless signs that he is waiting patiently for us, even while he passionately pursues us as the greatest of our lovers. Thus, God's love is the unseen hero in Greeley's stories. Grace, i.e., God's life in us, is ordinary before it is extraordinary. Our job, through the working of the Holy Spirit, is to develop the eyes by which to see the glory lurking in the ordinary world. Again, the second element involves a profound respect for all wisdom regardless of its source. Many of Greeley's characters discover and advance the importance of history with much of the sociological and political data entailed in it. Likewise, Greeley's protagonists discover and use the historical pluralism of the Catholic tradition, demonstrating that institutions change over time or die for the very lack of the ability to

---

[104] See Monika K. Hellwig and my discussion of her ideas in Chapter 2.

change. Embedded in this insight is an intellectual pluralism, which maintains that as human beings, we exist socially and politically with others. This often implies that no one ever possesses the whole of the Truth; to advance the truth, we need to test it with others. This often leads Greeley's characters to discover that there are many ways to the truth.

The compatibility of faith and reason, the sacramental imagination. In Catholic culture the cardinal sins are the "hinges" upon which all other sins hang. As the cardinal virtues mark the capacity for the goodness potentially available to all well-integrated men and women, the cardinal sins—the seven deadly sins—mark a propensity in human nature that can lead us to participate in evil by misusing or willfully ignoring what is good in things. Such is the framework for *The Cardinal Sins* (1981). Greeley writes in his opening note, "The cardinal sins result not from fundamental evil but from fundamental goodness running out of control, from human love that is confused and frightened and not trusting enough of love" (*The Cardinal Sins*[105] n.p.). Thus, the main characters embody and overcome their character flaws by living their lives according to their best lights. But they come to virtue and overcome their cardinal sins not through their own effort, but through the friendship they enjoy, betray, and find again. This novel tells a story of how we might learn to let grace be grace. It is a story of the common friendship of four flawed human beings and the moments of grace that save them for their friends.

Kevin Brennan is the prideful son of the newly successful Irish who, throughout his life, must catch the rebound for his friend, Patrick Donahue. Donahue is the child of a garbage collector, endowed with beauty and great charm, who suffers from a covetousness and ambition that takes him beyond his gifts. Ellen Foley is the daughter of a middling Irish family that burdens her with responsibilities beyond her years, and thereby, makes her abidingly angry. Maureen Cunningham is the daughter of rich but careless parents. She has the advantage of

---

[105] *The Cardinal Sins*. New York: Warner Books, 1981.

beauty and intelligence, but suffers from a slothfulness that keeps her involved with men who victimize her. This includes Donahue, who will be her lover while he pretends to be a celibate priest, archbishop, and cardinal.

The book begins with an accident and ends with a terrorist murder; the action takes place between 1948 and 1981, during which we follow the development of the four main characters. As adolescents, they are typical late 1940s Irish Catholics and they confront many of the major issues of that generation. As young men and women, they experiment with their awakening sexuality in the context of the Catholic dichotomy between lust and continence. It will take their friendship and their whole lives to discover what it means to see their sexuality as sacramental. Bound by the narrowness of their culture and Catholic Puritanism, they are forced to choose between marriage and religious vocations. Marriage is their gateway into the world of the laity; a religious vocation is a call to be beyond the world of men and women—this because celibacy is viewed as essential to the religious life. Their educations and their families initially imbue them with fear but eventually liberate them from the adolescent attitudes of their Catholic class. The miracle is that their Catholic faith, which in some sense is responsible for the narrowness of their option, when fully understood and embraced, serves as the means of this liberation. Here these characters establish a theme to which Greeley returns again and again in his fiction: our commitment to life and to love constitutes the means by which we participate in the grace that lies everywhere around us. His premise seems to be that life and love are the structure of the universe, but that it takes a certain trusting viewpoint to see it and dedicated hearts to discover it. Thus, the place of friendship in this novel. Friendship serves as the understudy for God as the novel's main character; hence, the connection of this novel to Holy Thursday. As God led Israel out of slavery into freedom at the Passover so, too, are we led from the slavery of our own isolated selves into the liberty that comes with knowing and loving others. What each of these four friends finds in his or her life is that ingratitude (the rejection of grace) is the greatest of sins and the very reason we live less than fully human lives.

As a teenager, Kevin Brennan is the responsible one, the boy who helps everyone and who finds in the priesthood an outlet for his caring. That sense of responsibility will become for him a source of pride, and therefore, it will limit his human development. Patrick Donahue is the star, the winner of all games, and a deeply disturbed person who transfers pressure into sexual rage. His covetousness becomes the source of his ambition as a churchman; his charm and good looks, the avenues to his success in the church. Between Kevin and Patrick, there is great love and apparent friendship. But as Donahue achieves ever-higher ecclesiastical dignities, Kevin learns Donahue's weaknesses, the most deadly being his lust. Donahue finally becomes a very successful bishop who plays the game of advancement for the wrong reasons. The result is that he ends a hypocrite of the worst kind: the apparent man of honor.

Ellen Foley, the child of an abusive family, loves Kevin throughout her life but gives him up because she does not want, what in her mind would be, to challenge God. Her first marriage begins with too many children, born too soon, and the early death of her husband. Her anger at Kevin and the church he represents nearly destroys her until Brennan helps her confront her self-pity. His talent is his steely determination and ability to name things for what they are. This determination and honesty eventually bring Ellen back from the brink. Maureen Cunningham, on the other hand, is the "loose girl," who seems sexually sophisticated, but remains the victim of Patrick's sexual confusion. Together, Maureen and Patrick present the image of thwarted love, the family that could never be because the rules of the church deny them their destiny. Behind their relationship is a codependency that advances his church career at the cost of Maureen's happiness.

Left to themselves, these four characters flounder through life, always aware that there is the possibility of happiness, but never sure of how to proceed toward it. When Kevin decides to become a priest, Patrick has a "religious" vision that directs him to do the same. The initial accident that begins the novel becomes the metaphor of their relationship: Patrick pursues his selfish desires; Kevin covers for him and saves him from their consequences. Ellen goes to nursing school, even though she wants to be a writer; Maureen takes advantage of her wealth and produces nothing. When her parents are killed in a house fire, she cannot, or will not, absolve herself (65). All of them initially follow rules, even against charity (64). Kevin becomes a good priest: "'strong on enthusiasm and energy, short on compassion and kindness'" (77). Patrick gives up service to the poor for power (92) (always with good intentions) and fathers a bastard daughter, whom he asks Kevin to watch over. Even though he loves the child, he does not know how to take responsibility for her.

By their forties, each has been successful in the view of the world: Kevin is a famous priest-author, who though exiled from his fellow priests by clerical envy, knows how to do what is right; Patrick becomes Cardinal Archbishop of Chicago; Ellen is a successful psychiatric nurse and a mother with a loving second husband; Maureen is an artist, the mother of a lovely daughter, yet a concubine to various church dignitaries, including Patrick. It is through their continued friendship, their communion with each other, that they come to discover the world of grace. Under a stern but wise spiritual director, Kevin learns that his well-being—both psychological and spiritual—depends on letting God be responsible for the world. When he complains about the *"papier-mâché"* character of the Cardinal Archbishop of Chicago, his director says,

> Is he the first *papier-mâché* cardinal? You will never denounce him, Father. You will keep tipping back rebounds to him, as you put it, for the rest of your life, if necessary. You must, however, give up this ridiculous conceit that if you were not around to save him, the Almighty would not find another instrument for using Patrick Donahue as an agent of His Plan. You indulge yourself overmuch in assuming responsibility for designs, which are the Almighty's and not your own. (255)

Kevin learns he must overcome his pride if he is to be truly responsible as a friend. In a sense, Ellen already has learned this, as she has become the lifelong confident of Maureen. Together Ellen and Kevin, by stealth and cunning, destroy incriminating evidence of Patrick's hypocrisy while he is in conclave to elect a pope. He looks to them to save him from being blackmailed into using his political power to elect an inferior man and follows his conscience, even though he does not know that he is off the hook. Donahue finally behaves as a person with integrity and a man saved by his friends. Yet, this salvation is not payback for doing what is right. He finally finds the courage to do the right thing for the right reason. Maureen is killed by religious terrorists in the final pages of the novel, but is reconciled with her friends, and therefore, with her church. Together her friends learn that they can mourn Maureen without brooding (306). The book ends, as do all things Catholic, with the faith of the *De Profundis*, the psalm that sings of the God who hears, who forgives, who waits, and who redeems.

Greeley's story of these four friends exemplifies the compatibility of reason with faith inasmuch as it corrects the impression that Catholic culture elevates the sacrifice of faith over the happiness that faith can provide. By developing the rationality of happiness, these characters learn that to the extent that faith is an impediment to happiness, especially to friendship, that faith is incompletely and imperfectly understood. The cardinal sins of these characters—pride, anger, lust, and sloth being the four greatest—are to be overcome not by sacrifice or blind obedience to rules or by renunciation of the world, but by the development of the real goodness that this world represents. In this novel, reason informs faith, corrects its inept realization in the minds of each character and helps that faith emerge for what it truly is—God's life in us.

This is further illustrated in *The Wages of Sin* (1992).[106] Sin is a word signifying a range of human activity that expresses in its totality the propensity of human nature to fail. Sin might be said to involve any activity that misuses what is good. In this sense, sin signifies the corruption of nature (human or otherwise). Sin might also be said to stand for the negative limits of finite matter. This latter meaning is what Catholics mean by original sin—the act that corrupted nature and introduced sin and death into a hitherto perfect natural reality. The former is what once was meant by "actual" sin—those freely chosen activities that misuse what is good and in doing so, corrupt not only the actor but nature as well. Both senses are involved in the psalmist's claim that the wages of sin is death.

---

[106] *The Wages of Sin*. New York: Putnam's Sons, 1992.

Greeley's title evokes these meanings, while the action of this novel seems to argue that even from sin God may produce something good. What might inform the reader of the novel's project is the old catechism's teaching about actual sin: there are two kinds—mortal and venial—mortal being the worst because it destroys all merit and makes of the person, God's enemy. Three conditions are necessary for there to be actual sin: the matter must be major, the person must know that the wrong is serious, and the person must fully consent to commit serious wrong. Venial sin results from doing something that either is not seriously wrong, or, and important to understanding what happens in this novel, the actor is unaware that what is done is seriously wrong. If one considers this idea of sin carefully, the idea itself might imply that hardly ever are most of us fully capable of committing serious, i.e., mortal sin. This would be so because of failures in knowing, or more often, failures to be fully free to consent.[107]

The novel begins with a suspicion of murder and an implication of incest, certainly mortal sins if there ever were such. Lorcan James Flynn, the scion of a family that would most surely qualify as psychologically damaged, finds himself confronted with the memory of a Labor Day weekend in 1954, when the house next to the Flynn's on Long Beach blew up, killing the entire Meehan family. Lorcan had lost this memory because of a serious meningitis fever. It was the last time he saw his beloved Maura. Years later, these star-crossed lovers are reunited through the impending marriage of their children to each other. The story involves the recovery of memories (the recovery of souls), and the discovery of who really killed the Meehan family; its resolution reveals that serious sin was never part of the tale.

The use of the word "really" brings to mind a recurring theme in Greeley's fiction, that of the Real behind the realities of our lives, the Being of being.[108] Is it ever possible that a human being can know with absolute certainly (Being) such that his or her actions (being) could be judged really virtuous or really sinful? Or, is it more the case that by virtue of our experiences we are more or less affected in ways that diminish our knowing and our freedom? This book treats the latter

---

[107] See the conversation between Lorcan and his priest brother Edward, 215*ff.*
[108] See especially the Noula McGrail novels below in Chapter 7.

as the more prevalent and suggests that our black and white attitudes toward sin and sinners ought to be reconsidered in light of our human and social frailties.

In this novel, nothing is as it seems. The characters occasion the issues of transparency and character: if we were really transparent in our actions and desires, others would know us well and respect or denigrate us accordingly. But we are never transparently real to others or even to ourselves—Lorcan is in the process of therapy for his failed marriage and has ambivalent emotions regarding his father and brothers. These characters seem to be transparently what they are, deeply disturbed and neurotically challenged yet, by the end of the novel, even they are recalled in terms of what they potentially might have been had they not been so harmed by life. Even Lorcan, the main character, has two identities, that of Lorcan the successful executive as well as that of his pen name as a sculptor.

Lorcan's task is to discover what happened on that fateful Labor Day in 1954; in the process of doing so, he comes to uncover the truth about himself. As in all of Greeley's comedies, this one ends with the possibility of happiness. The Meehan's house was blown up killing all except the foster daughter Maura.[109] Lorcan, wracked by fever, had been with Maura on the fateful night; otherwise, she too would have perished. The explosion was broadcasted as a gas fire, when in reality it was the result of a bomb constituted of high explosives and illegal guns. These facts seem to be connected to the memory of Tim Meehan, the long dead, Irish gunrunner and all around hero. Is he Maura's father? When Lorcan's family and Maura's family come together for the wedding, they are plagued by the recurring characters of Donald Rosco, US attorney, and Maynard Lealand, special agent in charge of the FBI Chicago office, who assiduously, though stupidly, continue to practice "functional" justice through press releases and publicity grandstanding. Added to the mix is the sinister behavior of members of the Order of St. Justin Martyr.

Lorcan returns to Long Beach on Holy Thursday, thirty-five years after the explosion. He meets James Quaid, who lives with his

---

[109] Even this character changes her name during the time of the novel's action.

wife in a house built on the Meehan's lot. On Good Friday, Lorcan is pressured into betraying Maura's family in exchange for immunity from prosecution for his own trumped-up crimes, and he learns that it was his father's money that had separated Maura from him after the fire. These memories liberate him from "two neurotic systems," that of his former wife and of his family (239). At the Easter Vigil, the omniscient Bishop Blackie Ryan preaches on the significance of the Vigil's symbols: when the Easter candle (male) is plunged into the new baptismal water (female), Jesus' love for his church is consummated; this passionate love destroys death and restores all things to life. The light of Christ overcomes the darkness of the fall; nature is sanctified (sanctifying grace) and restored to its original glory.

In the weeks after Easter, Lorcan witnesses the happy marriage of his daughter and Maura's son; Maura and he rekindle their passionate love for each other and with the help of his own resources, he defeats the combined machinations of the US prosecutor, the FBI, and the CIA. He establishes Maura's parentage and recognizes James Quaid, a.k.a. Tim Meehan, as the agent responsible for the explosives that destroyed the Meehan's home. He also learns that it was his psychologically damaged mother who started the fire that led to the deaths of the four Meehans. In the end, there has been a crime, but no sin has been committed. Each of the parties either were diminished in their mental capacity, or lacked the knowledge of matters at hand. Even the reason for gunrunning, the liberation of Ireland, might be morally justified.

On Pentecost, something more is revealed that has to do with our knowing what God might be like. The Holy Spirit, we are told, is much like Tinker Bell:

> who flits blithely about, sparking into life with her magic wand all matter of wonders and surprises and enchantments. So too with the Spirit of God. She spins about creation, calling forth and presiding over variety and diversity and uniqueness. She is especially responsible for that which makes each creature most particularly itself. Offer Her gratitude for the splendid, attractive, overwhelming diversity of God's creation.

> If one has the choice of accepting and rejoicing in the variety
> with which God's Spirit has filled the world and resisting Her
> Variety, one would be wise to accept and enjoy her playfulness.
> It is a mistake to try to fight the Holy Spirit. (343–344)

At one level, the novel is about a man who, on his own merit, must defend himself and his family by taking the law into his own hands. Living in a world where political agencies and agents serve only their own interests, where the common good is not only ignored but also not even recognized as part of the reason human beings find themselves organized in social and familial ways, he is not free to do otherwise. If this were the novel's only level, it would still be an interesting story, raising some important political issues, albeit obliquely. Its God-talk and Catholic imagery, however, suggest more. On another level, the novel is about appearances and about how much of what we think and believe is unreal. It is a story about recovering memory. In order to "remember" what occurred on a summer night in 1954, i.e., in order to save his soul, Lorcan Flynn must use all his resources to expose the truth. In the process of doing so, we learn how merely apparent things are. Like sin—the pursuit of only an apparent good—human agencies (like the FBI and US prosecuting attorneys) involve their denizens in activities that seem to be about what is good, but are, in fact, often really about the pursuit of personal and special interests. The question remains, whither the common good.

Here, Greeley's characters are at their best. Embedded in the language that Greeley's characters learn to reject are still some very important truths—truths that are revealed in the action of his novel. In the introductory lesson on "Actual Sin" in the Baltimore Catechism, we read:

> *Venial* sin is bad, but it does not deprive us of God's grace [...].
> We can avoid mortal and venial sins by using our supernatural
> and natural powers together. That is, we must *pray*, receive
> the *sacraments* (God's channels of grace), and remember the
> *presence* of God with us. At the same time, we must use our
> own will power to be always occupied, to keep free from the
> *capital* (chief) sins, and to stay away from the *near* occasions
> of sin. (35)

This is still solid advice Greeley's characters seem to suggest. We are prone to harm others and ourselves; the world as *sacrament* reminds us of God's continual presence among us; and we do have human resources, like reason and willpower that help us avoid such harm and repair it where damage has been done. The novel's ending, with the possibility of happiness for Lorcan and Maura, is an ending that seems to suggest that each of them, individually and together, have their own *natural* powers—powers that give them access to *supernatural* powers.

If, as Greeley's fiction seems to suggest, grace is ordinary before it is extraordinary, then the universe in which we live at least must admit the possibility of angels. Whether these beings are merely our better selves, or entities of a higher ontological order, the idea that an all-loving God has assigned a guardian to each person is evidence of the human imagination's working out of love as the foundation of all being. Greeley's angels are, indeed, just that. *Angel Light* (1995)[110] is a modern adaptation of the guardian angel myth, a myth with a genealogy no less than one of the books from the Catholic canon of the Old Testament.

The Book of Tobit, or The Book of Tobias, falls somewhere between the historical books and the wisdom literature of the Jewish testament and is accepted as part of the Catholic canon. A novel of sorts, it tells the story of devout, wealthy Jews caught in the captivity of 721 BCE. It is a story, at once, about the fidelity of the believer, and at the same time, about the reward that fidelity must certainly garner. Tobit, the blinded captive, sends his son, Tobiah, to recoup a large sum of wealth left in a far away land. On this mission, he meets Sarah, who has lost seven husbands to the evil one. Through the loving help of the angel Raphael, Tobiah and Sarah are wed, the wealth is returned to its rightful owner, and the father regains his sight—almost always emblematic of stronger faith.

---

[110] *Angel Light*. New York: Tom Doherty Associates, 1995.

Greeley's Tobit is G. Patrick Tobin of Chicago and his Sarah is Sara Tobin of Galway. "Toby" goes to Ireland to honor his distant uncle's will, which promises him ten million dollars if he woos and weds Sara. With the help of his guardian angel, Raphael—"God heals"—he finds his own talent and integrity, and thus, learns how to be a mature person capable of real love. The boy Toby, hectored by his older sisters and parents, becomes Patrick, and like naming in the tradition of the Jewish testament, he comes to have power over that which is named, i.e., himself.

This "Old-Fashioned Love Story,"[111] the subtitle of the novel, illustrates how ordinary grace becomes extraordinary through the power of God. In trusting himself, Patrick becomes who he is supposed to be, and in doing so, gains the respect of his father. Sara Tobin does not lose seven husbands, but suffers, perhaps, a greater loss. She was raped by a suitor and then raped again by someone to whom the suitor had sold her. Where Toby must overcome his family's penchant for seeing him as a bumbling fool, Sara must endure and overcome the psychic wounds of real violence. What "God heals" is Patrick's poor image of himself and Sara's self-hatred. How this is accomplished in the novel is not as important as that it is accomplished by God in "the integrity of their love." (37)

The story does involve, however, the extraordinary activity of angels. Sara and Patrick heal the ancient feud between the Tobins, and through their cooperation, save the family's property and good name.

---

[111] Greeley relates, "The book is certainly a love story, a quest tale like that in many other ancient cultures. The author has grafted on it many lessons for Jewish life such as loyalty, respect for parents, and concern for the dead, but these moralistic additions do not notably weaken the love story with its profound and powerful and modern, almost feminist, concern for respect of women. It is not the smoke that Raphael blows in the eyes of the demon that saves the young lovers, but the integrity of their love and the young man's sensitivity and respect for his bride. Raphael was probably a good spirit who figured in many Israelite folk tales because then, as now, readers like a touch of the occult. However, in the Hebrew Scriptures the Malek Jahweh, the angel of the Lord, is not distinct from the Lord Himself but merely represents God's concern for each individual person. Hence, the existence of a being named Raphael is fictional artifact. The angel may safely be considered merely a useful addition to the tale, but not the cause of its happy ending" (37).

The demon Asmodeus is played by the stupid rapist who allies himself with Northern Ireland terrorists, all of whom end up killing each other and generally making a mess of it. But in the most important sense, it is not the angels who deliver the innocent from the terrorist bomb. It is Toby become Patrick. Nor is it the angel who defeats Asmodeus, but the psychic work and commitment of Sara who must heal herself with the help of modern psychiatry. Like her music, her mental and moral health comes from inside her. God's extraordinary grace—his life in each of us—comes to us through ordinary means—human sexual love, the forgiveness of small and great sins, our loyalty to our families even when they do not deserve it, the beauty of Irish rain and the desolation of gray days—that we must come to see on our own. Angels are merely human blindness overcome by grace.

The respect for all wisdom regardless of its source. Greeley's notion of the Being behind all being implies that there is nothing per se in the world that cannot teach us something of value, hence, Catholic culture's insight that everyone and everything may be a source of wisdom. Three of Greeley's novels help us understand this: *St. Valentine's Night, The Search for Maggie Ward,* and *The Rite of Spring.*

In *St. Valentine's Night* (1989),[112] Greeley again employs part of the Holy Grail archetype to teach the relationship of human love to the love that is divine. On the morning of St. Valentine's Day, 1958, Cornelius O'Connor saves Megan Keefe Lane from a house fire. This act marks the beginning of a love that comes full circle. It defines his life and compels him to consciousness. The theme is of going out in order to return. The boy O'Connor must leave home—an apparent family disgrace—before he can return to learn the nature of real grace. When he returns to the neighborhood in 1987, he is a success in the media business but still an incomplete person. Having renamed himself Neal Connor—naming is an ancient mark of having power over something, indeed, the power to create—he learns of a lost beauty once revealed to him through art and music, the possession of which will make him whole.

---

[112] *St. Valentine's Night.* Warner Books, Inc., 1989.

The object of his sadness, the love not allowed between Megan Lane and himself, is renewed when he makes this helpless widow dependent upon him. Once, for lack of courage, he had run from guilt and shame, and she, too, had run from their love. Now they are reunited at a class reunion of the old neighborhood, a place that becomes sacred in both their memories (169). This is a story of incomplete selves finding the grace that completes them. Father John (Blackie) Ryan, scion of the great Ryan clan, which is church in many of Greeley's novels, plays the role of interlocutor.

> Consider those for whom we must mourn. Minimally. The little boy from another parish who moves into the allegedly affluent precincts of St. Praxides. He is big and bright and not unattractive, but he is shy and awkward and embarrassed by what he considers his inferior social status, a phenomenon to which the kids of St. Prax's pay no attention at all, whatever their parents might think. But he does not understand that. He wants to be friends, he wants to be accepted, he wants to belong. But he does not know how. So he is ignored and sometimes laughed at. He seems able to relate only to unusual types, a frustrated poet, a troublesome priest in the making [...]. From a far distance, he admires a girl whose cool self-possession dazzles him, but he dare not even talk to her [...].
>
> Now consider the other actor in our story: a little girl of the same age, the final fruit of a very odd tree. For reasons of nature or grace, not too distant perhaps from the miraculous, she has partially escaped the family subculture, which has been built up to protect their dignity against the image of working for the Outfit. They are silly people. The little girl knows this dimly and resolves not to be silly like the rest of them. She becomes very rational, controlled, candid, self-possessed, responsible. The exact opposite of the rest of the family. But she must struggle every minute of her life against them.
>
> Now, given your cosmopolitan experience, you perceive that we are grieving for unfulfilled and unexorcised dreams and the pain they cause. The little boy seeks happiness in a career

at which he is quite successful. The little girl marries a man whom she thinks is like the one she has lost. He turns out not to be, but as women are wont, she makes do. Neither has quite been able to experience the simple but often profound grief that comes from the end of childhood dreams, the termination of childhood crushed. (170–171)

Or so it seems. Could there be, however, "romantic passion"—a crush—that turns out to be "a higher wisdom" (172–173)? Indeed there can and is.

The plot of the novel is complex, as are most of Greeley's plots. Neal's task is to discover who killed Megan's husband, and whether or not there is any money left for the family. It involves not only Blackie Ryan and his Irregulars, but the Chicago Outfit—the mob—the Hispanic drug gangs of southeast Chicago, as well as a corrupt FBI and a federal prosecutor seeking to use power for personal, political gain. One might suggest that The Outfit, the drug lords, the US prosecutor, and the FBI represent what St. Augustine means by the City of Man, that world governed and motivated by cupidity and our lesser natures. This is especially evident in the section of the novel wherein Lou Garcia, the leader of the drug gangs, befriends Neal. Their relationship reveals that legalization of drugs, like liquor after Prohibition, might prove a more effective way to control the substance. Then, like The Outfit that came into being because of Prohibition, the drug lords could settle down and deliver a product much in demand. (See 257*ff.*) Human law has its limits, and alone it cannot change the human heart. This has been evident at least since Augustine. What Greeley's characters discover is that there is indeed a world of cupidity and violence and it cannot be escaped. But might it be transformed? Here Greeley's characters help us to a "higher wisdom." Chicago's crime and politics—there is very little difference between them in this story— stand as "[…] a maelstrom in which you didn't want to get caught" (402). Yet, it is within this maelstrom that our redemption is achieved: not because of it, but through it.

In this story, Neal works to keep his dependents—the Lane family—safe from the public prosecutor's misuse of the courts and the FBI's use of violence as a means of law. Two of the Lane children are hauled off to jail in public view on Christmas day—and out of the hands of The Outfit and the drug lords; yet cupidity and greed seem to win. When Neal finds the missing money among the effects of Megan's murdered husband, he is neither rewarded nor praised. Rather this discovery breaks asunder the delicate union between Megan and him, which to this point has been achieved by romantic passion, the love of children, and the approbation of the dead father's apparent ghost.

The truth of the story is revealed in the way the story ends and illustrates the ordinary places wisdom may reside. Neal uses his media savvy, his working relationship with The Outfit, his acquaintance with the drug lords—all experiences derived from being part of the City of Man—to save the youngest Lane child, Joseph,[113] who has been kidnapped by the *loco* Hispanic drug lord. It is Megan, who has been restored to herself by her fellows in the neighborhood, who saves Neal in the end. She pulls him from the ice of the Chicago River after their car is forced from the street by gunfire and the madness of Lou Garcia.[114] It is through a stuck-open sunroof, broken and inoperable throughout the novel, that he is pulled. Neal had saved her from fire; she saved him from ice. She has been delivered from the dependency of her flawed family, he from the "shame" of his past, both from the machinations of political and criminal violence. Freed from these dependencies, they are able to love one another. He had thought gratitude to be a trap (420) and learned that though it may be so, it need not be so. The wisdom these characters discover is that all is grace. We must develop the eyes to see it and the hearts to hold it.

"The harvest is over, the summer is past, and we are not yet saved." These words, placed in the mouth of the Prophet Jeremiah, signify the

---

[113] Greeley often uses biblical names and events to help the reader see his insights into a higher wisdom. For example, the key to finding the lost Joseph (the brother sold into slavery) is the character Maria Annunciata, whose brown eyes are "as old as sin" (407). Mary of the Annunciation is the biblical figure whose "yes" allowed grace to come into the world. Whether this use of terms is conscious or unconscious, it is still there in the novels for those who have the cultural awareness to use it. What makes Greeley a great storyteller is that his symbolism, though present, never carries the story's meaning. It only helps a good story toward a deeper meaning.

[114] If the play on the etymology of this Spanish word for grace is happenstance, the point still screams for recognition.

blindness of a people whose God is the God of second chances. One of the main characters in the novel *The Search for Maggie Ward* (1991),[115] Jeremiah "major prophet" Thomas Keenan, learns their significance as he searches for the ghost-like character, Maggie Ward. She is Andrea King at the beginning of the story and revealed as Margaret Mary Ward as this love story proceeds. They meet on July 22, the Feast of St. Mary Magdalene, in 1946, after war's ordinary brutality has had its effects on both characters. She is the widow of an abusive husband, whom she had to marry because she carried his child, an infant who died in her crib. He is a retired fighter pilot, who saw first hand the brutality of warfare and who learned how to hate it. Both are deeply influenced by these events and by their Catholic upbringing. She believes, he does not, and together they discover a God of love and of second chances.

But this book is more than a story of two lovers who overcome extraordinary psychological and social damage. She says early in the novel, "'I still want to die most of the time. But inside me, there's something stronger that tells me I want to live, something as powerful as the ocean or the sky [...]. I'm damned. But I can't and I won't die and it's almost not up to me ...'" (52). She also becomes the virgin and the spouse, and finally, the pietà. As such, Margaret Mary Ward signifies the church and her role in the order of redemption: at once, the emblem of Christ's mother at the foot of the cross and the woman taken in sin, who receives from Jesus a second chance and becomes proto-apostle,[116] the first to see the risen Christ. Jerry Keenan's search for Maggie Ward, his Holy Grail, is also his discovery of Andrea King/ Maggie Ward as the instrument of God's love in time. She possesses the ability to know things and to see things that others do not, and it is this power that will be the source of their insights into God's love, as well as the instrument by which they are joined as lovers. Their love becomes the mirror of God's love for creation, and their lives signify the universal story of such love.

---

[115] *The Search for Maggie Ward.* New York: Warner Books, 1991.

[116] The identification of the woman taken in sin with Mary Magdalene is based on a very old misreading of the New Testament. The mistake nonetheless remains widespread.

They meet in Arizona, where Keenan has come to explore the mining ghost towns of the area. She is running from her unhappy past. Together they discover the rewards of first love, their sexual unions prefiguring the love of the divine for all that is human. Together they experience what modern psychology would name a psychotic interlude, which in the sacred folklore of many religions follows a narrative about the war between good and evil, between heaven and hell: a contest that had been played out time out of mind.

In 1946, sex before marriage was considered a grave sin in Catholic moral thought, provided it was committed freely and knowingly as evil. Yet, even then, those who truly loved understood that sexual encounters between lovers could not be seriously sinful to the extent that such acts are truly acts of love. This ambivalence in Catholic moral theory—one cannot sin if one's actions are not free or if such actions are not understood to be seriously grave—produced either neurotic guilt, or more often than not, served as a way for young men and women to practice the art of loving each other in ways that image Christ's love for his church. Both the free commitment of the bodies of the individuals involved and the maturity of their understanding that married love is, indeed, the sign of Christ's unity with humanity are necessary for sexual love to become sacramental. Judging the moral character of their actions to be true and right, Keenan says,

> What would the various members of my family, experts on ethics each in their own way, judge about our romp in Picketpost House, should I provide them with the details?
>
> My daughter the clinician would say that it was a statistically probable event, and so long as no one was hurt, it might well have been beneficial for both. Still, there is always the risk in such hastily consummated liaisons of considerable dysfunction later on.
>
> My son the young priest would perhaps find it hard to understand why the question would come up; we were on an exploration toward a sacramental union (for which we

both hoped, despite our respective reservations and fears). In general, the more chaste such explorations are, the better for both parties. But who can say what is appropriate in an individual case? Finally, it is between the couple and God. (122–123)

Then, after the appearance of the war between good and evil, Andrea disappears.

Don Quixote's quest for his grail is on. Keenan's search for Dulcinea—he has named his car Roxinante—also entails the question of how his search is also about finding the church in our lives. Is Maggie Ward "Church" for Jeremiah Keenan? It would seem so. This is where Greeley's understanding of human sexuality as sacramental helps deepen our understanding of the story. The story is told after the fact, from some thirty years of experience. Thus, Greeley introduces from time to time the words of Keenan's wife, Maggie, even before he finds Maggie Ward and asks her to marry him. This is a voice of assured confidence and prefigures the presence of God in the lives of these characters. This voice, along with the knowledge of experience, gives to Keenan's story the depth of a history of salvation. While still with Andrea King on their first adventure, Keenan notes,

> The moon hadn't risen yet and the murky streetlights didn't illumine much of the town. In fact, however, neither of us was interested in sightseeing. Rather, we were afraid of the intimacy of the room and the demands and the conflicts that had already become part of our intimacy. I would have the same experience, not too often but often enough, in my marriage later on. In the rhythm of attraction and repulsion, communion fighting with individuation, bodily desire contesting with mental hurt, love struggling with resentment and anger, I would find myself drawn to my partner and repelled by her. And she would feel the same way. (149)

This insight into the psychology of sexuality takes a reader slightly acquainted with Catholic thought into the mystery of the church. Given to humanity as a sign of God's continuing presence on earth, it involves both glory and shame. Throughout his body of work, Greeley's characters say over and over that if God had wanted a perfect church, God would have given it to the angels. But God did not do so. The church, then, is like human sexuality, capable of both the miracle of love and the sinfulness of men and women. This seems evident in Keenan's summary of his sexual experience with Andrea King.[117]

> These last twenty-four hours have been the most remarkable day in my life. I am confused, uncertain, and terribly apprehensive about our trip tomorrow. I would get out of it if I could. She taught me how to love a woman physically and I'll never be able to thank her enough for that grace […]. […] It was grace, not sin. She also is nun-ridden, erratic, unpredictable, and possibly a little crazy. She thinks she will die soon and be damned to hell forever. Crazy, but, darn it, I still love her. (155)

Like the church, Maggie proves flawed and a little mad, as well as the instrument of Keenan's and her own salvation. She is the avenue of grace in the world and as such is virgin, spouse, mother. Maggie Ward Keenan becomes these for Jeremiah and Jeremiah becomes for Maggie Ward a second, indeed better, chance at happiness.

She also becomes the means by which Keenan rediscovers his faith. Having thought he had lost his faith when he witnessed the evils of warfare, it is through their love for each other that Keenan comes home to the faith of his mother and father. In an argument with Andrea about her self-damnation and need to expiate her guilt, Keenan says,

> I don't doubt God's love. I doubt his power. What's the point in having a God if He can't prevent the bad things from happening? But I'd never for a moment doubt that He wants to prevent them. The God in whom you believe is a terrible God. He doesn't love you, which is bad taste, since He made

---

[117] It may not be consciously the case, but Greeley's ironic naming of many of his characters might suggest that Andrea—from the Greek root for humanity—King—the *dominus* or lord of creation—might signify more than the pseudonym for a young girl.

you so loveable. The God who may exist for me is a sweet, nice old God who means well and thinks you're irresistible [...]. [A]sk which God is the one Jesus talks about in the Gospels: your powerful God who hates or my sometimes weak God who loves. (162)

He continues,

What's God like? He's like me, you gorgeous little nitwit—loving, inept, and dumb. Run from that if you want but don't make up an imaginary hanging judge who won't give you a second chance.

[...] Just keep this in your thick little skull: the God Jesus talked about is not interested in damning you. He's like me—say that over and over—and right now He wants to do the divine equivalent of finding a quiet corner somewhere, taking off your clothes and making love to you all day long. And into the night. Any other God is a faker. (163)

In the face of this theology, Andrea King runs away; Keenan experiences a psychotic interlude in which he witnesses St. Michael's banishment of Satan and discovers in himself something of the power of God (191).

A drunken Irish priest tells him that Andrea is a succubus from hell, but Keenan's experience tells him that this cannot be true. The search for his grail is on. By learning the personal history of Maggie Ward, Keenan discovers the truth of his experience much like most Catholics discover that the history of the church tells a story revealing the truth of its mystery. They stay part of the church on their own terms because their experiences teach them that in spite of human failure, Christ remains present through it. And Christ, more than any other figure in history, stayed with humanity and remained true to his father on his own terms.

What Keenan discovers while searching for Maggie Ward is a rumor of her death. It seems she committed suicide and her body buried in unhallowed ground. But like the story of Mary Magdalene, what is discovered is an empty tomb. "*Nolle me tangere*" Jesus says to the Mary in the Gospel narrative. Don't cling to me as though I am dead. The women at the tomb discover "He is risen as he said." This is the news the church is destined to proclaim from the housetops in season and out. Kneeling at her grave, Keenan asks, "Had her assignment been to recall me to my faith before she went to heaven? Was part of her purgatory the terrible fear that she was already in hell? Did she have to conquer that too?" [...] "All right, Maggie [...] you win. I believe again. I don't promise that I'll bounce back into Mass next Sunday, but I'll make my peace with God because you said I should" (286–87).

This rediscovery of the church and her ancient faith involves Keenan in a deepening of both his love and his faith. He comes to know Dorothy Day and the Catholic Worker Movement. That experience and his commitment to it lead him to the awareness of the perfect law of love: "It does not matter where we come from or who we are. It only matters who we become by the ways we love others" (319). This insight that we cannot say we truly love God if we do not truly love our neighbor makes all the difference in the world. After resisting his law-school's retreat, Keenan learns from its Jesuit retreat master something about his universal destiny: "We live, my dear child, in a universe filled with wonder. My colleagues in physics are now ready to admit that ours is a mysterious and open cosmos which we will never completely understand. The more we know about it, the more we know that we don't know" (329). Assuring him that his psychotic experience in the desert was not without significance, the Jesuit says, "You did battle with [...] evil. Perhaps you did not win completely, but surely, you did not lose [...]. [T]he forces of good and evil which lurk in our cosmos, of construction and destruction, are locked in combat, in a way in heaven [...]. Always we are involved in that war, in some rare moments of peril and grace, much more explicitly than is normal" (330). Lest we think that the church teaches a Manichaean dualism, Greeley's characters turn to the mystery of the church as evidence of God's victory over sin, death, and evil. The priest tells Keenan, "You will never stop searching for Maggie Ward. She is a suggestion of another world, a touch of the numinous, the wonderful, the surprising. One never forgets such hints of grace as long as one has a hunger for the numinous. No, you will always search for her [...] Maggie Ward as Grace, how about that!" (331). On the Feast of the

Immaculate Conception,[118] December 8, the day that prefigures the great "yes" of a human being thus, enabling God to work his plan of redemption, Jeremiah Thomas Keenan goes to Mass and receives Holy Communion for the first time in years.

This saying yes becomes an important theme in this novel and throughout Greeley's fiction. At the end of this novel, Keenan's imaginary guardian, who seems very much like the Archangel Michael, responds to Jerry's "Why don't you take care of yourselves?" by saying "You know we can't act without human cooperation. That's you [...]" (447). This is a human insight into the idea that "grace does not force nature, but perfects it" through the working of men and women. It is also about the realization that the mundane is the aperture of true wisdom.

What Keenan discovers is that Maggie Ward lives in Chicago, is not completely sane but on the way to being so, and needs others to help her become psychologically well integrated as a person. When an envelope with eleven one-hundred dollar bills is delivered to Keenan at his family home, his brother (a seminarian) helps him discover the clue[119] that reveals Maggie as being in Chicago, almost as if she were waiting and hoping to be found. This attribute of God as waiting and hoping for our response to his great love for us is tied here to the church as the witness of this great love. The postmark on the envelope reveals Maggie to be in Chicago; the church is always home. Keenan pursues her once again only to find her involved with an unsavory

---

[118] The Feast of the Immaculate Conception of Mary is not about the conception of Jesus (that is the Feast of the Annunciation, when a young girl freely chose to cooperate in God's plan of salvation by saying yes to being the Mother of God). Her Immaculate Conception is the consequence of that salvation. She was conceived without original sin, according to theologians, so that she might bear the Godhead. As a theological conclusion, this feast marks a kind of dogmatic logic. It must have been so because of the plan of God. But the Feast of the Immaculate Conception is also about Mary as a real human being, who with God's grace was able to say yes and to be a model, like Jesus, of human perfection.

[119] The money came in an envelope Keenan has torn up and thrown out without knowing what it contained. The scene in which Jerry and "Packy" search for the bits of envelope in the garbage is Greeley at his best (340). The significance of a soon-to-be-priest helping a newly mature Catholic layman find what will lead to that layman's happiness ought not be lost on the reader.

bully, who eventually tries to kill him. The question involved in this part of Keenan's pursuit is what Maggie's yes will be. It comes at Christmas with the Keenans (370). But in spite of Keenan's defeat of her false lover, beyond the love of the Keenan family for her, Maggie must decide on her own terms whether to love in return. The novel ends in the subjunctive mood, with Maggie not getting on the train that will take her back to Philadelphia and her newly returned father.

> "She looks shy and kind of frightened and all tired out and he says something real intelligent, like why didn't she get on the train, and she says she couldn't and might she please have just one more chance, and he says a couple of thousand and she says one will do for the moment; then though there is no reason to think he has to revert to caveman behavior, he picks her up and carts her off—his choice of words—to Roxinante, his car, you know."

"I know."

Such is the grace that is Maggie Ward.

The Rite of Spring (1987)[120] expands the extended family of the Ryans to include Brendan Herbert George Ryan, someone who has always felt himself to be an outsider. He is from a different branch of the Ryans, and his grammar school and high school friends had no tolerance for Ned Ryan's family. These friends soon disappoint Brendan when he most needs them—in his adulthood—and prove false. Part of his unease with his life is the fact that he possesses a sensory characteristic,[121] which the Irish call being fey, i.e., he sees things no one else can see, both from the past and into the future (10). Like most of his contemporaries, he dismisses this characteristic as illusionary and part of his mental breakdown. What he learns is that this characteristic is part of his being, and therefore, something that should be part of him. God does not make junk after all. This knowledge gives Ryan the courage to accept another essential part of

---

[120] *Rite of Spring.* New York: Warner Communications, 1987.

[121] Greeley notes at the end of the novel, "Brendan Ryan is part of that three or four percent of the population, men and women perfectly normal in every other respect, for whom these phenomena are a routine part of life" (Endnote n.p.).

his being, his passion. As Blackie Ryan tells him, "passion is but one manifestation of hope, the trickiest of God's games [...]" (278).

This brings us to the title and to the time the novel begins.[122] "Rite of Spring" refers to both Matisse's primitive painting, "Dance," and to Stravinsky's music for Diaghilev's Ballets Russes, premiered in May of 1913. Ryan's first date with Ciara Kelly is to hear this music. The novel begins in the last week of April, "the beginning of my fall from grace" (3) according to the main character. What we shall find by the end of the book is that Ryan has quested for the Holy Grail and won, but only after he comes to trust himself and God. This trusting is worked out in the heroic action of the final rescue of Ciara from the hands of maniacal terrorists, but the real action of the book involves Brendan's coming of age regarding his passion for Ciara. She is a mystery throughout most of the book—sometimes we are almost told that she is a fiction of Brendan's confused mind—but she is and has been real throughout the work and the reader finds that this reality is very like the reality of God. Brendan's "fall from grace" proves also to be his "happy fault" by which he is redeemed as a human being.[123] This redemption involves having his daughter, Jean, restored to him both in terms of their love for each other and in terms of her rescue from terrorist demons.[124] What Brendan "gets back" is nothing less than himself in quite the same way that the world gets itself back[125] by the rite of spring.

---

[122] The novel consists of five parts: "A Morning in Spring," "The Adoration of the Earth," "The Dance of Sacrifice," "The Quest for Ciara Kelly," and "The Strand at Inch." Stravinsky's work consists of two parts: "The Adoration of the Earth" and "The Sacrifice."

[123] Brendan says to himself, "Thus, did I fall from grace. Or maybe, I don't know, fall into grace" (51).

[124] Lest one think this is more than the novel can bear, note Greeley's guidance: "Some readers may observe that the Strand at Inch was the locale for the climax of my first novel, *The Magic Cup*. The similarity is not accidental. This story of spring, like the story of the earlier book, is a retelling of the old Irish version of the quest for the Holy Grail, a story which in its primordial form as a liturgical cycle, was also part of a spring ritual. In the ancient story, the quest is for a cup and a woman who represent a divine power that operates not so much by creating and ordering, but, long before Alfred North Whitehead, by inviting, calling, alluring, enticing. Slavic music and Celtic story."

[125] See 188*ff.*

Yet, dances and spring's renewal are never singular events. They require others and the whole complex of natural systems that are what we mean by nature. So, too, in this novel, Brendan Ryan does not find his Holy Grail by himself. The Ryans are Brendan's community after his wife, best friend, and priest have betrayed him. Without Mike Casey, the Ryan clan at Grand Beach, the Ryan siblings, Bishop Blackie, and his colleagues at work—Eileen Ryan and Nick Curran—Brendan could not have proved his innocence in the death of his wife and priest best friend, nor could he have procured the material necessary to overcome the terrorist who had kidnapped first his daughter and then Ciara. Clearly, the social thesis of this novel is that by ourselves, we are without hope, but with others, through others and because of others, we have hope in abundance and thus, faith and love.

Brendan's change comes in three parts: first he finds the lovely Ciara Kelly and they fall passionately in love. This passion holds the same place in this novel as in all of Greeley's fiction; it is the sign and the symbol of God. Only when we find our grounding in God—it is not as difficult as professional religious make it, for it is planted in the depth of our being both in our bodies and in our souls—can we become who we are supposed to be. In this great love, Brendan learns that he is much more than his lifelong friends have made him out to be, an outsider who waits to perform the role his friends have defined for him. He learns that he is loveable and that he is a great lover. Second, he discovers that his lifelong friends are, in fact, terribly diseased in hearts and minds and bodies. His wife, Madonna Clifford, divorces him to become her own person. She merely succeeds in becoming nearly anorexic. His broker, King Sullivan, defrauds him of a million dollars, King's wife, Patsy Walsh, tries to kill him so he does not give evidence to convict her husband, and his best friend, priest Ron Crowley, sleeps with his wife. It is this last betrayal that puts Brendan in jeopardy. When his boat is blown up, killing Madonna Clifford and Father Crowley, Brendan is suspected as the murderer. It is only after this betrayal that he becomes who he really is. Like the resurrected Christ, Brendan is raised to new life. This new life, found in the friendship of the Ryan clan,[126] takes him to Ireland and to his third epiphany of change, the rescues of his daughter and his soon to be wife. Brendan gets back the life God had intended for him all along.

At the heart of this novel is the message that God's love takes form in our lives to the extent that we live them fully and lovingly. This message is found throughout the book but especially in two characterizations: the first involves the negating of this message as characterized by Father Ron Crowley; the second is revealed in the counsel of Blackie Ryan. Father Ronald Crowley was Brendan's best friend in grade and high school. Always the leader of the pack, his decision to be a priest changed the balance within the group of five friends. After it, Brendan was seen as the mate for Ron's girlfriend, Madonna. Their marriage would prove to be very unhappy. In Ron's character, Greeley delivers his critique of the human hold on power. Certainly not the only time such a critique is raised in Greeley's work, but this time it is very succinct and disturbing. Here is Ron Crowley's advice to Brendan:

> "It's natural that men should dominate women. We always have. It's structured into the nature of things. They're weaker and we're stronger. Okay, the world is slightly civilized now and we have to pretend that everyone is equal, but deep down they want to be dominated. This feminism business is only a transient thing. You can't say that in public or there'd be hell to pay. But it's true. Anyway, they want to be dominated. It's

---

[126] See 193. "A strange, quixotic bunch, a throwback, perhaps, to more ancient Irish days of loyalty. The Ryans had family problems like all families; at various times many of their marriages were in jeopardy (including her own, according to Eileen's brief hints). They knew, as do all families, the meaning of suffering, tragedy, and premature death. But unlike most of the South Side Irish of our generation, the Ryans did not approach life with cautious prudence. They did not minimize the risks or hedge their bets or play the conservative percentages. They did more than meet life halfway—they charge into it aggressively, embracing every possibility, every challenge, every opportunity that came anywhere near them. As my mother had once remarked long ago, 'They're a bit much, but they're never dull'" (192). That Greeley has equated the Ryans with the church takes on a new meaning in light of these words.

in their nature. Find yourself a well-built widow and push her around a little. She'll love it.

Was this really the Catholic peace activist of a year ago? The militant civil rights and antiwar protester of the seventies? The "Third World" enthusiast so often celebrated in the pages of the *National Catholic Reporter*? Had the pastorate of a rich suburban parish completely transformed him, or was Ron a burned-out case?

"Doesn't that legitimate rape and sexual harassment?" I asked dubiously.

He quaffed half his martini at a single swallow. "No woman," he licked his lips, "is ever raped who doesn't want to be raped. You can't say that these days without offending the nutty nun feminists, but that's the way it is (63)"

This attitude toward women is also his attitude toward those with whom he works. As pastor, he is the autocrat who must be obeyed; obedience itself is his idea of the most important virtue for everyone else. He, however, is radically disobedient in relationship to the authority of others. Part of the novel's heart is that we cannot be happy with this idea of authoritarianism. Authority is not about fawning before higher ups and abusing those beneath us. God's equality is that of love and mercy. Ron Crowley is killed in the embrace of illicit love on Brendan's boat.

Thus, we come to the positive heart of this novel revealed through the character of Monsignor John Blackwood Ryan. It is Brendan's anger during the Clifford's wake of their daughter, Madonna, that gives us the first of Father Ryan's readings on hope. He says to Brendan, "'Never underestimate the immensity of God's mercy or the lunatic passion of His love.'" To which Brendan replies, "'I'm sure that's true, Monsignor, but I still don't understand why God does something like this.'" Blackie's response tells us much about hope. He says, "'The youngest first grader in Holy Name Cathedral doesn't call me Monsignor [...]. And I don't accept that God is responsible for the tragedy of Ron Crowley and Madonna Clifford. He wanted their stories to be very different, and He was unable to write them the way He wanted. I reject all other explanations.'" Ryan then goes on to say that when the Greek philosophy in which much God talk is encased conflicts with what we know of God from the Gospel, we must reject Greek philosophy, i.e., God's omnipotence cannot be cause for blaming God for the failure of human freedom. According to Blackie's gospel of hope, "'God is the great improviser, the great player-by-ear. When bad things happen, or we do bad things to one another, He simply adjusts His game plan and achieves His goals by an alternative path. Humans are responsible for the death of your wife and your friend. God isn't'" (197).

This sense of hope is further characterized in Madonna's ghost, who comes back through Brendan's fey self and suggests forgiveness and mercy. He sees her several times after her death, and we are led to believe that she is instrumental in helping Brendan save Ciara from harm. Brendan's rebirth is accomplished by his acceptance of the universe as it is supposed to be. Blackie Ryan says to Brendan,

> One either lives in a universe where absolution and new beginnings are possible, indeed a matter of common-place occurrence, or one does not. The burden of your interlude was that you and Madonna could still forgive each other and still begin again despite the absurdity of death. It is surely not the first time you've heard that message. If the message is true, then all things are possible. But the issue—is it not?—is whether the message is true and not whether a particular phenomenon is possible, a phenomenon which, in the nature of things, does not admit of easy falsification or verification. (226)

And thus, we come to Blackie's homily (directed to children) on Memorial Day, the subject of which is courage.

> Courage is nothing more than generosity in time of crisis and risk. It is nothing more than powerful hope translated into action when others desperately need our help [...]. Life is an exploration of hope, an enterprise of risk taking, a journey of ever-renewed challenge. Generosity, hopefulness, courage are not options on such a pilgrimage. If we wish to be able to respond spontaneously and heedlessly in moments of crisis, [...] then we, too, must develop habits of generosity in our daily lives. We must take out the garbage when we're asked, put gasoline in the

car when we're asked, clear off the table when we're asked, pile up the dishes in the dishwasher when we're asked, and run to the store to buy milk, bread, and charcoal lighter when we're asked. It is of these small heroisms, and sometimes at the moment they don't seem very small, of which great human courage is created. (268)

God's attributes, especially hope, are found in the little things we do that add up at the end into who and what we are. Brendan is able to find his grail because of who he is, i.e., who he has become throughout his life. And this is the score God uses to play this rite of spring.

Chapter 7: Other Wonders of Greeley's Fiction

The Catholic imagination's reliance on the compatibility of reason and faith, with its corollary that wisdom can be gleaned from the world in all its diversity, implies three further notions about the world: it should be non-elitist; it must respect the continuity of persons in community; and it depends on more than knowing how the world works, it requires wisdom. Greeley's best characters, especially the ones who compose the families and neighborhoods that so delight his fictional world, insist that everyone has a right to use the truth as he or she sees fit. This means that we must trust that others will get it right. Greeley's negative characters are usually marked by or produced by envy, today's greatest sin (See Chapter 2). Envy produces mediocrity and mendacity, which corrupt essential institutions of society, causing untold damage to persons and their chances in life. Greeley's characters are at their best, moreover, when they understand the continuity of persons and community. Greeley's fiction reveals that life is a comedy, and that this means that there are limitless second chances. These are vouchsafed as grace. Often they are evidence in human affairs of the formal principles of subsidiarity and solidarity. Sometimes his characters must learn this continuity through experience, but precisely because experience teaches their lessons, these two principles are affirmed as valid. Finally, Greeley's best characters learn how to integrate knowledge (the things they know) into wisdom (they use what they know for the right reasons and to the right effects). This implies that reality is dynamic rather than static, and it entails an intellectual approach to the world that respects the dynamism and contingency of God's world. Greeley's commitment to the social sciences, their study and uses, exemplifies the Gospel's insistence that the truth will makes us free.

A non-elitist, perhaps, egalitarian approach to the world. We can see the Catholic preference for non-elitism in *The Cardinal Virtues* (1990). [127] Set in Chicago during the late 1980s, *The Cardinal Virtues* is a novel about the habitual failures of human nature and their magnification when religion masks or hides them for what they are. The first of three opening epigrams are the words of George Bernard Shaw from St. Joan: "Must Christ be crucified in every generation by those who have no imagination,"[128] and they convey the thematic thrust of this story. Of course, in every time and place, Christ will be required to accomplish the effects of his salvation of the world from sin and death: that is Christ's mission, that is God's plan—the "Deep Magic" referred to by Lewis in the Narnia tales—and that is why, in Catholic thought, Christ gave himself in the church—that he remains with human beings until the end of time. Thus, the human characters who make up the church ought to know better than they do the tremendous responsibility of service that being church requires. That, too, is why the failures of these men and women cause so much damage and why the scandal of the humanity of the church proves to be so great. Toward the end of the novel, its main character, Father Lar McAuliffe, asks how parish life, which has become so meaningless to him in his disillusionment, could "contribute to the salvation of a single life?" His answer helps us understand both how the cardinal virtues are present in human beings and why knowing how this is so is important. "The parish community, bound together by whatever means we could find, provided patterns of meaning, directions, and goals for human lives. It existed so we could all of us together practice the skills of offering ourselves in service to

---

[127] *The Cardinal Virtues*. New York: Warner Books, 1990. Greeley tells us in *Furthermore! Memories of a Parish Priest* (128) that this novel was originally designed for a TV series.

[128] The character Cauchon says "'Must then a Christ perish in torment in every age to save those that have no imagination?'" (St. Joan "Epilogue" 154).

others" (377). Without this service and these skills, Christ is destined to be crucified over and over again.

The parish as community moves the novel along and binds its characters, the good and the bad, into a drama that ends ambiguously. If we see the ending as a comedy (Greeley's comedies of grace), it appears that life remains flawed but meaningful. If we see the ending as tragic (as those do who see life as a death sentence), life seems to be grasping, mean, and violent. Lar McAuliffe, whose zeal has grown cold, lives as though it is the former, not the latter. His religion, his faith, and the meaning of his life are all tied to his vocation as a priest. His resistance to the bureaucratic idiocy of the church's political structure—embodied in a good but weak, conniving cardinal archbishop—stands as the sign and symbol that Christ is present in a wounded world. McAuliffe's love of the church as a mystery marking God's presence in this world mirrors his political and personal virtues.

In Catholic thought, the four cardinal virtues: prudence, justice, courage, and temperance, are called "cardinal" because they are the hinges upon which all other virtues depend. Without them and their habituation in each person's life, there can be no other characteristics that reflect our higher natures. To these virtues are added the three "theological" virtues of faith, hope, and love, which are marks of God's life, Catholics would say God's grace, in our lives. These seven virtues, four which develop over the course of a life through our own efforts and habits, and three which are radically dependent on God's giving them to us, mark both the goal and the process by which a person acts well in God's great comedy of grace. The cardinal virtues mark our attempted responses to the great gift of love that is God's grace. Our responses, like these virtues, take place in community. Thus, the character of Lar McAuliffe is the sum of his relationships. He is who he is, for good or ill, because of his role as pastor of St. Finian parish. Because of this, he cannot be seen as better than, or more important than, all the others to whom he is connected. Those with whom he works and for whom he ministers are all essential in telling his story. Each has his or her own dignity and worth. The question becomes, how do the cardinal virtues manifest themselves in their consequences?

Behind this question, in good Celtic style, is the real question of the book, how might salvation be accomplished?

Greeley, therefore, recalls another work of fiction that treats the same question. It is a story referred to often throughout the novel, especially when describing the new priest sent to help Father McAuliffe with the work of the parish: Jamie Kennan is referred to as Billy Budd. It seems that *Billy Budd* reveals the structure of this novel. The parish, like the ship in Melville's novella, is the bark upon which life takes place and depends. That life is revealed through a range of human types—conservatives, liberals, reactionaries, Marxists, bright, stupid, cunning, and holy—and is measured by the perceptions of the parish staff who make up the core of parish activities. The season is fall to winter, days of "infinite sadness" and terrible cold. The subplots involve the violence of spousal abuse and incest, with the psychological destruction these entail: envy hidden in a secret reactionary society and its un-Christ-like denizens; the injustice of corrupt government agencies that ignore basic human rights; autocracy and incompetence in the chancery and its clerical buffoons; burnout from overwork and its diminishment of vision; suicide with its devastation of the living; hatred disguised as parental love and its calumny against the innocent—all the marks of an unredeemed world. In the working out of each of these problems, the reader witnesses the temperance that rebuilds self-images marred by incest, abuse, and alcoholism; the courage of those falsely charged when facing their tormentors; the justice involved in protecting human beings, especially the least among us; the prudence required to confront the secrecy of envy and its lies; the faith that motivates even a burned out and exhausted vocation; hope in the face of death and the resiliency of the young; love that is the reason for friendship and an essential quality of a humane life.

No plot summary can capture the brilliance of this novel. It is so tightly written and its subplots are so well integrated that only the dialogue among the characters, and especially, the interior dialogue of the main character, can convey the richness of this comedy of grace. At best we can say, it is a novel about friendship, especially between an old pastor and a new curate—a relationship that usually does not produce friendship—and that its action reveals hope as the major characteristic of our better natures. Hope and friendship function together.

The action begins in a suburban parish where "[t]here is nothing left that we priests could do that we have not done to drive them [Catholics] out" (48). Jamie Kennan takes to his new assignment much like Billy Budd does to his; he is loved by everyone and is able to accomplish anything by working with everyone. Well integrated as a personality, he is the last child of Maggie Ward—a character of great psychological insight and power—and Judge Kennan—a courageous war hero, Solomon-like judge, and novelist (See *The Search for Maggie Ward*.) But as his mother and a wise old priest both remark, he is an innocent. As such, Jamie confronts a world defined not by virtue but by every vice known to humankind.

We see this world through the exhausted eyes of Lar McAuliffe, the pastor.[129] It is a world where the church has lost its ability to employ its rich teaching on human sexuality because that church's henchmen have used sexuality as a means for asserting autocratic authority over the faithful, a faithful that merely ignores the church on this point. Early in the novel, Father Kennan remarks, "'Sexual love is no solution to any problem [...]. It may make solutions possible—motivation for therapy, courage to grow, faith to take risks'" (93). This, in part, foreshadows the depth of the church's true understanding of this most important aspect of the world's sacramentality. It also serves as an insight into the character Dr. Jeanne Flavin. Her need to expiate guilt for being incestuously abused by her father is a sign of her intemperance, a characteristic she overcomes through her friendship

---

[129] I quote only two of McAuliffe's inner dialogues about his moral and psychological condition. This novel is a profound meditation on the abilities of virtue in the face of the most debilitating personal anguish: "I'm equally bitter at the guys [who] ran out on their commitments. Some of them told the whole world that all the good priests were leaving and that only the sick and the sexually neuter were remaining. They destroyed the image of the priesthood; they destroyed vocations, and they made it much harder on those of us who kept our promises" (158). "I'm pissed off at all the false prophets who come down the pike with the new answers that were supposed to solve all our problems—salvation history, sensitivity training, Kerygmatic catechetics, client-centered counseling, the Third World, fundamental option for the poor, the Rite of Christian Initiation for Adults, etc., etc" (159).

with both the old and the new priest. She is like many recurring characters in Greeley's novels, a victim of the forces of change which would sweep through the church as a result of the imprudence of its leadership immediately after the Second Vatican Council. She had been a member of a religious order that like so many during those times, lost its way. As McAuliffe views what happened to religious congregations after the Council, "'The idea was that you stopped doing what you did well for people who wanted it in this country and went to the missions to do the same thing badly for people who mostly didn't want it'" (94). One of the results of this mistake, he argues, was that like many religious men and women of the time, Jeanne Flavin left Christianity to "'become a dedicated Stalinist, convinced in theory—not in practice—that justice can be achieved through ruthless violence'" (96).

The forces of autocracy, envy, and injustice, common to human beings without well-developed virtue, are arrayed against the parish and its community of friends. There is George Wholey—hardly an unintentional pun—a member of the Corpus Christi Society[130] that works to terrorize the church into following its reactionary religious agenda. This group is the agent of most of the sinful behavior in the novel; above all else it is emblematic of the vice of envy—one of the capital or cardinal sins—in Greeley's fiction, perhaps the greatest of these sins.[131]

> The Catholic Church with its centuries of rich tradition, the Archdiocese of Chicago with its immense resources and horrendous problems—both were at the mercy of a small-minded, petty, ignorant suburban real estate developer. He held his power to disturb and disrupt not because he represented anyone, not because he was important or influential, and not because the Cardinal and his stooges believed his complaints.

---

[130] Those unfamiliar with Catholic culture might miss the irony here. Corpus Christi, the Body of Christ, refers to a central doctrine of Catholic Christianity: that Christ's body is present in the Eucharist, which itself is a sign and symbol of unity and love. The agenda and the machinations of this society hardly mirror this doctrine.
[131] See *The Cardinal Sins*.

He was a problem because he belonged to a secret society of which they were frightened. (153)

George Wholey is the pawn of Father Louis Almavivia, and he uses his teenage son to perjure himself by charging Jamie Kennan with child abuse. His wife, Jill, finds the courage to contradict these charges.

The reader finally comes to the confrontation between Father McAuliffe and the chancery. Father Joseph Slone, vicar general of the archdiocese, a Claggart-like character whose stupidity serves the cardinal archbishop, attempts to confine the fallout produced by the calumny against Jamie Kennan by transferring him out of the diocese and replacing McAuliffe as pastor of St. Finians. But as the main character says, "'This year [...] they don't hang Billy Budd; they don't burn Joan of Arc, and they don't crucify Jesus of Nazareth'" (424). Using Jill Wholey's testimony, which saves her children from her husband's folly, McAuliffe confronts what is behind Slone's *auto da fe*: his quest for dominance (the sin of pride), a confused idea of power. The novel demonstrates that the Holy Spirit's guarantee that the "gates of hell" shall not destroy the People of God is not patent against the consequences of failed virtue. McAuliffe knows what any good man or woman knows after working in the world:

> He [the cardinal] would have deported Brigid to Ireland[132] when there were legal grounds for her to stay. He would have shipped Jamie out of the archdiocese with a cloud over him that would have lasted all his life. He would have done both of these ugly deeds "for the good of the 'Church.'" He would have ruined two lives "to avoid more public scandal"—by which he meant media reports that would attract the attention of his masters in Rome and diminish his clout. (443)

Yet the novel does not end with a temporary victory of the cardinal virtues, though these wins do sustain us. The novel ends on the Vigil of Easter, the highest of Catholic holy days. After Father Keenan sings the Exultet, "the hymn heralding the Resurrection" (448) and the

---

[132] Referring to an earlier episode in the novel involving the injustice of the immigration authorities' attempt to deport the rectory's cook.

oldest extant Christian hymn praising "the happy fault of Adam by which we merited such a redeemer," McAuliffe

> preached about the symbolism of the fire and the water—the story of a God who, despite all good taste and right reason and plain sanity, had fallen in love with his creatures. God's passion for us [...] first sensed by the Hebrew prophets, is like that of a man and woman falling head over heels in love with one another. The only difference is that God's passion is more violent and more reckless than the strongest of human passions. Easter is an invitation to renew that romance between God and us and to simultaneously renew our romances with one another. (448)

Then his mind turns to a couple who have reconciled and fallen in love again and speaks directly to God:

> You sent an irresistible sign to one of those priests, one who has been wallowing in a hot flood tide of grace since the day his New Priest arrived, and didn't have the sense to comprehend that he had been swept up in the surging current. It's not only Jamie's encore for which I'm waiting around Saint Finian's. I want to see Your encore too. (448)

To the Catholic imagination, these words evoke not only the words of the great scholastic thinker, Thomas Aquinas: "grace does not force nature but perfects it," but they also connect us to the abiding truth found in all of Greeley's fiction that grace is lurking everywhere, and that we have the eyes to see it and the character to embrace it if we let ourselves be embraced and if we habituate ourselves to do so continually.

This theme of lurking grace is connected to the idea that life depends on social relations. The characters in Greeley's *Fall from Grace* (1993)[133] are many and varied. Using the multiple voices of these characters, Greeley constructs a novel of deep sensitivity for the human condition. The characters are revealed in layers of relationships, which prove true and which indicate the profundity of human love. As

---

[133] *Fall from Grace.* New York: Putnam and Sons, 1993.

always, human passion is a metaphor for God's love for creation and for human beings especially. Yet, in this novel, God seems absent. Where in many other Greeley novels, characters pray to a silent, yet communicative God, in this work God is invoked only rarely and then in the most pedestrian of ways. It as though the author has come to be almost completely secular in his art. (This does not mean that Greeley's novels are secular, but rather, that he hides his main character, the God of infinite love, in the relationships his stories depend upon.)

The first layer of relationship is that of Kieran O'Kerrigan, Kathleen Leary Donahue, and her brother, James Leary. O'Kerrigan has returned to Chicago after an eighteen-year absence, to reestablish his love for Kathleen. She is now married to Brien Douahue, who is a rich, successful, but hardly politically savvy candidate for the US Senate. James, the auxiliary bishop of the Archdiocese of Chicago, is the right-hand man of the cardinal. Interestingly, the cardinal does not appear in this novel except as representative of the archdiocese as a "corporation sole." This status as a legal entity has significance because James is involved in a pending lawsuit about child abuse in the priesthood. That the church is only its legal self signifies the depersonalization that transpires in social organizations when their true warrant is forgotten and when they depend on legalized elitism.

The relationships of Kathleen to Brien and to her brother James reveal her role as mother of three teenage daughters. (Note should be made here that for Greeley, teenage daughters are often a powerful symbol of God's agency in the world. They also are the most non-elitist of his characters.[134]) Kathleen's marriage is in shambles: she is a battered wife who learns that her husband has engaged in a homosexual affair. James Leary's role in this relationship seems to be that of support and compromise. Indeed, James is the compromiser par excellence in this novel.

Brendan McNulty is a priest of the archdiocese who, to the great consternation of Bishop James Leary, serves as a lawyer to the abused victim's family. McNulty's role is that of the gadfly who stings the great beast into action. He also introduces a subplot involving a satanic cult

---

[134] See for example, Noele in *Lord of the Dance.*

intending to sacrifice a child on All Hollow's Eve. The reality of this plot remains ambiguous until the end of the novel. Kathleen confronts her husband, the scion of a fading but still politically active family, and makes him agree to therapy. That therapy reveals to Brien his homosexuality, and more importantly, his hatred of women. It seems as if he might be happy, but the responsibilities laid upon him as the last best hope of the Leary-Donahue patricians intervene. And they intervene through James, Brien's childhood friend. In fact, James is the common denominator in all the relationships. James is the good Catholic gone wrong without knowing it.

Throughout the novel, it is Bishop James Leary who bears the responsibility for the good name of the church, so much so that he participates in suborning perjury in the sexual abuse case in which he and the archdiocese's lawyers are involved. He tries to mediate the failed marriage of Kathleen and Brien, not only for the good of the sacramental character of their union, but also because of the political impact a divorce might have on the upcoming Senate race. Bishop James is also the voice of discipline in the priesthood. He is very much irritated that McNulty is both acting pastor and practicing lawyer. He sees this practice as both un-priestly and as dangerous to the archdiocesan defense against the charges of sexual abuse. James Leary is also the voice of loyalty to the church, its representative for and defender not only of its good name, but also of its good. James cannot believe that a priest he knows well could possibly be involved in homosexuality and pedophilia. Nor can he understand why the laity might question the impartiality of the archdiocesan administration and the agencies it employs. Bishop James is a good priest fortified by the prejudices of his class.

Thus, we are surprised when, after Brien has nearly killed Kathleen in a drunken rage—she is saved only by the martial art of one of her daughters—we learn that it was James Leary all along who has played God from the beginning. O'Kerrigan had been forced to leave Chicago as a young man because his father was convicted of a crime he did not commit and because O'Kerrigan was accused of stealing money held for a charity function. James bailed him out with a personal loan so that the money could be returned and restitution made. Yet we learn

James had set up O'Kerrigan so that he would not marry his sister, just as we learn that the Leary-Donahue clan had set up the senior O'Kerrigan. More surprising is the revelation that the authorities have uncovered and arrested a plot to sacrifice one of James' nieces and that a trusted priest was Brien's lover and the agent of the plot. Even more surprising is the fact that James and Brien had been engaged in homosexual behavior as adolescents, and that James' injustice to O'Kerrigan was motivated by James' desire to have his best-loved friend, Brien, marry his sister.

Revealed as sins, in the end all is forgiven with a wave of the hand. This sacramental forgiveness is embodied in the timing of the action. The Feast of All Saints follows Halloween, and it is during this sacred time that we witness O'Kerrigan's forgiveness of James Leary and Kathleen's forgiveness of Brien and of his family. Such forgiveness seems divine in light of the human characters who are its agents. We are forced to asked how this could be so. That answer is found in another, and a greater sacrament, that of the marriage of Kathleen and Kieran. The reader discovers, from a bit of theological logic, that the bodies of the man and of the woman are the sign of this great sacrament. They administer the sacrament to each other, even though their formal, civil contract will not take place until well into the future. Just as the unavailability of a priest may mean that two persons may marry each other without that priest, so, too, the moral absence of clergy, the proximity of their marriage to the death of an important person and the putative scandal that might be involved in a celebration at such a time, means that Kieran and Kathleen can begin to heal through their love for each other before the benefit of clergy. It is Kieran's love, Kathleen's intelligence, McNulty's expertise, and an overarching respect for these characteristics that ground Greeley's political world. The assumption throughout is that love, intelligence, and expertise constitute the warrants for the action. Anyone possessed of them is entitled to act and assumed to act validly. It is not status in an elite—Bishop James' role in family and church—but the love, intelligence, and expertise of those who act that move the Catholic imagination.

Two of Greeley's Bishop Blackie Ryan mystery novels further illustrate the negative connotation of elitism, one at the level of the local church—*The Bishop and the Beggar Girl of St. Germain* (2001)—and, the other at the level of the universal—in this case international might be a better adjective—*The Bishop Goes to the University* (2004). Each provides a fast-paced story involving the intrepid Bishop Blackie Ryan.[135]

In *The Bishop and the Beggar Girl of St. Germain,* the local church, represented by the Archdiocese of Paris, finds its cardinal archbishop at wits end because of a troublesome priest, the Dominican Friar Jean-Claude. He is the most admired priest in all of France, having become popular through the medium of television. His preaching has brought many back to their religious roots. When he disappears, foul play is suspected, and as soon as he disappears, the miracles begin, and his saintliness becomes the archbishop's problem. One might think a good Catholic preacher—the very charism of the Order of Preachers—and the priest's sanctity would be welcome news to the administrative church. Such is not the case here, and Greeley uses the theme of an envious priesthood and the venality of high ecclesiastical dignitaries to critique an elitist ecclesiastical organization.

As Bishop Blackie Ryan goes about his investigation of the priest gone missing, he has the help of a young woman, who serves as the voice of the believing church even as she is alienated from her society—she and many others like her are too poor to practice their teaching vocations and are ignored by the French state—and from the church. She cannot see a reason to envy or malign Friar Jean-Claude. Together they interview all the usual suspects and find in them the same expressions of fallen human nature that seem to be everywhere the same. In fact, both his order and his archbishop would rather he stay missing, while those who have learned about the infinite love of God from his preaching want him home. The mystery is solved when Ryan finds the priest's twin sister. After Jean-Claude had died of a rare disease, his sister took on his identity. The person who became the great and holy preacher was, in fact, a woman all along. This raises a set of very interesting theological problems and gives the characters the

---

[135] *The Bishop and the Beggar Girl of St. Germain.* New York: A Forge Book 2001, and *The Bishop Goes to the University.* Thorndike, ME: Center Point Pub., 2004.

occasion to address issues related to the role of women in the Catholic Church. Although not the central theme of the book, these issues, for example, the sacraments administered by "Jean-Claude" as valid but not licit, occasion consideration of the politics behind them. Are the effects of God's love and grace in those who hear and heed "Jean-Claude's" preaching, altered by gender? And, are the rules regulating gender in the church about doctrine or about power?

Whatever the answers might be, the questions afford the characters the chance to demonstrate that God's grace can never be boxed or cornered and that this grace works sometimes through our openness to it, and more often than not, sometimes in spite of us and of the administrative church. At one point in her story, the sister says she "prayed before she believed," a sentiment that epitomizes her journey of faith. Here we find grace working in persons unaware of or opposed to its effects. She became her brother out of love for him: the greatest commandment in Christianity is to love God above all else and show it by loving our neighbors as ourselves. In becoming her brother, she loved God perfectly. In spite of envy and ridicule, in spite of the politics of power, in spite of a doctrine's propositions, God is lurking everywhere.

It would seem that the sheer abundance of grace, of God's life in all things, and inasmuch as all things are a means to God's abundant love, the church, which is supposed to celebrate and guard this truth, would be a beacon of goodness and humanity: a holy place set apart, in which to express our gratitude. Yet, as Greeley's characters continually suggest, God turned the church over to fallible men and women and not to his angels. Thus, the church as the mystery of Christ's presence among us and as the Spirit's life in the world, too often is marred by human machinations—the Machiavellian politics of earthly realism. To be sure, the church must work in the world. How this is so, however, makes all the difference to those living in this world. History indicates that many times the church, through its corporate activities and the actions of its officials and members, has failed to be witness to God's grace.

The machinations of this temporal church are the backdrop against which the action of *The Bishop Goes to the University* (2004) unfolds.[136]

---

[136] *The Bishop Goes to the University* Thorndike, ME: Center Point Pub., 2004.

The role of the church in the collapse of the Communist empire in the late 1980s and early 1990s and its collaboration with other states in this historic event is a story that remains to be told in its entirety. It is at least historically correct to say that Pope John Paul II, as a son of Poland and a stalwart anticommunist, recognized the Solidarity movement in Poland, an organization that was the beginning of the end of Soviet domination in Eastern Europe. And it is suspected that through the institutional church he played a greater role than most know about in the undoing of Communism. This work of fiction suggests this history and suspicion.

Bishop Blackwood Ryan again is sent by his cardinal to deal with the murder of a visiting scholar at "The" University. The secret to the locked room murder is quickly solved only to introduce the history of one Brother Semyon Ivanivich Popov, the supposed murder victim. In his life, we witness the political in its negative international sense, and we are asked to judge whether the inherent dignity of the human person—the guardianship of which is the church's particular warrant—is more important than the machinations of international intrigue.

Blackwood discovers that the murdered scholar is not Popov but someone in the employ of either the CIA or its Soviet equivalent. Brother Semyon, however, has survived, but at an incredible cost. We learn that as a Polish seminarian in Rome during 1965, he was approached by high Vatican officials and asked to live secretly as a Russian Orthodox monk as an experiment in the Vatican Council's newly minted ecumenism. In the process, Popov becomes a scholar and is forgotten until asked by the pope to be an archbishop *in pectore*, i.e., secretly known only to the pope. Faithful to this secret and to underground Catholics in the Soviet Union, Brother Semyon leads a double life. The demolition of the Soviet state makes his work no longer feasible since Russian Orthodoxy burgeons forth upon its newly won freedom in Russia and the former Soviet states. What he has learned as a Christian "double agent" is that although the beliefs of the Catholic and the Orthodox churches are basically the same and they could with very little effort subsist in unity, the history that runs between and against them is too much to allow that unity. The international Machiavellianism that determined the life of the good Brother Semyon proves to have produced no fruit. Once again, we learn through the characters of Greeley's fiction that playing fast and loose with the means, employing means that produce evil rather than good, ends in the failure of the good. Popov has been made a cardinal in the Roman Catholic Church even as his life has been wastefully used. God's work, it seems, is never the sole property of elites, even the best intentioned.

In a third novel in this series, *The Bishop in the Old Neighborhood*,[137] John Blackwood Ryan, auxiliary bishop of Chicago, is yet again called upon by his cardinal archbishop to solve a "locked room" murder, this time in the church of St. Lucy, a parish in an integrated neighborhood. The character of God as love reveals itself in the tender love story of Declan O'Donnell and Camilla Datillo, a police officer and a prosecuting attorney, respectively. The mystery involves the question, who would gain from the desecration of a church, and is it tied to the deaths of six teenagers from the parish sixty years ago? With the support and help of his community, Blackie solves the crime: the recent murders are the work of the O'Boyle's, owners of a firm tied to the redevelopment of the neighborhood, and more to the point, to the sixty-year-old crime. Through the good office of his deceased father, Bishop Ryan uncovers a government-sponsored murder of six beautiful children in the interest of the national security of 1944. They were killed to keep them from revealing one of the government's many special projects—in this case the development of chemical death.

The role of God's justice is played out by the community of other good Catholic men and women, e.g., O'Donnell and Datillo, who help set in motion the process by which the crimes are uncovered. That justice, as we know from the Greeley characters who populate this and other of his novels, when it comes from God comes as mercy. The final scenes in the story involve the confession, absolution, and happy death of the culprit O'Boyle, who has suffered from guilt for sixty years. One of his victims, Annie Scanlon, greets him upon his death and takes him to the many-colored land of God's infinite love. What makes this novel new as a Blackie Ryan mystery is that the old

---

[137] *The Bishop in the Old Neighborhood*, New York: Forge Books, 2005.

neighborhood comes alive through several contemporary issues: urban redevelopment and the elitist interests it entails—racism, both black and white, and the role of the parish in such development—Catholic schools and their effectiveness as an alternative and excellent form of education for all; and Homeland Security that gives witness to the elitist idiocy of security over personal freedom. These are developed along with the regular Greeley issues of church politics, clerical envy, city politics, and police corruption, all to very good effect. Since Father Greeley has studied the sociology of these matters in some detail, this fiction helps enflesh these issues and makes them real on the human level. The real surprise in this novel is that the Ryans' Cardinal Cronin has collected his markers in Rome and caused the elevation of John Blackwood Ryan to coadjutor with the right to succession. He is to be the next Archbishop of Chicago. What this means for his sleuthing remains to be seen.

The continuity of persons and community. *Death in April,* (1980)[138] Greeley's second novel,[139] is the story of a second chance at love, where the courage of the truth is used to counter the law's misuse

---

[138] *Death in April.* New York: Dell Publishing Co., 1980.

[139] Greeley's first novel, *The Magic Cup: An Irish Legend* (New York: McGraw Hill, 1979) is the story of a pilgrim's quest for the Grail. The journey through Ireland and to the Western Isles involves the protagonist, Cormac MacDermot, in the process of human maturation through which he discovers hope, love, and forgiveness. His slave girl, Brigid, turns out to be his princess, who he only finds after she has been lost. Through her, Cormac comes to confront evil, and with her, and because of her independence and power, he confronts evil, subdues it, and finds life. "Who needs a magic cup when he has a magic princess?" MacDermot asks.

To this point in the narrative, the man and his dog have come through much suffering; he is the king returned, but a king hardly capable of ruling justly. His sufferings have made him cold and tired, and his self-pity blocks his view of others. It is Biddy—the Irish woman with the right to interrupt the ponderous work of men—who teaches Cormac that love begins with hope and carries us to forgiveness. This pagan Biddy teaches Christian Ireland because she has a secret relationship with the King Jesus and his Mother Mary. "Waiting is praying," she learns from them both: God does not so much speak to us as he waits for our reply to his love and providence. This kind of faith does not escape the world or the sufferings men and women sometimes make from it: this faith seeks to come to love through the hope that can be born of such suffering. Such hope is found in laughter and song and dance. Here, the God who creates, the God who speaks, and the God who calls—Greeley's portrayal of the Trinity—works

of justice. James McCormac O'Neill is a successful writer living in Paris, who returns to his Chicago past to resolve issues of his midlife and rediscover his long-lost love, Lynn Conroy. James O'Neill must come home to find himself. His daughter, Clare, knows this even as he does not. O'Neill must return home because he had left it by running away. Even though his dream of writing in New York was his perceived reason for leaving, he left to escape the lowliness of his social status.

On a layover in Chicago, O'Neill drives to the summer lake community of his youth and literally runs into his old sweetheart, now a widow with five children and a successful real estate company, which she has saved from the wreckage of her husband's poor stewardship. Like God, she is ready to be foolishly in love (78). The two have a second chance with each other. It is, after all, April when the action takes place.

Both find their second chances through each other and through their common search for justice. Lynn Conroy faces indictment because of the political machinations of the US attorney, who misuses his authority (his power to use the grand jury system for his own political purposes) in order to gain power through public opinion. A character representing the intellectual elite of Chicago explains this idea

---

through the human agencies of intelligence, poetry, and song. These characteristics of Irish culture are visited throughout Cormac's and Biddy's adventures—adventures that teach both how to be together without one obliterating the other. They become persons together, each with their own weaknesses and strengths, so that in the end, the magic of pagan culture is transformed into sacrament. Grace abounds everywhere.

"Prisoners of pride" (228) are what men become when left to their own devices. Virgil's great epic, *Aeneid*, ends with the missed moment: when Aeneas kills Turnus in revenge for the death of his protégé. Mercy rather than justice—an eye for an eye—would have shown man's higher angel, but true to human nature, we today might say, the hard wiring of the human psyche, Aeneas' lesser side, "wins" the day. Perhaps Virgil was giving Augustus, his patron, a lecture in the failed policy of mercy initiated by Caesar in a time of civil war. Greeley, however, has his hero hoping to the end that he might defend this life and allow the aggressor to live. This aggressor, Aed MacSweeney, kills himself by lunging on Cormac's raised sword (230). Another missed moment, but one that accounts for the human propensity to pride. "The God of mercy and love" (235) triumphs in the end through the mercy shown to his enemies as well as the love of his marriage bed.

of justice. In response to O'Neill's proposition that the diminishing of anyone's rights involves diminishing everyone's rights, especially when prosecutors try and convict individuals through the press, the character Stern says, "'[…] the corruption in this city is so evil I find myself convinced that technical indictments and immunized witnesses are a necessary aberration we must permit for a short time'" (152). A little evil used to realize a greater good! Such utilitarian rationalization undermines the Catholic idea of the continuity of personal rights with the social protection of these rights.

At issue in this novel is the question of how far a good person may go in collaborating with the fallen world and the evil implicit in it, as well as the corresponding question involving the moral danger to those who rule and believe themselves to be just. One character remarks, "'We want to govern so badly because we are smart and moral. Should we ever gain power, I personally would migrate to California or some other safe place. I fear the rule of Robespierre […]'" (155). The form of elitism this character fears threatens the rights and well being of persons, and in doing so, destroys the integrity of the community.

The church as an institution (the Archdiocese of Chicago) is involved in Conroy's case because the cardinal archbishop has in his files a memorandum that were it made public, would vindicate Conroy. The church's power to reconcile seems implied here. O'Neill obtains the memo through his own talents and the assertion of personality against the corrupt, and perhaps, insane cardinal. It is through O'Neill's art as a writer that Conroy is saved. This comedy of grace (206) ends when the prosecutor's political claims are placed in jeopardy by O'Neill's new novel about a project that involves a dishonest prosecutor's misuse of authority—a tale within a tale. The novel is too true to life and Conroy is not indicted. Art imitates life.

The story ends ambiguously. In the penultimate scene, Lynn and O'Neill argue until he strikes her. In the last scene, on Pentecost, the action having lasted from Good Friday, we find Conroy showing up at the airport, planning to fly to Paris with her victimizer. She has forgiven him "[w]ithout confession or contrition" (250). His question about the Holy Ghost is now answered. She has pursued him and been his second chance; she has allowed him to be angry (253–54), and they still go on together. Grace never forces nature; she always perfects it through love.

The idea that persons require human and humane communities in order to survive and that such communities are prerequisites of personal freedom, is part of the sacramental message of Greeley's Passover Trilogy (*Thy Brother's Wife* 1982, *Assent into Hell* 1983, *Lord of the Dance* 1984).[140]

The Easter Triduum marks the three days of the highest holidays in Catholic culture. They come at the end of the season of Lent—a time of self-assessment, penance, and longing. Holy Thursday celebrates the communion of the Lord, the Lord's Supper, where he gave his great mandate that we love each other as he has loved us. It marks the foundation of the Eucharist and of priesthood, the sacraments of unity and of service. Good Friday marks the day of Christ's suffering and death, his crucifixion. This is the penultimate day of salvation, when Christ laid down his life for his friends, for friends certainly not worthy of such love but in being so loved, are redeemed once and for all. It is the mystery of Christ's death and resurrection, reenacted in every celebration of the Lord's Supper, in every Mass. This day marks the claim of God to all history, past, present, and to come; the emblem of the cross becomes the archetypical sign connecting the world and heaven. Holy Saturday and Easter Sunday mark the ultimate day of our salvation. The resurrection of Jesus from the dead—the promise of God that life is greater than death—is the moment that contains all time and all promise.

Greeley tells us about the three essential components of the Jewish and Christian versions of Passover: community, freedom, and new life. (*Assent into Hell* xi). The first novel in the series, *Thy Brother's Wife*, is about a family and the community that makes up their lives. It is a story of secrets and the fears that thrive on and derive from such secrets. Michael and Mary Eileen Cronin have two sons, Sean and Paul. After the death of Mary Eileen, a foster daughter, Nora Riley, comes to live with them. Michael, the product of post-World War II wealth, is a man driven by the need to be successful, and he has plotted

---

[140] *Thy Brother's Wife*. New York: Warner Books, 1982. *Ascent into Hell*. New York: Warner Books, 1983. *Lord of the Dance*. New York: Warner Books, 1984.

the destinies of his two sons as part of his own: Sean is to become a priest and Paul a lawyer. Ultimately, he wants Sean to be a member of the Catholic hierarchy and Paul to be President of the United States. Such are the ambitions of the Irish Catholic middle class. Michael uses sex as a means to exploit women and his first son, Paul, is no better. Both Paul and Sean fall in love with Nora.

The novel covers the period from 1938–1977. Against the backdrop of American cultural and political history, Greeley constructs a story that reveals the role commitments can have, both for good and for evil, in the building of community. More to the point of the novel's action is the intimate connection of community and communion. The eight books of the novel are organized around Christ's discourse of love from the Gospel of St. John (John 13–17), a discourse central to the Catholic liturgy of Holy Thursday. In this discourse, the doctrine of love is made explicit and serves as the foundation for the Catholic understanding of Christ's divinity. The Great Mandatum, from which Maundy Thursday derives its name, is embodied in Christ's command that like him, we wash the feet of others. As Jesus washed the feet of his disciples to demonstrate his love for his friends, so too, Christians are called to be servants to each other as the sign of their love for God. This raises a critical point about loving God and neighbor. Jesus says, "You are my friends if you do what I command you" (John 15:13). The critical point is in how these words are to be understood: is friendship with God the reward for doing what we are commanded? Or, is doing what God commands, i.e., in serving others in love, identical with friendship with God? These questions, and how they are answered, mark a great divide between kinds of religious behavior. This certainly is behind the meaning of this novel. Greeley writes in a Personal Afterword, "This particular religious story will be successful if the reader is disconcerted by the tale of commitments that are imperfectly made and imperfectly kept—but that are still kept. And by the image of a God who draws straight with crooked lines, who easily and quickly forgives, and who wants to love us with the tenderness of a mother" (351). Nora will be the key character in bringing us to this understanding. From being an object of love for Sean and Paul, she becomes the sign of God's Motherhood. Like all good mothers, she comes to know that the rules directing the lives of her children and of herself are merely instrumental in bringing all persons into a community of love.

Paul, who will become Nora's husband, is, like many of us, only apparently good. He is a war hero, yet in fact, he proved a coward in battle and ran from danger. Only he and one other person know this. That other person will use this information to blackmail him, and eventually make a murderer of him. But before there is Paul's secret, there is the secret of Mary Eileen's death. The boys and Nora grow up believing that she died in a car accident in 1934. Her husband, Michael, will play sexually with other women, but until this secret is revealed, he will never love them or be loved by them. Michael's duty to his sons blight their relationship with him and with each other: Paul is duty bound to become a public man, Sean is duty bound to be a priest, Nora is duty bound by her status as an orphan. Though comfortable in a middle-class way, essentially their lives are driven by the rules and the fear of what might happen when these rules are broken. Sean is ordained; Nora and Paul are married and have children; Michael pursues power and wealth as a hedge against death. They are all slaves in some way. The seminary life, for example, that Sean must endure in realizing his duty constitutes a world of pettiness and fear:

> The seminary held one principle of priestly training absolutely sacred: no one ought to be too good at anything, much less successful at a number of things. Athletic ability was tolerated, so long as it did not include every sport or accompany "too much" intellectual curiosity. High grades were viewed with suspicion, especially when combined with a propensity to read too many books. Intellectualism was taken to be almost a sure sign of pride. Affluence, especially the rumored great wealth of the Cronin family, was also a grave danger to a priestly vocation, because it made a young man think he might be independent of Church authority. (53)

Anyone familiar with Catholic life in the 1940s and 50s, or perhaps even later than this, will understand this fiction.

But in spite of such personal and communal deficiencies, is it the case that we are good enough to be loved? Is Christ's command to serve only a command to sacrifice? Might that command also mean that to serve is to love, and to love is to be worthy of being loved? John's Gospel is clear: Jesus "fully aware that he had come from God and was going to God" washed the feet of his disciples (John 13:3–5).

Book III begins with Peter's denial of Jesus' offer to wash his feet. What does Peter have to learn about loving? Paul, Sean, and Nora pursue their individual vocations while feeling more and more worthless. Sean serves in a poor parish where there is no time for anything but work. He becomes a priestly slave. Paul becomes a successful lawyer and a politician who must remain on the make. To realize his ambitions he breaks the law, to satisfy his sexual desires, he uses others. Nora is a mother who is unloved by her husband. The rigidity of their lives leads them to suspect that they have been manipulated and robbed of happiness. Even when Paul and Nora save Sean from parish servitude and get him assigned to Rome during the Second Vatican Council, he finds no liberty. Is serving the instrument for being loved? Are our commitments fetters or do they free us to love? What can make a servant into a friend?

Together these three characters learn the answer to these questions. What they discover is that love knows no duty and commitment sets us free to be who we really are. They learn the continuity of the person with community. Even though each of these characters breaks their commitments and fails to follow the rules perfectly, they love and are loved nonetheless. This is the great mystery of God's love and of God's redemption. Sean discovers that keeping his duty to the church has been at the cost of himself and those he loves. When called to become the cardinal archbishop of Chicago, he says no until Nora shows him how that service also involves loving others, especially her. Paul, whose moral life has declined as he cheated his way to success, is not so blessed. He dies in a boating accident during a terrible storm while all his crimes are revealed to those he loves. Crippled by strokes, Michael turns his business over to Nora, who demonstrates great talent in this regard. She discovers his secret—he has had Mary Eileen institutionalized to keep her insanity secret. Amid all this sorrow, Nora rediscovers herself. At Mary Eileen's funeral, during the consecration of the bread and wine—the sacrament established on Holy Thursday whereby Christ remains with us as food and in service—she has what might be called an ecstatic experience:

> Then, suddenly, the Presence, gone for so long, returned. There was no forgiveness, no blame, no lifting of burdens of guilt, no message that at last she was forgiven. Rather, the love that surrounded Nora behaved as though it had never left, chided her gently for not noticing its presence, and enveloped her in caressing and tender warmth. Embraced by such love, Nora realized how irrelevant was forgiveness, how foolish was anger, and how ridiculous was guilt. The part of her that had been numb and dead was alive again, so vital and so happy; the numbness seemed only to have been a very minor part of a faintly disturbing dream she had had long ago.(282)

God's friendship is revealed to her; she had had it all along, as all of us do.

"Do you understand [...] what I have done for you? [...] I have given you an example so you may copy what I have done to you" (John 13:12–15). The book ends on Holy Thursday after Paul's funeral. Sean must wash the feet of his servants to make them his friends. Love and commitment are one and the same thing, he has learned this from living. And this is the freedom celebrated on Holy Thursday. He continues to serve but does so freely (349). The final words of the book are from the hymn often sung on that day, "Ubi Caritas," "Where charity and love prevail, there God is ever found [...]" (350). Where God is found, there is no duty.

The second novel in this trilogy, *Ascent into Hell*, tells the story of Hugh Donlon and Maria Manfredy. Hugh is a man who gives up the active priesthood; Maria is the representative of God who saves him from himself. At the heart of this story is the false assumption often made by Catholics that we can walk to heaven on our own. Pelagianism claims that human freedom is such that it does not require God's grace.

We are free, the argument goes, and therefore able to save ourselves.[141] This error inheres in the human propensity to "exempt" ourselves from God's grace—Hugh's greatest sin (371). Thus, the book's title, *Ascent into Hell*, suggests that our *rise* in this world and our control over its means of existence may be synonymous with the *descent* into that nether world where we are completely helpless and hopeless.

Organized around the last words of Christ on the cross—a traditional Catholic devotion for Good Friday, the only day in the liturgical year when the Mass may not be said or sung—the novel takes us step-by-step into the decline of a person of faith, a decline that will also be his means to salvation. The first of these words, "Woman behold thy son." traditionally mark Christ's giving the church to humanity in the guise of his mother, who was first to believe and the first to carry Christ in the world. She and John, of all the apostles, stayed at the foot of the cross. Hugh Donlon was promised to God when he came into the world. The son was exchanged by the father for his mother's life. Book I, under the words "I thirst," introduces Maria Manfredy, who will be the exemplar of God's love throughout Hugh's life. It is a story of both slavery and of freedom.

"I thirst." Maria Manfredy makes simple things into sacrament (21). This is in contrast to the Catholic ideology which maintains that the best things are always the most difficult. Hugh Donlon thirsts from a lack of everyday graces, because for him doing what is difficult and doing what is good are tied together. He is the son of a stern judge with an Irish conscience. Maria calls him to love by loving her, but he retreats into the difficulty of his vocation to the priesthood: satisfying the notion that if it is hard or impossible, it is what God wants (44). Hugh's brother, Tim, is his opposite, someone who takes the easy way and serves himself before all others. Tim uses his freedom to give it

---

[141] Greeley includes a translation of the condemnation of this error by the Second Council of Orange (529 AD): "If anyone says that mercy is divinely conferred upon us when without God's grace we believe, will, desire, strive, labor, pray, keep watch, study, beg, seek, knock for entrance but does not profess that it is through the interior infusion and inspiration of the Holy Spirit that we believe, will, or are able to do all these things in the way we ought [...], he contradicts the words of the apostle: "What hast thou that thou has not received?" and "By the grace of God I am what I am" (372).

away while Hugh thinks that freedom will be his means into heaven. His sister, Marge, leaves the church only to become the family's most strident representative of that church after her marriage to a loveable Irish lord.

"Father forgive them for they know not what they do." Under these words, Maria happily marries someone else, and Hugh doggedly pursues his labors as a priest. He must learn the truth of what he himself preaches:

> We must remember [...] that we do not earn God's forgiveness by our sorrow or by our reparation. God's love is a given. It's always there, waiting patiently for us. We need only turn to Him to receive it. He is pleased with our efforts, but He is even more pleased with us. That's why He made us. You cannot earn God's love because He gave it to you before you started to earn it. No more than any love can be earned. Love is always given before the effort to win it or it will never be won. First grace is purely gracious. (94–95)

Hugh buries his love under a mountain of rules (104) and with the institutional church, uses these rules to alienate the People of God. He has only an uncertain sense of this, but when he acts from love, God's people come back to the church.

"This day you shall be with me in Paradise." Working with Sister Elizabeth in his parish, fighting the worst an unstable parish can impose, Hugh discovers the world of the Fowlers—an abusive husband, a wanton wife and daughter, as well as a community of religious men and women in search of themselves—selfish individuals who can see only their own pain and who disguise their own self-interests by the shallowest psychological nonsense. Hugh's degeneration begins:

> After his Mass the next morning, Hugh remained in church to pray. He should not be saying Mass without confessing his sins. Yet he'd made love in a different order of reality from that in which he said Mass. The body of Christ was one thing, the body of Sister Elizabeth Ann something else. God would

not mind his saying Mass while he tried to straighten out his convictions and emotions. (165)

As he so often does, Greeley ties his characters to a half-truth so they are never truly outside of God's love. Trapped by Sister Elizabeth's pregnancy, he leaves the active priesthood to become a very rich commodities trader. Hugh defiantly stands against his family and his church, knowing as he does that the difficult choice presented by their pregnancy calls him to such a stance. Elizabeth's pregnancy, however, proves to be false!

"My God, my God, why have you forsaken me?" So begins Hugh's ascent into hell. With his brother Tim, he becomes one of the best and riches traders in the Chicago Mercantile Exchange. To placate his wife, they have their marriage blessed by the church. But they never prove to be happy: "Something had gone wrong with his ability to love, to bring others happiness and himself joy" (220). In his disease, he is unfaithful to Elizabeth, fails as a father to his children, and even becomes a sexual sadist. He destroys and humiliates his financial enemies, especially the Fowlers—making Ben work for him while he fornicates with both wife and daughter. Confessing to an old priest friend, he hears,

> "sin morality doesn't work. I'm not saying you haven't sinned. You'll understand, however, only when you find what you're looking for."
> "Which is ...?" [....]
> "God ... who else?" (246)

"It is finished." Hugh's brother finally ruins him by arranging for him to be convicted of a ten million dollar silver fraud. Then Tim, Elizabeth, and Hugh's children are killed in a plane crash while on vacation together. Hugh's prison is not nearly as awful as the ice that has taken the place of his soul. It is Maria who works to prove his innocence.

"Into thy hands I commend my spirit." On Good Friday, freed from the false charges of fraud and refreshed by the love of Maria, Hugh finds himself giving absolution to an old Irish woman who has collapsed before him in the street. "God has forgiven everyone already" (365) he tells her. And as she finds her eternal freedom through the church's absolution, he finds his freedom in "an implacable and impulsive Love, one that forgave without being asked, never turned away from the beloved, and wanted only that the beloved surrender to love and be happy" (366). His freedom is the freedom granted to creation on Good Friday.

Imagine a world so exact in its justice that any violation of the law entails strict vengeance. All human failings would be balanced by reciprocity in kind. To live in such a world would be to know that we end in a pit of Godlessness, in absolute despair. Greeley's third novel in the Passover trilogy, *Lord of the Dance*, is about the possibility of such a world and the forgiveness that save this world from that pit. It tells the story of the Farrells: the effete intellectual, Roger; his pompous priest, brother, John; their eternally adolescent cousin Daniel, and the insecure Irene. All of them are prisoners of the actions of their parents. Only the Christmas child, Noele Marie, is able to tell their story without deceit. Ultimately, Noele is able to bring her family together so they might begin to live their lives in freedom and in truth. Such is the mystery of the church and the glory of Holy Saturday. Such also is the continuity of persons in community.

From the point of view of these characters, Holy Saturday is the beginning of the entombment of the dead, an entombment that will seem to last forever. It is the beginning of the apparent absolute end. From the point of view of Noele, however, entombment entails resurrection. The family has a terrible secret. Daniel, presumed dead somewhere over China, was believed to have killed his uncle Clancy, the father of Roger and John, after a fight over the good name of Irene. The action of the novel reveals that Clancy's wife, Brigit, is responsible for the death of Daniel's mother so that her sons might inherit the family wealth. Daniel's sudden return to life becomes the occasion for overcoming guilt and insecurity, a second chance. He must, at one and the same time, protect the family from their own guilt—this he does through absolute forgiveness—while giving all the characters the chance to free themselves from the memory of who he was for each of them—an object of desire for Roger, a best friend for John, and a lover for Irene. In Daniel, we find the protection of God embraced by the forgiveness Jesus showed his tormentors from the cross.

Noele is the fair child of the Farrells. She is probably fey in the best Irish sense, she drives a red automobile she has named Flame. In her character, we find the Holy Spirit enfolding the church. First, the car is harmed by members of the Mob who are hell bent on keeping the secret of the murder of Daniel's mother. Next, caught be the evil of "our friends on the west side." Noele is brutalized and raped while her boyfriend is made to watch. Unable to protect the Farrells from the evil in which they have involved themselves, the police helplessly wait for the next assault. In self-defense, Daniel and Noele's boyfriend kill the culprits. This deliverance from evil does not solve the problems of the Farrells, however. They must forgive themselves for the decisions they have made throughout their lives. Roger must forgive himself for his misuse of sex, and more importantly, for abandoning his political ideals in the name of intellectual ideology. John must forgive himself for defending his mother from the blows of his father—a defense that led to the father's deadly fall down the stairs—and he must come to understand that his worth does not depend upon what his brother priests, his cardinal archbishop, or even his family think of him. Daniel and Irene must be reconciled as the true parents of Noele, and Noele must begin life again. Finally, Brigit must let her husband, Burke, forgive her for the deceit that led him to attempt to kill Daniel as a means of defending their love.

The theme running throughout the novel is the theme of the dance. Since the Middle Ages, the Lord of the Dance has been associated with the crucifixion, the dance of death, which promises us forgiveness from our immoral attempts to defend ourselves from evil. The promise of Holy Saturday is that in a world that surely seems to be a world of reciprocal payback, a world where vengeance is justice and the best social organization we can hope for is that of the ethics of the Mob, there might be a rumor of the kind of forgiveness that reconstitutes broken relationships, love gone terribly wrong, and even allows the victims of the worse kind of violence to rejoice. The Farrells go into the time of the entombment believing that they all must go down into the pit, only to learn that Holy Saturday, when even God seems absent, is like every day, the day of surprises, when rumors of grace prove to be true, and when forgiveness is easy.

Greeley points the reader to two key passages. The first is Noele's homily as she leads her parish in the singing of "Lord of the Dance." She says,

> Our lives are a dance, and our friends and families are our dancing partners, and God is the head of the dance. He calls the tunes, and directs the music, and invites us all to dance. Sometimes He even interrupts the normal dances so that He can dance just with us. Let's all sing it like we were dancing so that God will know that we are ready to dance with him whenever he wants. (79)

Reflecting on Noele's prescience, Father McNamara ponders its rarity:

> What a curious crowd to have produced Noele: Brigit, with her guilt and her superstition; John, with his transparent but harmless vanity; Roger, with his faintly bent ideals; Danny, a doomed genius; Irene, drifting ever more deeply into a dreamworld where she mourned for something she had lost.
>
> So much promise and so much possibility when they were young. And all the opportunities wasted. Happiness offered and rejected. And the damn Neighborhood, with its magic hold on anyone who had experienced it [...]. (84)

All of us are entombed by our failures. But forgiveness comes regardless of them.

The second key passage, according to the author, reflects the healing of Noele Marie:

> Then Noele was a broad beam of sunlight moving lazily down Jefferson Avenue, like a sophomore girl slouching home from the Ninety-fifth Street bus on a warm, Indian summer afternoon, daydreaming about a senior boy to whom she had never spoken a word in her life. Dark clouds moved ahead of

the sun as though running from it, and Jefferson Avenue was bright all the way to Ninety-fifty Street.

Noel knew the demons from hell could still touch her, perhaps even hurt her, but they would never prevail against her. She heard [this] in her memory of Mary O'Hara's voice and imagined the little Irish kids dancing on the Courts with the Lord of the Dance. (378)

Like the church, we are promised that evil will not win; it may do its damage, but it will not prevail. For this reason, we can forgive and forget, even as God does. Whatever belies this promise keeps us entombed. The promise of Holy Saturday is that it need not.

The integration of knowledge as wisdom. Diana Marie Lyons and Conor Clement Clarke of *Love Song* (1989)[142] come from two different worlds. She is the daughter of a Sicilian mother and an Irish father; he is the scion of a wealthy and corrupt Irish family. She is an assistant prosecutor for the State of Illinois; he is a venture capitalist. She works for a politically ambitious district attorney who uses his staff to achieve "functional justice," i.e., any means is justified if it produces a conviction; he uses his wealth both to make money and to improve the economic situation of the blue-collar working class. That class envies his money and power, an envy that enables Diana's bosses to try individuals in the press and manipulate the legal system so it seems to be producing justice when, in fact, it does just the opposite. This inversion of the agencies of the good—the state should be the agent of justice, while the economy, the agent of personal well being—is indicative of Greeley's treatment of community as the agent of the common good. It takes wisdom constructed from experience to realize social justice and personal well-being.

These two young people fall in love, fail in that love, and come to unhappiness from summer through spring. Each part of the story is introduced by sections of the Song of Songs, the great Jewish love song considered canonical by Catholics and Jews. The essential action of the novel revolves around the liturgical seasons of the church year.

---

[142] *Love Song*. New York: Warner Books, 1989.

Through them the two lovers live and suffer: from the ordinary time of high summer, throughout the declining light, renewed at Christmas, into the frigidity of winter in Chicago, which is, its seems, a reference to Dante's center of hell. Their reconciliation comes on a Good Friday in spring. This symbolic overlay helps both move the action and explain the meaning these characters reveal.

As in each of Greeley's novels, God is the main character, revealed in the passion and love of men and women. The story is, like "Romeo and Juliet," a tale of love betrayed. Diana Lyons is a woman, a virgin like her Roman namesake, dominated by the exactitude of the law, and overwhelmed by the duty such exactitude demands. She loves Conor Clarke yet, uses this love to entrap him for a crime he did not commit. She does this in response to her father, who is embittered by his own failure to achieve prominence in the legal profession. His embitterment controls Diana's life. In loving and respecting her father, she comes to consider herself worthless. Conor's reaction to the false accusations is both psychologically realistic as well as the reason he cannot win. His attempt at justice is really and merely the realization of revenge.

Diana's sense of worthlessness and Conor's realization of vengeance set the stage for the novel's resolution. The recurring character of Monsignor "Blackie" Ryan occasions this resolution, which is itself a moment of extraordinary reconciliation. Recall, we are at Good Friday, Jesus' forgiveness is the model, and Ryan's homily is the means. To wit:

> The worse of Judas' sins was to refuse to accept the forgiveness that was offered him twice—once at the Passover supper and again in the Garden of Olives. It was, one may reasonably assume, not easy for Jesus to offer forgiveness to the loved one who had betrayed him. We know from our own experience that the first impulse when faced with the treason of an intimate other is to even the score or to store up the memory of the other's offense in the careful account book we keep to treasure our dearly loved grievance against those who we love.
>
> If it is difficult to offer forgiveness, it would seem, on the basis of the evidence, far more difficult to accept it. Thus, the

mystery of Judas. Poor, dumb, blustery Peter, the most humble Pope in history, a man with much about which to be humble [....] accepted forgiveness, if not quite with grace, at least with becoming alacrity [...]. Why not Judas?

He certainly had his regrets. Throwing the reward for his treason on the floor of the temple treasury was a more public acknowledgment of his offense than any of the other first bishops were willing to attempt [...].

Having thus dramatically denounced his own guilt and responsibility for injustice, why did not Judas hasten to Calvary to accept the proffered forgiveness?

To be offered a forgiveness we do not deserve—and if we deserve it, then it is not forgiveness but justice—is a terrifying experience as each of us can testify from our own lives. We cannot claim forgiveness, it is pure gift, pure grace, pure mercy, and—ah, there's the rub—pure love. If we have betrayed the intimate other, only absurdly foolish love can possible forgive us.

[...] The trouble with being the object of a love that is too absurdly foolish to resist is that it is terrifying to be that loveable. It is an assault on our consoling self-rejection and our soothing self-hatred. If Judas was the focus of such a love, if he were really that lovable, then he would have to live again, love again, try again, laugh again, despite this own conviction of ugliness and worthlessness. That was no mean challenge. Judas, we may have learned in school, was the victim of pride. Doubtless, but pride meant a self-rejection and a self-contempt which told him that he could never have earned again the love which he betrayed.

Judas, you see, represents that part of our personality which wants only the love that it can earn and thus control. Peter represents that part of our personality that realizes love is unearnable and therefore surrenders helplessly to a love which is beyond merit [...] . (426–428)

Blackie Ryan goes on to say that Good Friday is when Peter wrestles with Judas. How that contest ends determines whether we are like Diana, dominated by obligation, or like Conor, able to risk everything to become who we really are. In the end, the couple laughs over the tragedy of their betrayal of each other, and the novel ends in hope: the hope that perhaps, they will be happy. In this novel, we see how the knowledge of religion is transformed into a wisdom that enables community. It is a wisdom supported by the knowledge that persons are the ontological substance of any community based on love.

This wisdom of communal love serves as the basis for the two main characters in Greeley's Nuala McGrail novels.[143] With the development of the characters Nuala McGrail and Dermot Coyne, Greeley continues his meditation on the characteristics of sexual love as it functions in the married state. Sexual love continues to serve as a metaphor for divine love, and in this sense, the love between Dermot and Nuala remains an attempt to approach the mystery of the triune God—the God who creates, the God who speaks, and the God who calls. But in this series, this image of God is not only embodied in the relationships between the characters, as in earlier works, but also in the thematic content of the relation of the past to the present. Nuala McGrail—the fey, dark pre-Christian goddess—serves as the human embodiment of the divine, while Dermot—the lumbering, large boy child possessed of both an adversary and an irrational demon—serves as representative of humanity itself. How the divine and the human come together in these stories is explained in the coming together of the characters' knowledge brought to bear on the past and present mysteries that each novel presents. Throughout these stories, it is Dermot's knowledge integrated into wisdom that serves his faith, just as Nuala's near supernatural powers crystallize Dermot's knowledge into wisdom. Both are essential in each story. Greeley's characters here seem to suggest that grace and human effort are required if love is to have effect in this world.

---

[143] *Irish Gold*. New York: Tom Doherty Associates Book, 1994. *Irish Lace*. 1996. *Irish Whiskey*. 1998. *Irish Mist*. New York, Forge Book, 1999. Irish Eyes. New York, 2000. *Irish Stew*. 2002. *Irish Love*. 2001. *Irish Cream*. 2005. *Irish Crystal*. 2006.

In *Irish Gold* (1994), Dermot Michael Coyne seeks the truth about his Irish grandparents, William Ready and Nell Pat Malone, and their role in the Irish troubles (1919–1923). Recently deceased Irish-Americans, the Readys came to the United States and prospered. Could it be that they never returned to the old sod because they had been implicated in the assassination of Michael Collins in 1922? Dermot's question is not welcome, but his grandmother's diary, written in Irish and translated by Nuala who has taken on an especially personal relationship with Nell Pat, leads him deep into the past.

Both the death of Collins and the mystery of a treasure of gold, serve as backdrop for the love affair between the main characters. The past is a tale of treason, civil war, and personal corruption. Could it be that in the present, the British are plotting to reaffirm their domination of Ireland? Could the ghost of Michael Collins be roaming Dublin in search of vengeance? To his great relief, Dermot discovers that in their own self-defense, his grandparents were instrumental in killing the killer of Collins. Their exile is the result of violent times. With the help of Nell Pat's diary, Nuala and Dermot find the gold, and discover the probability that the person who ordered and paid for Collin's assassination was none other than Winston Churchill. The novel ends in the peace of All Souls' Day. Yet, the grail, Dermot's love, remains to be found.

One of the thematic questions presented by these characters, especially the characters who serve as antagonists, is about what happens to human beings when they either fail to feel or cannot feel for others. Cut off from human community, they suffer and become the agents of evil. They are never to be despised, but they must be rendered ineffective. Thus, all of Greeley's characters carry the weight of a larger question, and this is the question of the relationship human beings have with each other and with their world. Is it to be a world of love or of violence, a world of knowledge and wisdom or of ignorance and fear? Moreover, and more problematically, can human beings escape either love or violence?

In this sense, then, these characters raise many of the same questions raised by St. Augustine in both his *Confessions* and *The City of God.* What is the source of the human heart's restlessness? Is this restlessness a sign of our condemnation or of our salvation? Do we find the source of peace by ourselves, or do we find it only with and through others? One might say that Greeley is asking these same questions in a way that will make sense to those who experience the same insecurities as Augustine. At least we might say that his characters are expressions of universal human emotions and seem to be on the same search as the fifth-century saint. As one of *Irish Gold*'s epigrams, Greeley quotes Patrick O'Connor:

> Young lovers think they have forever
> Hormones, however, have social origins
> Intent and consequences.
> Private minutes of affection
> Celebrated in ecstatic interludes of spring freedoms
> Inevitably involve the family from which they come
> And the family toward which they are going.

If this is the case, then it follows that as the theology of Augustine involves a political theory—since the Christian finds himself or herself in this world but not, necessarily, of it—so too, certain political ideas might be found in Greeley's stories. Perhaps without intentionally doing so or even knowing it, Greeley's Irish series is a reflection on the connections between our private selves—the love story of Dermot and Nuala—and the public persons we become.[144]

The question of violence is certainly overt in these novels. The story of the murder of Michael Collins implies the political problem of revolutionary violence. In any revolution, an older system of rule is replaced through a violent imposition of a new form of rule. Violence is the essence of any revolution. In the case of the Irish revolution, Collins was the founding father, who had accepted a less than perfect solution to the Irish question in the hope that the limited freedom of the Anglo-Irish Treaty of 1921 would be a step toward greater independence. His involvement in its negotiations and his subsequent attempt to protect the new government from those who would not

---

[144] I, however, doubt that one as well-read and well educated in the Catholic tradition as Andrew Greeley is unconscious of these connections. It might be so, but I doubt it.

accept the treaty's terms (the IRA) were his death warrant (48–49). Revolutions involve the use of arms, and those who live by them also perish by them.

Is, then, violence necessarily a part of human society? This is the question embodied in this novel's dialogue between past and present. Those who see political solutions as less than acceptable argue that it is. It is this argument that has sent good men and women into exile, and in fact, may explain the bloody history not only of Ireland but also of the whole of the twentieth century. The protagonists in Greeley's fictional world are not free to answer thus. Their task is much more difficult. Theirs is the message of love, not of arms. The gold that is this novel's treasure was initially intended as payment for armaments. Nuala and Dermot discover it, as did his grandparents, and it becomes a means of escaping violence—Nell Pat brings one bar with them into exile—as a resource that will be used for education. Nuala and Dermot turn the treasure over to the Irish government for use in schools. What had been a source of violence and death becomes an occasion for life and recovery. The past is redeemed by the present.

Irish Lace (1996) continues Dermot Coyne's quest for his Holy Grail. Like Charles O'Malley, he is in need of direction. Like O'Malley's photography, Coyne's writing requires a muse. Like Rosemarie Clancy, Nuala McGrail knows what Dermot needs. Unlike Rosemarie, who is imperfect and in need of redemption, Nuala seems to be extraordinary in everything, almost like a changeling: "She merely becomes the person the scenery demanded" (49).

McGrail has moved from the west of Ireland to Chicago as an accountant, but unlike most accountants, she sees the dead. In this case, the dead of the American Civil War. Together the couple will raise the dead through their knowledge of history in the same way they had raised the dead of the Irish Civil War in *Irish Gold*. What this fey character and her besotted friend reveal are the violent episodes that constitute Chicago's history: perhaps, again, the violence implicit in all human attempts to live together—what St. Augustine names as the City of Man. Greeley's characters recognize the role violence plays in human history while they work to overcome it, i.e., to build the City of God.

Camp Douglas became a prison camp for Confederate soldiers in 1862. This image of a concentration camp—not a killing camp as some concentration camps became under Hitler—is particularly apt in light of twentieth-century history. Dermot and Nuala's love story is informed by their historical research, and by an ominous mystery involving themselves and the IRA. The experiences described at Camp Douglas in 1862 are those of men deprived of their humanity: violence ruled, but there were exceptions that proved the rule. The official history of the camp describes a conspiracy to break out of the prison camp and to burn Chicago. This conspiracy serves as a connection to the mistreatment of Irish immigrants by a violent legal system both in the past and in the present. (An unscrupulous US prosecutor on the make illegally deports Nuala.) What becomes the "Lace" memo, written by a nineteenth-century woman known for her Irish lacework, tells the tale of moral conscience in defense of life, even the life of the enemy. Although never a real conspiracy, some of the citizens of Chicago sought to ameliorate the suffering of the Confederate prisoners held at Camp Douglas. When amelioration proved impossible because of the venality and corruption of those in charge, several political interests collude to plan a mass escape. This "plan" is never realized and the lace maker, Letitia Walsh, leaves her memorandum for posterity. It becomes Nuala and Dermot's tasks to verify its historicity. At odds in this story are power and mercy. The reader discovers that Abraham Lincoln, had he lived, would have granted clemency to all the Confederate prisoners. But this is not to be. Like Lincoln, mercy is struck down by corrupt power, and the world goes on. By extension, the question of violence is again raised by the present's efforts to discover the past. Is all power merely subject to human cupidity? The official history of the conspiracy at Camp Douglas would suggest that this is so, but the love story of Nuala and Dermot would argue otherwise.

Irish Whiskey (1998)[145] involves the story of Prohibition and one Jelly Roll Sullivan, who Nuala McGrail discovers missing from his grave. Again, the love story of Dermot Coyne and Nuala McGrail involves them in the past. What is the explanation of the empty tomb? And

---

[145] The etymology of "whiskey," Greeley tells us in a note, is "water of life."

what good will come from finding out? The answers to both questions are contained in the subplot, which involves a corrupted legal system in which moral bigots use the law to enact their own judgments of what is right and wrong. Like most private judgments, these prove to be crooked (139–140). At work in these characters is the Catholic perception of human nature as fallen, never lost, and always redeemed.

The public prosecutor, using reform of the Chicago Mercantile Exchange in a bid for publicity and political gain, charges Dermot with financial misdeeds. At the same time as his public humiliation, he must endure the private investigation and interference of Nuala's brother, Lawrence, a newly rich social snob who believes Dermot to be a bad match for his youngest sister. Both persecutions, public and private, are indicative of the fallen character of human kind. What are states but gangs of robbers without justice, Augustine asks in the *City of God*, and what evils are not evident in families without love?[146] At work here is a particularly Catholic notion of the social order. Justice is the prerequisite of politics: trust is the foundation of the family—the basis of all society. Truth is the prerequisite for justice. Love is the basis of all trust. Freedom is the fruit of these four virtues.

As the action of the novel proves, it is the network of interconnecting relationships, articulated in Greeley's fiction by the family relationships of his characters, that makes it possible for the protagonist to save himself from ruin. An example in this novel is Dermot's chance meeting with Mike Casey,[147] who is both artist and detective, that helps save Dermot from the State sponsored tyranny.[148] This novel, too, calls upon academic intelligence as embodied by the university, to restore the past to the present and demonstrate the truth necessary to hold evil at bay.

In this story, the Chicago Mob serves to represent the private tyranny that develops when the law is corrupted by moral fervor—in this case, Prohibition and private interests—here the public prosecutor's run for political office. A press unconcerned with the truth of what it publishes aids such corruption. In an interview with

---

[146] *City of God*, chapter IV, book 4.

[147] See *Angels of September*.

[148] See *Irish Whiskey* 147.

a university professor who has studied Chicago's history of the 1920s, Dermot learns of the correlation of crime to private self-defense. Al Capone, he is told

> was just a businessman, providing the public with something they wanted. He deplored the violence which Prohibition caused and denounced the corruption of law enforcement. He probably half believed what he said, more than half when he saw how eagerly the press bought it. He was right about the corruption, you know. He and his allies spent a million dollars a week on bribes. Government paid its Prohibition agents $2500 a year, the Outfit paid them a thousand dollars a week. Chicago was wide-open. The bootleggers' problem was not finding customers, so much as finding and making the product. (144)

Hence, Dermot discovers that Chicago's history has been one of consistent corruption of power:

> Gangs fought one another for turf from the beginning of the city. Extortion, vice, gambling were their cut of the expanding city. Capone and Torrio's contribution was to attempt to organize it, to "systemize" it, to use their word, from an Italian word which meant what our professors of business administration mean when they say "rationalize." Capone tried to "restructure" crime in Chicago. His principle was that there was enough money for everyone, so why kill one another? He failed to convince the others for very long. Hence the killings and especially the Saint Valentine's Day massacre. (145)

In this manner, the City of Man is rationalized. People can live by the principle of cupidity just as they can live by a moral code. The key question here involves the distinguishing characteristic between them. Greeley's characters, like Augustine, find that characteristic to be love.

The resolution of the novel is just short of miraculous—perhaps as love itself is miraculous. Sullivan's widow reveals the story of his faked death. By "dying," Sullivan came to live in love. Sullivan and his wife had a good life together and *mirabile dictu,* one of their grandchildren is the dishonest witness who stands against Dermot's vindication. It is his grandmother's threat to disinherit him that makes him reveal the truth about Dermot. The empty tomb revealed new life.

Irish Mist (1999) begins with an attempt to kidnap Nuala McGrail while she is singing at a charity event in Dublin. In this tale, like every story in this series, the past and the present become one. The 1927 assassination of Kevin O'Higgins is the subject of Nuala and Dermot's investigation. Forgiveness and passion form the core of these books. How can Kevin O'Higgins forgive his killers on his deathbed? How might Nuala and Dermot live, not their love, which is a given, but their passion? Do both questions presume an integrity unknown to almost all of us? Or, could forgiveness and passion be the reality behind the things we think of as real?

One of Greeley's recurring themes is at the heart of this novel: how do we who are the children of violence—for what other characteristic is so universal since the nineteenth century—escape it or at least, hold it at bay? This question is behind both the investigation into the assassination of O'Higgins: "the man who made Ireland a peaceful democracy" (185), and the fiction of Castle Garry.[149] Greeley connects fiction and history by making O'Higgins a hero, one even capable of escaping the sexual wiles of Lady Laverty. As in all foundation stories, he becomes mythic. Likewise, both the Downs become heroic—he in war and she in life—while the historic Hugh Tudor is humanized as a man of a violent age. Behind this fiction and this history, indeed, behind Nuala's attempts to overcome her sense of inferiority both as a person and as a wife is the proverbial truism that violence begets violence. Thus, the foundation of every city involves some form of violence because every action that seeks to establish a political state requires at least the escape from violence.

It is here that the Christian message of forgiveness *and* passion as divine actions makes the difference. The Old Testament's ascription

---

[149] Using this fiction, Greeley asks the perennial question of politics: Can a polity be established without the use of violence? The historical O'Higgins followed the use of terror by Michael Collins with an attempt to escape the violence of that usage.

that unless the Lord keep the city, the watchman wakes in vain, applies here. It is as though human beings are caught between heaven and hell, but still required to make a choice. Greeley's characters learn that human passion, especially sexual passion, may move us to love, just as it may move us to exploit others. They learn that love can move us to forgive and that forgiveness is how we guarantee our human integrity. Nuala gains an articulate sense of her integrity as a person precisely because she knows that God is involved in O'Higgins deathbed act of forgiving his IRA murderers, just as that God is caught in Augusta Downs' forgiveness of Hugh Tudor and his Black and Tans. Living as a Carmelite, Downs finds that human love has a divine counterpart (300). Her life after the Irish troubles, which cost so much in terms of human suffering, testifies to the power of forgiveness (314). As she was forgiven—she had committed adultery with Tudor when he saved her life—she forgave Tudor in exile. Before such a miracle, the envy that occasioned the attempted kidnapping of Nuala McGrail seems hardly to count. That Dermot and Nuala learn how to make love by abandoning themselves to their passion for each other makes all the difference in their marriage. And from it all, "a child is born."

Irish Eyes (2000) brings the Coynes back to Chicago and Grand Beach, where their infant daughter sees a ghost ship. Again, the question is about the Reality behind the real that we see and sense. In this novel, three stories come together. The tale of the 1898 collision of the *Charles C. Campbell* with the *City of Benton Harbor* and the consequent deaths; the machinations of Nick Farmer, a self-righteous bigot who ends up murdered, and the family troubles caused by the Coynes' mentally unsound sister-in-law. The key to the three mysteries is that in each case something is stolen and requires restitution. In the case of the manic in-law, her personality lacks the psychological integration necessary for full personal relationships. She cannot function except by tearing others down. This lack is remedied by Nuala's friendship—again a case in which the victim rises above herself to forgive. In the case of Farmer, his murder is the act of a plagiarist hoping to hide his crime. Farmer's reputation is restored through the kindness of the Coynes. Finally, in the case of the ghost ships, an ancient grail is found by the infant Nellicoyne and restored to Ireland.

In each case, violence of some kind had to be overcome before ghosts could sleep. God is again the main character working through the human love of these characters. As Nuala says,

> Don't I think that God is always singing lullabies to us? Hasn't God brought us into the world just like mothers do? And hasn't He fallen in love with us? And don't mothers have to sing lullabies to their children? So I think when we mothers sing lullabies to our children we are imitating what God does all the time—and especially when His children are loud and noisy and cantankerous! (85)

Once again Dermot and Nuala overcome obstacles to their love—in this case, their daughter's demands on their relationship—just as God overcomes obstacles to his love through human errors and flawed personalities.

In the eighth Nuala McGrail novel, *Irish Cream* (2005), two models of fatherhood confront each other. John Patrick O'Sullivan is the paterfamilias, Notre Dame graduate and immensely well-to-do businessman. His family is everything to him, and he has taught them that loyalty to the family is the single most important virtue. Together the O'Sullivans suffer a common neurosis: sons and daughters, daughters-in-law and sons-in-law, all are radically dependent on the father's love and acceptance. John O'Sullivan can tilt any playing field to favor his family. All except the hapless Damian, the last child, artistically gifted, out of sync with his brothers and sister, who are successful professionals or members of the O'Sullivan firm. Damian is the family scapegoat, the son who is sacrificed for the well being of the family. In short, the collective neurosis of the O'Sullivan clan is an apt description of a form of Catholic spirituality that thrives wherever the Catholic religion becomes something other than the vessel of Catholic faith. The father becomes the terrible God of Kierkegaard's Abraham as he ascends Mount Moriah. The son is the victim of the father's need for vengeance.

The Reverend Richard James Lonigan, DD, on the other hand, is a nineteenth-century priest assigned by his cardinal to the wilds of Donegal. His job is to bring the Irish to the truth of their faith through the suppression of ancient pagan customs and the restoration of education to his people by establishing schools under Catholic auspices, formidable tasks that would seem to call for the same attributes and neurosis as those of the O'Sullivan clan—at the very least the nineteenth century must have been more repressive than the twentieth. Such is the myth.

What we discover in Father Lonigan, however, is a priest who knows how to love, not merely in the intellectual sense of willing the good for others, but also in the sense of emotional connections with the varied and sundry characters in his parish. He is a father who enables children to come to their full potential, who knows that the love between a man and a woman involves human sexuality and that this sexuality is, indeed, the metaphor for the love of the God Lonigan serves. His work in the Donegal parish does not produce a collective neurosis but a community of values, one that can withstand oppression by the British. He learns these qualities through respecting his people and through understanding the pagan practices of the rural nineteenth-century Irish as the continuity of their culture. There is nothing in the world this father fears as much as the diminishment of persons. As the father of his parish, he lets his people grow to fullness. Lonigan is a man of faith; O'Sullivan is a man of violence. Greeley's novel asks the reader to consider the differences in the communities each creates. Each represents a model of community. The question is, which is appropriate in a world that is much like the world of the Irish émigré? How many left their homeland, turning back to see the "diminishing church steeple."

The reader comes to the story of Father Lonigan through the diary of Ned Fitzgerald, who readers will recall from former novels in this series. The incomparable Nuala McGrail Coyne and her "spear carrying" husband, Dermot, read this diary as they work to solve the problem of Damian O'Sullivan. He has been convicted of manslaughter in the case of the death of his father's business partner. His family has worked the legal system not to Damian's advantage, but to punish him for a crime he did not commit. What are the consequences of a model of parenthood that must commit manslaughter in order to be redeemed? What possesses a parent to destroy a child? In many ways, this novel raises the same kinds of questions Kierkegaard asks in *Fear and Trembling*: what was Abraham's attitude toward the God who demanded sacrifice of that which he most loved? One attitude surely must have been fear, fear that if he did sacrifice Isaac, he would violate the order of creation that keeps him safe. Such a God could not be loved, only feared. A second attitude might be despair, despair of an existence that allows the evil of human sacrifice to pass as religion. This God must be hated as well as feared. The final possibility is that of a God of faith and trust: faith and trust that even as Abraham could not understand what God was asking of him, he nonetheless hoped in a God and a creation imbued with love. This attitude is what makes Abraham a "sojourner in the land of promise" (Hebrews 11:9). This is the father of the people of the book.

This novel ends with the observation that the Coyne's two-year-old child, Socra Marie, has learned to speak using "I" instead of "me" as the subject—a sign of the child's development of an integral ego. Without this verbal integrity, she would remain the object of the world in which she lives, just as the children in the O'Sullivan clan remain perpetual objects of their parents' machinations. Unlike Coyne's two-year-old, they remain dependent on the false reality of O'Sullivan's violence; they are perpetual children in a world made by others. What Damian comes to know through the good offices of Nuala and Dermot, is the real world in which his talents may prove his happiness. Damian learns what Father Lonigan learned nearly a century before him: "the love, which would, with the grace of God, sustain [...] and bind them together no matter what troubles they might undergo" (276).[150]

In the end, we learn that the Irish émigrés, those Father Lonigan gives up because he loves them, are the forbearers of the O'Sullivans. Implicit in this connection is the truth that the church, no matter how often she falls victim to collective neurosis, remains true to her people, and thus, to her God, by insisting on the transcendent dignity of each

---

[150] These words are specifically about two individuals who are to be married. I use them, however, because the God of marriage is the God who loves and sustains. He is the God who carried Abraham on his road to Moriah.

person—Damian O'Sullivan is not be sacrificed for the good of the family—and on the good news that God is love.

What do a neonate named Socra Marie, a corrupt businessman named Seamus Costello, and the Haymarket massacre of May 4, 1886, have in common? The answer is fond in this sixth Nuala Anne McGrail novel, *Irish Stew* (2002). This is a story of the workings of an unjust legal system and its consequences in society. Socra Marie is hardly a candidate for a full and happy life. Her doctors tell her parents that it would be understandable if they consented to a "do not resuscitate" protocol inasmuch as prematurely born infants are subject to terrible disabilities in their future lives. "'It would be better to let her go and try again sometime in the future. I don't think there would be much quality of life for her'" (29). Seamus Costello is a bad man who knows how to use his talents to make money: "'a brilliant, complicated vulgar man, with perhaps a heart of gold'" (196). Dermot Coyne thinks, "So there we were on May 4, a fragile little girl in our house, a loud and sometimes obnoxious lawyer whose life we were supposed to save, and the Haymarket bomb alive in our midst" (37).

The story involves a great deal of worry and speculation on the part of the main characters. The title, *Irish Stew*, evokes the Irish penchant for worrying about the great issues that confront us. In the telling of these three tales, the characters stew about what is wrong in the world and what they are called to do about it. The basic question of human imperfection and how much of it we are condemned to endure remains the root of all three. First, in the case of Socra Marie, the attitude that anyone not like us must not have as much going for him or her seems deeply flawed. Our "quality of life" is imposed as a sentence on others who may be different from us. What could neonates be to us who have been born healthy? Second, Costello is dishonest in his business practices, but he does not deserve to be killed. Third, the Haymarket massacre of seven police officers and the wounding of seventy protestors remains a mystery to this day. Greeley's characters serve to show the monumental injustice of the trial of the several anarchists involved that fateful day in May, 1886. The historical record reveals that their trial was unfair, and in all fact, those condemned to prison and to the gallows were not guilty. What this dimension of the story reveals is how civil society breaks down when it unjustly begins killing or exiling those who are different or those with whom society disagrees. Certainly, the anarchists who were railroaded through a trail the outcome of which was a foregone conclusion were not given the full protection of the law's justice. What occurred in the aftermath of the Haymarket massacre was a reign of terror in which the law and the courts were used by the police and the plutocracy to enact vengeance and send a message to those who would reform society.

This novel, published in 2002 and certainly fiction in all its parts, takes place in 2000, one hundred fourteen years to the day after the Haymarket riot. But a historically sensitive reader might not be wrong to ask if this novel might have anything to teach us post-September 11. The social panic caused by the Haymarket massacre and the subsequent injustice of the trial of the anarchists, who favored the eight-hour day and the rights of workers, is very close to the Homeland Security panic which followed the attacks of September 11, 2001. In fact, many of the sentiments are the same in each case. The anarchists are not found guilty of throwing the bomb that killed the police officer (the other six police officers were killed by the friendly fire by their compatriots); rather they are convicted of being anarchists, which was seen as the same as being a murderer. This is very similar to the invention that anyone who does not support the American president in his fight against terrorism aids and abets terror everywhere. This is never posited in the action of the novel, but one might legitimately raise such questions in light of the novel's main theme.

At the baptism of Socra Marie, Bishop Blackie Ryan preaches on who Jesus is:

> Jesus [...] had a very bad habit of refusing to fit into anyone's paradigms. He learned a lot from the Pharisees, but he wasn't one of them. He may have hung out with the Essenes, but he was not a compulsive hand-washer. He was surely a Jew, steeped in the Torah, but He put a very different spin on it. He was charming and even witty and told wonderful stories but He refused to be a celebrity. He dealt politely with those in authority, but did not sign on with them. Half the time He

reassured people and the other half of the time He scared them. He told all the old stories but with new and disconcerting ending. He was patently a troublemaker. Which is why they had to get rid of Him. (98)

This portrayal of Jesus requires that Christians carefully make judgments about what is wrong with the world and about how they will address those wrongs. They are not permitted to condemn others who have decided these judgments for themselves. Just as Nuala and Dermot accept as their own bit of God's grace their new child with all her potential limitations; so too, we are called to accept what is right about the world even in the midst of a great deal of wrong. Thus, the reader hears a bit of Catholic social teaching in Ned Fitzgerald's diary about the Haymarket trial. This social teaching stands against the ideology of the rich and the violence of the police when they are used by the rich to effect that ideology.

> Anyone with eyes to see is aware of the terrible suffering of working men and their families in this city today. They are forced to work hours that are too long, in unhealthy places, for little money. They are treated little better than slaves. In some ways, their plight is worse than that of slaves because the slave masters have some interest in keeping their property alive. The plutocrats have no such interest [...].

> While the Catholic Church does not approve of violence and condemns all violence in the relationship between workers and employers—on both sides—it is not so blind as to believe that situations like those currently existing in our factories do not create strains and tensions which lead to violence [...]. [T]he Church also believes in justice. (124–125)

Given this teaching, the reader is asked implicitly, "What would Jesus do" in the case of the Haymarket anarchists?

The case of Seamus Costello personalizes the need to make judgments amid the ruins of all that is wrong in the world. While investigating the attempt on Costello's life, the Coynes discover that he has many enemies, all of them afraid of him. Nuala remarks, "Maybe they want to be afraid so they can hate your man even more" (187).[151] This need to be afraid so we can be free to hate hits home to all of us affected by September 11 and its aftermath. Just as the police chief involved in the arrest, trial, and execution of the Haymarket anarchists used fear of them to keep others in line with the plutocracy's agenda, so today, there are many ways in which fear is used to keep people in line, and more significantly, silent. As it turns out, Seamus was shot, first by a woman he scorned, and second, by an irate and mentally unstable former business associate. There never was in his case an evil deserving death. Perhaps that is the truth of this tale. Human beings are imperfect and become really dangerous when they begin to define the possibilities of life—as in the case of Socra Marie—or, when they collectively lose their ability to judge right from wrong—as in the trial of the Haymarket anarchists. In Costello's case, we are what we are and need to be better.

The 2006 addition to the Nuala Anne McGrail series, *Irish Crystal*, involves two mysteries: the historical question of how Robert Emmet, the leader of the Irish 1803 Rising, was betrayed and the solution to the crimes committed against the Curran family. In both cases, the answer has to do with spies. In telling the tale of the 1798 and 1803 Irish uprisings, we learn of the attempts by Wolf Tone and Robert Emmet to lead Ireland to independence through force of arms. As with almost all Irish tales of violence, these end in failure. As Greeley writes in an Afterword, however, these attempts were about the usual means to ending colonialism: first, those who were oppressed fought, and then they negotiated until a peace of sorts emerged. That the Irish are often condemned for doing what most indigenous people have done to enact justice in their political lives reveals a prejudice in need of examination.

Both the God of love and the God of peace are found in the characters of this novel. Nuala McGrail, her husband Dermot Coyne, and their children work with the Ryans and the Murphys to protect the Currans from violence. McGrail and Coyne play the part of God as love in their ongoing marriage, while the God of peace is invoked through the telling of the tragic endings of the Irish patriots of '98

---

[151] In a note at the end of the novel, Greeley writes, "The behavior of the police, the courts, and the press in Chicago in those days is a disgrace to the city". (301).

and '03. In Catholic thought, peace is about right relationships within the self, within society, and in relationship to God. That the colonial exploitation of the Irish by the British constitutes impediments to each of these relationships becomes evident in both the historical tale and in the contemporary mystery of this book. Of special note is the sacrifice of Wolf Tone and Robert Emmet in terms of what was required of them—they were condemned to die as a result of the treachery of spies. This indicates the extent injustice has for both personal and social relationships. Emmet, especially, must give up his great love to serve as an example of patriotic love. The bind is that without a well-ordered society, there can be no individual good or prosperity. Love depends upon justice for its beginnings.

Likewise, we find the Curran family threatened by the mental instability of an in-law—one who has developed neurotic notions of religion and sacrifice for family. In solving the mystery of who threatens the Currans, Greeley's characters rely on the well-integrated families of the Ryans (the model for church) and the Murphy's (a model for inclusiveness—Cindasue McCloud Murphy being not from Chicago but from Stinking Hollow, West Virginia, and a Baptist by conviction). The mystery stems from the disintegration of a personality, one who has gotten religion wrong, rather than from any overt evil like British colonialism. In either case, however, relationships are not right, and hence, are the engines that drive to the story's violence. The malignity of such relationships sometimes is embodied in the idiocy of many who involve themselves in Homeland Security. As in the Ireland of Wolf Tone and Robert Emmet, the United States—once the bastion of the rule of law and of personal civil rights—seems to be degenerating into a land of spies and legal treachery. Just as England had no right to colonize Ireland, nor make her people suffer the loss of their human rights, so too, one might suggest, the United States has no right to colonize the Middle East, or to deprive citizens and immigrants of their basic human rights in the name of national security.

In all the novels of this series, the wisdom necessary for the solution to their mysteries is the result of the knowledge acquired by the main characters from all kinds of diverse sources. It is knowledge that is intellectual and emotional, religious as well as sociological. It comes from the learned, the unschooled, and many times from children. What it accomplishes is never the result of an isolated individual; rather, it comes to fruition through the communities that support it. This is its integration into wisdom.

Chapter 8: Falling into Grace:
Greeley's Social Philosophy

The word "grace" and the idea of its superabundance serve as constants throughout this book. That God's life (grace) is always and everywhere available to each human being, that God initiates intimate relationships with all of us, and that God passionately pursues us, granting over and over new chances and new life, these are the substance of the theological insights of Greeley's fiction. But there are important social and political implications to such a theology. In the tradition of Catholic social theory, such implications mark the practical and temporal effects of a God who loves. This chapter outlines the social philosophy embedded in Greeley's characters.

In *Patience of a Saint* (1987),[152] we meet Redmond Peter Kane, his wife, Eileen Anne Ryan Kane, their two daughters and their son, following them from the Feast of All Saints (November 1) through Christmas Eve. Redmond is a successful Chicago reporter, and Eileen is an even more successful lawyer. Their life is typical of the upper-middle-class Irish. The problem is that God ambushes Kane after Mass on All Saints Day. He experiences what some might call an ecstatic experience, an experience so intense that he is changed.

Red Kane, we learn, is a reluctant war hero—a title he denies—a child of a union organizer father murdered by police in 1937, and

---

[152] *Patience of a Saint.* New York: Warner Books, 1987.

a long-suffering, vindictive mother who blames her children for her unhappiness. Needless to say, Kane is not the healthiest of selves. Yet his experience of God, renewed several times throughout the novel's action, is transformative. He brings down the murderer of a teenage prostitute; falls in love again with Eileen; recaptures the love and respect of his children; and completely falls apart. He loses his job, alienates his family, and ends where he began, hoping to start over at Christmas.

As should be obvious from the discussion of his other novels, Greeley's characters teach us much when they are considered in the context of the symbols of Catholic liturgy and belief. That Red's transformation begins on All Saints' Day signifies the possibility that each of us is called to an intense, personal, loving relationship with God. A saint is anyone who remains open to grace—God's life in us—and through individual effort makes that grace obvious to others, i.e., loving all those who are placed in our way. The Feast of All Saints is the church's way of celebrating the possibility that everyone can respond to the promptings of grace. All of us are called to a mystical union with God, even if sometimes, as in the case of Red Kane, God must hit us with a ball bat to get our attention.

All Saints Day is preceded by Halloween, the day of the damned, and followed by the Feast of All Souls—all those individuals who have died. All saints and all souls, living and dead, constitute the Communion of Saints. It is on the Feast of All Souls that Red begins to be haunted by the ghost of a murdered child prostitute. That the church has sanctified All Saints and All Souls, but not Halloween, indicates that no authority, not even the church herself, may put limits on the mercy of God by claiming to know who is or is not saved. The prostitute is not condemned but considered a potential candidate for sainthood. There may be a hell for those who freely turn away from God's love, but whether anyone is in it belongs only to the judgment of God. This last point raises in Greeley's fiction a particular set of issues around the relationship between justice, which is the prerequisite for human society, and mercy, which is the logical consequence of the God who loves. As in all of Greeley's works, the tension between justice and mercy marks a particular territory that everyone must somehow traverse: territory that is religious and political. Part of Red's role as a reporter involves his judgments about the public's right to know and his responsibility to inform; in this case, to expose Harvard Gunther's murderous crime even though the culprit has bestowed great wealth on the public good and has only months to live.

Red tells the truth: Gunther murdered an adolescent girl for the pure pleasure of doing so, and Gunther kills himself, unleashing his goons on Eileen and their daughters. Yet, the world—the organized opinion-making media and its public—blames Kane for injuring an old, dying man. That everyone turns against him prompts Kane to reject his newly found sanctity and to reestablish himself so that the world will no longer see him as crazy. Embedded in this action are several important issues.

The first is that ecstatic states are most often considered episodes of schizophrenia. Both Kane's therapist and his priest think of Red's experience of God's love as psychological and moral maladies. His therapist counsels acceptance of his destabilized state of mind, and his confessor tells him that his only Christian duty is to identify with the poor! All other experiences, they maintain, are false. Kane, however, recalling Hopkins, thinks the Holy Spirit might somehow have captured him. Confronting Kane throughout this novel is the relationship between his love affair with his wife and his love affair with God. The reader is asked the distressing question of whether human sexuality tells us anything about who God is. This is distressing, in large measure, to the puritanical approach to sexuality offered by agents of the church throughout the middle of the twentieth century, the period of Red's upbringing. We learn, for example, that as an adolescent, his mother's best woman friend sexually abused Kane. Later, a priest tells him that he is not culpable for his actions because of a diminished freedom to choose, and that if he cannot be a celibate priest, it is better to marry than to burn.

One of the reasons Kane has been alienated from the church is its failure to teach the positive, indeed, the sacramental character of human sexuality. Through sexuality a couple constitutes a sacramental bond, and as in all sacraments, marriage brings us intimately into contact with the divine. Sacraments are signs of the secret that God lurks everywhere in creation. Human sexuality, then, is one of the bonds that connect the world with God. To denigrate it as much false spirituality and vocational propaganda did in twentieth-century American Irish culture, is to commit heresy. This is what both Red and Eileen labor to discover, "The passionate attraction between humans reveals what God is like" (Greeley in Pasquariello 139). Part of the dramatic content of this novel is that the main characters do not quite get this.

Greeley is often pilloried by critics for writing novels with sexual content. As a priest, he knows that it is his duty to teach the truth about human sexuality, and his novels are a way of doing this. They are part of an attempt to create a positive sexual anthropology derived from a theology that can speak to contemporary culture. In the novel, Eileen is to Red "a creature of light," which is the meaning of her name in Irish (203), and part of Red's mystical experience involves falling in love with her again. The sexuality in this novel is a sign of grace: something some people who spend a great deal of time discussing God do not often admit. The resistance to such an anthropology of human sexuality by the Catholic ecclesial community—some of the People of God, i.e., the hierarchy—has had profound import in today's politics. In fact, it may be argued that the dehumanization and commodification of sex in American life is partly attributable to this resistance and failure to construct a more scientific and psychologically convincing human anthropology, especially in matters of sex education.[153]

Kane's self-assurance and confidence in his new self, what he believes is grace forcing and controlling his nature, will prove false. As the narrative progresses, the "new Red Kane" falls to pieces, endangering his family. Yet, this decline into his lesser nature is not his fault. He does not decline through himself alone. This is where we see Greeley's understanding of the importance of community and of church, conceptualized in the principle of solidarity that underpins the Catholic idea of human nature as social and as political. Kane realizes that his ecstatic experience may be something he needs help

---

[153] Without fully engaging the argument here, it may be argued that the Catholic resistance to abortion was weakened by the Catholic pro-life identification of birth control with abortion.

with, and he turns to the church as represented by a friend, who serves the poor as a parish priest. Red needs the social approbation of his church to understand the process of development and change he is experiencing. This particular priest, however, fails him; the priest's version of Christianity is that of the liberal social gospel gone too far. The only thing Red should be concerned about as a Catholic, the priest tells him, is helping the poor. His excursion into ecstasy is merely psychological selfishness. Here Red relies upon his community (the church), and through the error of this priest, he experiences the failure of that community. But, as Greeley's characters constantly remind us, God never leaves us to our own devices. Red still prays and finds in God's silence something essential to his well-being. God does not speak directly to Red, yet Red's talking to God gives him something that has been missing in his life.

This can be seen in the relationship he has rediscovered with his wife. Eileen reveals to him her sense of inadequacy, very much like his own, and learns that she is afraid of losing him. As a symbol of God, Eileen tells us something more about the silent God with whom Red has collided. Like every passionate lover, God, too, is afraid to lose us. "He is standing around patiently biding His time until we are ready to return His love" (344). This vulnerability of God has significance for Red. Vulnerability requires the self to be open to its own destruction. The images of death that haunt this novel—the murdered teenage prostitute, Red's dead mother, the suicide of Harvard Gunther, Red's awareness of Eileen's premonitions of death—all lead to the central mystery of baptism, of life dying to be reborn. In giving himself sexually and completely to his wife, Red's "being began to disintegrate. *Each time this happens,* he thought, *I feel like I'm going to die and at the same time live forever*" (374). Like Jesus' gift of himself to the People of God, the groom and his bride, Red comes to the resurrection.

> He perceived, with absolute clarity, or so it seemed to him then, what he must do and be and say in order to make Eileen a happy woman and keep her happy. His insight went far beyond physical skills. He would not only make love to Eileen, but he would love her, and being loved, she would be happy and his. The pride, the enormous shattering pride that went

with that realization, was not a pride of possession, but rather the pride that comes from knowing at long last who one must be and what one must do (375).

Red again experiences the ecstatic presence of God. The sexual love between a wife and a husband is a hint of the love of God that waits silently for all of us. He says to Eileen, "'Neither one of us is ever going to die. And I'll never leave you!'" (377).

It seems Red has gone off the deep end. Those who experience the love which is God, are almost always seen as mad. The "new Red" does not fit into his world. His family finds fault with his new way of acting. His son, for example, resents him because of the favorable impression he makes on his girlfriend; his colleagues in journalism fault him for revealing Gunther's murder—they say it caused Gunther's suicide— and his wife becomes livid about the way he tries to save her from Gunther's revenge. In the end, Red is a perfect failure. Here, Greeley's narrative reveals something important. It recurs throughout his fiction. The truth that in this world no good deed ever goes unpunished becomes obvious in Red Kane. Finally, talking to Eileen's brother "the priest" Blackie Ryan helps Red see why the "new Red" is viewed either as a madman or as a fool. It is the truth bound into all friendships: to love another is to will the good for the beloved as he or she is, and at the same time, it is to be the good for that friend. When friends live up to their full human potential, they become exemplars of our own better selves; they demand that we live up to our own potential. As such, friends are judgments of how good and how loveable each individual could be. And this is very disturbing to this world. True friendship is a form of saintliness; the "new Red" has become a saint! And saints are evidence that grace lurks everywhere, surprising us in its abundance and effects. Yet saints are always vulnerable because, like God, they demand of us our freedom.

Such is too great for this world, and the silent God will not tell us what to do. Here, it seems, Greeley is showing us something about original sin. The temptation is not to be who we really are, to appear to be someone else. Made in God's image, like Adam and Eve, we chose not to be that image. That image is too vulnerable, too weak, and too difficult. Yet, this "happy fault" by which humanity merited its savior[154] need not defeat us. Red Kane fails in the end because he cannot abide the vulnerability of love: "He was afraid of too much love [...] (469);" yet, he is still changed. We leave him on the eve of Christmas, the Feast of Incarnate Light. In Catholic thought, Christmas is the feast of the beginning of the Incarnation, a feast completed by the feasts of the Resurrection and of Pentecost. The reader is left to imagine what shall happen to Red Kane.

Principles of Catholic social justice. What, then, does this love story tell us about Greeley's social philosophy? To answer this question, it is necessary to return to the tradition that supports Greeley's worldview, the Catholic intellectual tradition, and to the social theory derived from that tradition. The social teaching of the Catholic Church formally begins with the papal encyclical *Rerum Novarum* of Leo XIII and continues up to today through a sequence of papal letters and pronouncements. Yet, what is often forgotten when viewed in terms of its historical chronology is that the social teaching is rooted in the theological truth that the church claims as its special warrant. Thus, it may be argued that the social teaching is as old as the church and must be found in the historical circumstances of that church's development.[155] Nevertheless, that tradition has a core of principles, which may be summarized as follows.

Social justice, the church teaches, is a consequence of the inherent dignity of the human person. As reasoning[156] beings, human persons are capable of discerning right from wrong and acting upon this discernment; as believing beings—persons of faith—human beings are made in God's image, thus possessing an extraordinary dignity. Following the Hebraic and the Greco-Roman intellectual history of justice, Catholics understand that justice consists of giving to each what is due to each as reasoning and believing beings—a simple definition

---

[154] This is a rough translation of a line from the Exultet hymn from the liturgy of the Vigil of Easter.

[155]See, for examples, Rodger Charles, S. J. *Christian Social Witness and Teaching: The Catholic Tradition for Genesis to Centesimus Annus.* Vol 1. *From Biblical Times to the Late Nineteenth Century.* Herefordshire: Gracewing Fowler Wright Books, 1998.

[156] In Catholic thought, reason is not the same as rational.

with a very complex set of implications. What this definition consists of depends on the philosophical, social, and theological definition of the word "each." In Catholic thought, that definition consists of the reasonable and biblically revealed claim that each person is possessed of an inherent dignity independent of his or her actions, class, race, ethnicity, gender, socioeconomic state, religion, or belief. Each person has a claim to be treated according to this ontological dignity.

Following Aristotle as amended by Thomas Aquinas and the school of natural law, and latter of natural rights, all persons have a claim to justice, both in the arithmetic sense of contractual obligations, as well as in the distributive sense by virtue of their relationships to other human beings, i.e., as a part having a share in the whole of the social community. These kinds of justice, commutative and distributive, take the form in society as law—legal justice—and as a set of social assumptions about what is owed to every member of the human community—as social justice. Thus, in the Catholic understanding of justice, our humanity makes claims on both our own initiative, in terms of what we are capable of achieving in and providing to society, and in terms of what we have a right to claim as part of society.

Supporting this view of justice are several theological principles with important social implications. The first is that the created order has a universal purpose ordained by its provident Creator. Catholic thought is directed toward and by the promise of the Gospel. God has a purpose for all that is created; all that is created is essentially good; and human beings are the stewards of this goodness, not its lords, but its caretakers. Thus, the second theological principle is that there is a *universal* common good[157] that ought to direct human actions, taking into consideration the contingency of history and of culture in terms of its expression. The human task is to understand the world well enough to apply the good news of salvation to it in the most appropriate way.[158] A third principle is human solidarity defined by

---

[157] The formal definition of the common good is, "The sum of those conditions of social life which allow social groups and their individual members relatively thorough and ready access to their own fulfillment" (*Pacem in Terris*).

[158] This is why in Catholic thought the virtue of prudence (wisdom) is the highest of the practical virtues.

respect for human subsidiarity. Human beings are properly human when living in community. Yet, they may never use community as an excuse to diminish their inherent dignity as individual persons. They must respect the individual person as the primary agent of his or her own good. This entails, too, a knowledge of the appropriate decision level at which the good can be accomplished, as well as an understanding of the historical and social circumstances in any given society if this respect is to be actualized.

The character Red Kane is himself an allusion to the church's teaching on the right to organize labor and to the idea that we can overcome the effects of our upbringing. His father's death in the cause of unionization is an overt reference to the role the Catholic Church played in defending the right of workers to unionize and the right of workers to associate for the purpose of giving them some power vis-à-vis their employers. His mother's neuroses have not stunted his power to define his freedom in terms of his journalistic bosses. Like Father Hoffman in *The Priestly Sins*, Red Kane has created his freedom through his power to initiate action, action that defends him from overweening authoritarians.

Like most of Greeley's main characters, Red Kane stands solidly in the middle class. Unlike their parents, Red and Eileen have the economic resources essential to a life of full development. This indicates the Catholic assumption about the common good. Without the material conditions that all persons need for real human and personal development, there can be no real chance to develop as individuals. The child prostitute whom Red avenges against the powerful and rich Harvard Gunther represents two categories of human beings: those who have lacked the traditional resources of American society, children and women, and those who have had the power to victimize them. The differences between the economic status of the Kanes and the adolescent girl forced into prostitution by circumstances of her birth, measure the injustices that exist in our world. Yet, as Red's own success indicates, these measures need not determine our place in society.

But material well being is not the whole of it. Implicit in Greeley's story of Red Kane, as in almost all of his stories, is the Catholic distinction that this world is created and as such is not all there is in the universe. As created, everything in this world is good, especially human beings, but as created, we are *in* but not *of* this world. This implies that there is more for Red Kane than this life and the good that he can initiate during it. God has a purpose for Red Kane and it is to be loved now and forever. This is the promise of the resurrection. It follows, therefore, that there should be no disconnection between Red's faith—not the strongest nor the best tended at the beginning of his love affair with God—and how he lives in the practical everyday. What he discovers through this love affair is his purpose as a husband, as a father, as a citizen, as a man of faith, and he does this by finding God in friendships. His wife, children, church, and colleagues demand that he be his better self—that he live up to his true potential as a child of God. Through his community, even as it fails him, he learns how to be a saint. Central to this community is his sexuality and marriage as signs of his union with God. Red and Eileen Kane, with their children, represent the foundation of all society, the family. He prospers and declines not by himself but in the context of others. His sainthood involves a social process, and hence, the institutions of society: in this case primarily the media, but also the legal arm of government. These either support or when not properly functioning, as in this story, hinder his sainthood.

We can view further this notion of hindered sainthood in a novel that critiques the liberal idea of social justice, *Virgin and Martyr* (1985).[159] Greeley cautions the reader at its beginning, writing,

> My tale is [...] of a temptation. Paul Tillich called it "idolatry"— the confusion of temporal and contingent political goals, however laudable, with the transcendent and the absolute in religious revelation. G. K. Chesterton called it "heresy"—the confusion of part of revelation, however important, with all of it. Msgr. Ronald Knox called it "enthusiasm"—the confusion of emotional fervor, however necessary, with religious conviction. This temptation is as seductive to the right as it is to the left, to the traditionalist as to the modernist, to the conservative as to the liberal. (*Virgin and Martyr* n.p.)

---

[159] *Virgin and Martyr.* New York: Warner Books, 1985.

We have already seen in the story of Red Kane, this "enthusiasm" in the priest who tells him that the only thing a Christian need do is identify with the poor and the oppressed; this "heresy" is also evident in the failed politics of the anti-Vietnam era protests that serve as background in the O'Malley saga. In *Virgin and Martyr*, it takes life in the form of many of the changes that took place after Vatican II. This religious "idolatry" and its secular doppelganger, liberation politics, form two corrupting poles in the development of the religious consciousness of Catherine Collins, the novel's main character. As such, she reveals a malignant form of group membership—solidarity without subsidiarity—often misidentified with the Catholic teaching on authority—an authority without freedom.

One of the reasons the church cautions against the temptation to make our reading of the requirements of the Gospel into the only reading the Gospel might sustain is its wisdom on human nature. More often than not, we sin by misusing the good rather than acting evilly per se, and more often than not, we do the right thing for the wrong reason. This implies that doing good, although the action of an individual agent, must be considered in light of an entire community. Merely because I intend to do good does not necessarily mean that what I intend is, indeed, good. We are by nature required to make our judgments in communion with others, thus, the ideas that wisdom comes from all kinds of sources, and that it is our vocation as reasoning beings to use knowledge well. For this reason, the church admonishes that no one may appropriate the church's authority to serve political purposes: there is in Catholic thought, no preferred culture, or system.[160] This is true both for the conservative forces that worked against the changes in religious life during Catherine Collins' early religious formation and for the liberation theologian who corrupted and betrayed her missionary service.

The novel traces Catherine Collins' development through the perspectives of her best friend and would-be lover, Nick Curran; her childhood friend Blackie (Punk) Ryan; her psychological mentor,

---

[160] See paragraph 43 of *Gaudium et Spes* (I. Chapter 4).

Mary Kate Ryan Murphy, as well as through a series of letters written by Catherine herself. These perspectival directions give a non-definitive description to this character, based upon the mythical mystical character of St. Catherine of Alexandria.[161] Through this device, Greeley entertains the possibility that life and fiction may not be all that different. Hence, like her mythical namesake, Catherine Collins is a mystery throughout the novel. She is both the friend known by the other characters, as well as the mythical saint martyred in the cause of liberation. It is through this mystery that we view two dismal parts of the American Church before and after Vatican II: the solidarity without subsidiarity of some religious communities—in this case of women—and the solidarity without subsidiarity of some liberal politician guised as experts in theology. In both cases, we confront a form of fascism that makes the person secondary in value to the group, a fascism that hides the Führer Principle and Fatherland above all else behind the veil of religious authority and obedience.

Catherine's sense of religious vocation is captured in a conversation between Blackie Ryan and Nick Curran about what went wrong in the renewal of some religious congregations called for by Vatican II. Blackie says, "'The religious orders? They had a wonderful ideal, which, toward the end, they imposed mostly through power and envy. Then when the big changes came in the church and power and envy were turned into different forms, they found they no longer understood what the ideal was'" (75). He continues,

> You can't expect to maintain order among a group of seventy novices, young women filled with bodily energies, unless you claim a monopoly on knowing God's will and unless you use group control to keep the aberrant and the gifted in line. That's how it was done. You went through the motions teaching them what the religious life was and helping them to freely assimilate its principles. You talked about the spirit of the Holy Founder, whoever he or she was. But in practice, you governed through fear and thought-control and group pressures. You wanted internal conviction and commitment, but you settled for external conformity because you had so

---

[161] See *Virgin and Martyr* 64–64 on Catherine of Alexandria.

many classrooms to fill with teachers, so many hospitals to staff, so many Latin American missions to maintain. Cathy's talent with a brush was a luxury you couldn't afford. You didn't need art teachers, and special training for her, [it] would have created unrest among those who were less talented. Even if you didn't have an excuse like sending her to South America, you had to repress her special gift. It all worked fine until someone said there were changes going on and you began to examine what you were doing. Then you destroyed the old power structure, denied that the superior was the voice of God, wiped out the old tools of social control and discovered that there was nothing left to love and hate, to lean on and rebel against. The very people who destroyed the old mother in the name of the new mother found that with the old mother gone there was nothing left, and departed in droves. And those who remained shaped the new mother in the image and likeness of fashionable liberalism—social advocacy or the peace movement or feminism. And you don't have to be a religious sister to support any of those things." (74–75)

The accuracy or inaccuracy of this as a description of religious life in the decades leading up to and immediately after the Second Vatican Council remains a matter of sociological investigation and data. In the context of this novel, however, this description is meant to serve as an example of solidarity—the virtue that binds us to other human beings by virtue of our duty or promise to live together—without its reciprocal virtue, subsidiarity—the virtue that respects the person as an individual who must be involved in the decisions that affect his or her life. This principle of subsidiarity would respect Catherine's unique artistic gift and would have involved her in decisions that affected her life. Without that respect and consideration, the demands made on her by her religious congregation prove to be onerous and destructive.

Such solidarity without subsidiarity survives on weak selves, i.e., on persons with diminished senses of their own worth. Catherine's mother had been a woman in search of miracles because she lacked the sense of her own worth to see the love and grace she represented to her family. Such selves often use duty without rights as the indicator of a religious vocation. Catherine, for example, reveals in one of her letters that she failed to follow very good advice, advice to the effect that "the best sign that we're doing what God wants us to do is that we're happy in it" (93). Rather, she follows one of the all time worst ideas associated with Catholicism, her sense that she is letting God down (94) by not following the perfect life of a professed religious.[162]

Like many who are infected by low self-esteem because of their religious formations, after her absorption into her religious community has failed to enable her happiness, Catherine looks to a form of solidarity that promises liberation from the state of being part of this world. The version of liberation theology she experiences argues that political compromise is always a form of complicity in evil. In this version, our moral responsibility in matters of economic and social injustice must be all or nothing. Hence, she falls victim to the most facile of political ideologies: "As Marcuse says, there are some circumstances in which the hope of freedom and happiness for future generations justifies the violations of freedom and rights and even life, so long as the end is present in the actions. We kill when we have to, not out of hatred, but out of love and with a sense of repentance" (310). She finds herself used by others, this time not in the service of a religious order but in the service of a political agenda.

It is an empty tomb that reveals that Catherine is not dead, nor martyred, nor a saint in the misconceived meaning of someone who sacrificed her happiness in the service of a God always on the lookout for failure. In spite of herself and a false identity, Catherine comes home to those who love her and through them, to the God who has always loved her. Blackie says to her "'you have always wanted to be a remarkable woman. I suggest that now you realize that you have sought for remarkability outside yourself when it was always lurking within you, unformed, nascent, but ready to blossom'" (408). Catherine's story would have been greatly different had the leaders of the groups she depended upon known this truth and been willing to help her make decisions appropriate to her human dignity.

---

[162] Note Sister David Mark's dirge on Holy Obedience, pp. 116–117.

The hindered sainthood of Red Kane and Catherine Collins may be viewed, again, in the often recognized corruption of the Catholic imagination found in two other Greeley novels, *Angels of September* (1985) and *White Smoke* (1996).[163] These novels will serve to conclude this discussion of Greeley's social philosophy.

In *Angels of September*, Father John Blackwood Ryan (Blackie) investigates putative diabolical influences said to be taking root in the art gallery of Anne O'Brien Reilly. What he discovers and helps his friends to see is a God "dragging all of us into heaven by the skin of our teeth" (4). Anne Reilly is haunted by a remembered guilt which has pursued her throughout her life. Patrick Michael Casey, who went to grammar school with Anne, meets her again when he investigates an explosion in her gallery immediately before an opening of a show of art by a "mad" priest. What they shared as children was fear and a sense of worthlessness. As adults, this sense of fear remains. The action begins in September, the time when these characters reconnect. The novel's action hinges on the relationship between evil as the work of a diabolical agent and the evil of psychological illness.

Are Anne Reilly's experiences those of the devil, or do they result from her psychological history? The pre-Vatican II Catholic American Church had been severe and relentless in its doctrine of sin and damnation—a severity more recently admitted and corrected—by a God who relentlessly judges and catches out all and every deviation from the rules, especially the rules governing sexual behavior. Anne Reilly is the product of this older church and is haunted by an unnamed guilt, even as she attempts to live as a life-affirming person, who is yet unconscious that her own life is graced by God's love. Anne's guilt stems from a sense of responsibility, ingrained through her Catholic education, for her personal salvation: this, as we have discussed above, often was translated into the notion that, on our own, we can walk to heaven if we have the will for the effort. Her immediate question is, whether it is the devil or human beings that account for evil in this world. If it is the latter, do human beings possess any higher angels of their nature? Are there angels of September?

---

[163] *Angels of September.* New York: Warner Books, 1985. *White Smoke.* New York: Forge/Tom Doherty Associates, 1996.

Yet this novel is also a love story about Anne Reilly and Mike Casey; in being so, it is also a story about how God works in this world. When they find each other again—indeed, they had always known they loved each other—they discover that grace has surrounded them from the beginning, but their eyes could not see it. Greeley writes, "The mystery that had bound them did not [...] demand revelation of terrible secrets. It did not pry into the dark origins of guilt. Rather it sought out suffering, and exorcised it" (225). Against this beneficent power is a world that has misperceived it as an implacable judge.

The action comes to a head by the Feast of St. Michael the Archangel (September 29). The diabolical events that have driven Anne Reilly into almost losing herself, we learn, are the result of abuses in her childhood coupled with the tragedies of her life. She first lost her family, and then her son. Her sisters died in a terrible grammar school fire; her brother in World War II; her parents in a plane crash, and one of her sons is a Vietnam MIA. Abused by a priest, she has personalized all these losses by feeling responsible for them. Yet, her great intelligence and strong will have benefited from her sense of responsibility. This sense is the result of her Catholic education, an experience made up of the positive forces of the Catholic intellectual tradition, as well as her own judgments in the face of a flawed moral teaching about sex and gender. This flawed moral teaching, in spite of Anne's attempts to judge it for what it is, becomes the gate through which her demons come.

The Ryans, in this novel most clearly identified as the church, become the agents of affirmation that Anne needs to escape her misapplied responsibility. Mary Kate Ryan, the psychologist, Blackie Ryan, the priest, and their cousin Mike Casey, the lover, hear Anne's story. They function as the Trinity does in the Catholic explication of the mystery of God: the one who creates, the one who speaks, the one who calls. These three, along with a woman patrol officer,[164] save Anne from her false memories and help begin the healing that will treat the evil effects of a church all too human in its sins. Her guilt about

---

[164] In the Author's Note, Greeley writes, "[...] the four principal "angels of September—priest, lover, psychologist, and patrol officer—represent the Church at its most effectively caring best" (n.p.).

the fire that killed her sisters turns out to originate in a false memory that she had been its cause. The facts discovered by her four angels refute this false memory. Anne learns that the terrible things that have informed her life are not her responsibility. Thus, she is free from the burden that she has been their cause. Evil remains a mystery, and why it occurs in the lives of good people stays unanswered. The novel ends with a message that while we do require of ourselves and of others a sense of informed responsibility, at the same time, we must guard against the psychological and the social influences that can distort that responsibility into debilitating guilt. We do have a responsibility to stand up to evil and to a world that is less perfect than it might be, but we are not God, nor are we to render judgments of the absolute kind. Rather, it is best if we work with our better natures—our angels—and leave the rest to God, knowing always that we have a responsibility to cooperate with God, but that it is God who will finally and lovingly save each of us, even from ourselves when we get it wrong. As in all of his novels, in this one we find a person who was raised with the dark prejudices of the old church, who can, and indeed, does have the capacity to change from darkness to light. That capacity is the ability Greeley finds in every person, the ability to love. As a lesson in social theory, the novel emphasizes the power of individuals to contribute to their own well being, even as it cautions against the power of the individual as absolute and autonomous.

In *White Smoke* (1996),[165] Dennis Michael Mulloy comes to Rome to cover the papal conclave. There he rediscovers and falls in love again with his estranged wife. This love story takes place within a larger story of papal politics, Curial chicanery, financial scandal, and attempted assassination. We meet again the Cardinal Archbishop of Chicago, Sean Cronin, his faithful alter ego, (now) Bishop Blackie Ryan, his sister Mary Kate Murphy, all of whom have functioned in other novels, as they do in this one, as parts of the People of God. Politics plays center stage in this story of the political forces that fight for control of the Catholic Church. Cronin leads moderates to elect another John, overcoming the lies and authoritarianism of Curial incompetents dressed in cardinal red. Throughout we find the God who loves life much more than anti-abortionists and pro-lifers, a God

---

[165] *White Smoke*. New York: Forge/Tom Doherty Associates, 1996.

who writes straight with crooked lines and who promises that life will always be stronger than death.

In an Author's Note, Greeley observes that his fiction contains only the plausibility of human nature and human history. Obtaining here are several key notions: The first is that secrecy in the church often results in a viciousness and vindictiveness that isolates and destroys good individuals. Second, money when added to power that is secret, is a combination that always corrupts and the institutional church is always the poorer for it. Third, historically the Catholic Church has been administered in many ways, for many reasons, and through many stages. It once nearly became democratic and was most certainly more just then, than when it moved toward centralized and unaccountable monarchy. Fourth, women have suffered incredibly from the male-egoistic view of them as inferior, and the church has more than once been in the trawl of secret societies. And finally, most Catholics remain in the church because she is their mother; there is no easily scandalized simple laity, save in the minds of clerics who have no clue of the power of Catholic faith. That faith is, after all, God's life in us.

An Appendix to this novel includes an article Greeley wrote for the *New York Times* in 1994 on why Catholics stay in the church. In it, we hear not from Greeley the novelist, but from Greeley the sociologist. He begins by confronting the nativist prejudice that intelligent people simply do not remain in an authoritarian church founded on infantile fantasies. To the contrary, they remain Catholic Greeley contends, because of the imaginative power of Catholic metaphors, the power to explain and to sustain human life more fully than others: "Religion is experiences, image, and story, before it is anything else and after everything else. Catholics like their heritage because it has great stories" (379). This Catholic imagination explains more of reality with more and better stories. These stories are rooted in the sacramental view of reality: "the conviction that God discloses Himself in objects and events and persons of ordinary life" (379). Thus, it covers more deeply the moments of birth, death, reconciliation, community, and government, if not better than other religions, at least as profoundly. Part of this is due to Catholicism's ability to incorporate the past—even unto pagan times—into stories that help explain the lifecycle and sustain hope in the face of the human condition: the parish, the school, the family, and the person all celebrate what it means to be human. The faith of the Catholic is not infantile, Greeley insists, but it begins with an infant, his mother, and the poverty of his birth. From this story, we discover God, not only as Father, but also as Mother and as Child: "The Catholic imagination sees God and Her grace lurking everywhere and hence enjoys a more gracious and benign repertory of religious symbols than do most other religions" (381). Catholics believe, as Greeley says, that if he or she cannot get into heaven through the front gate, the one guarded by priests and popes, they can go round to the back door and God's Mother will let them in (383).

The points Greeley underlines in Dennis Mulloy's story are important to understanding his social thought. First, Lord Acton's adage that power corrupts and absolute power corrupts absolutely, is so simply true that most ignore it. All power tends to diminish those who hold it. For this reason, Catholic thought invented the idea of office early in the thirteenth century to provide a means for authority and power to be joined in a limited and accountable way. The holder of the office is to be judged by its constituents in terms of its constitutional use, i.e., by how it is used vis-à-vis them. Greeley's reference to a democratic church is to the fourteenth- and fifteenth-century attempts to limit ecclesial government in conformity to the Gospel's warrant for the church. Second, secrecy only complicates and enables the ineluctable corruption of power. Third, by supplying the social-historical evidence of why Catholics remain part of the church, Greeley indicates the imaginative function the church plays in the human condition. We remain because we derive something essential to our humanity from being part of an institution that only partially lives up to its Gospel warrant. It is the best we can find this side of paradise. Finally, the reality of these observations points to a realism in Catholic thought: a realism that sometimes is part of the corruption of power, but is also sometimes a sign of our being *in* but not *of* the world. Thus, it marks our transcendence amid the immanence of being human; beings who are called to work imperfectly in this world to perfect it, even while we wait for the perfection that is rumored to be beyond it. We do this because it is part of our humanity, and we know that our humanity is something that might also be shared by God. Red Kane, Anne Reilly, and Dennis Mulloy are examples to be heeded.

Chapter 9: Understanding the Critics of Greeley's Fiction

Critics of Greeley's fiction are legion although there is no locus to which we might go to find that criticism. Two kinds of criticism are particularly inchoate: criticism that essentially argues that Greeley did not write the kind of book or create the kind of character the critic wanted him to write or create, and criticism that claims of a character something that cannot be found in the text.[166] Both kinds of criticism are nearly impossible to refute. The first because the critic holds Greeley to an impossible standard—"you didn't write the story as I would have liked you to do!"—and the second, because such critics either do not, cannot, or will not read the text as it is written because of some intellectual or political agenda on their part. To wit: Greeley's use of sexuality exploits women because all male examples of sexuality are necessarily exploitative as the consequence of male patriarchy!

Like many authors, however, Father Greeley sometimes alludes to his critics through the characters he creates. A survey of his fiction would include the following in any summary:

---

[166] See, for example, the treatment of Blackie Ryan in A. W. R. Sipe and B. C. Lamb, "Chesterton's Brown and Greeley's Blackie: Two Very Different Detectives." *Commonweal*, 14 August 1992:18–19; 25–25, and Anita Gandolfo, *Testing the Faith: The New Catholic Fiction in America*. Greenwood Press, 1992.

- Characters who know an academic discipline well are often opposed by antagonists who argue that those who know a substantial discipline like sociology, church history, or theology should not write fiction. Priests, especially, should stick to what they know—sacred doctrine—and not muck about in other disciplines, especially popular literature.

- Characters who are priests are often opposed by authorities who argue that priests should not write about, or even know about, human sexuality. Such antagonists are particularly hard on "dirty-minded" priests who seem to know about sexual love but ought not to because of their celibacy.[167] Indeed, anyone who argues that human sexuality demonstrates something positive about how the Godhead might work in the world ought not to tempt or tax the minds of the simple laity.

- Priests and laity who need hierarchy for an ideal of church and their contrary, who see in hierarchy a humane order of authority (potentially capable of being independent of patriarchy) rather than a privileged arrangement of power.

- Characters who understand how culture and ethnicity may serve as a means of understanding those they serve are opposed by those who see culture and ethnicity as divisive.

Such characters and their interchanges in the novels might be seen as a self reflection on the general reasons critics give for judging

---

[167] See Anita Gandolfo, *Testing the Faith: The New Catholic Fiction in America.* Greenwood Press, 1992, wherein she writes that Greeley's praise of the Catholic priesthood is not surprising "in light of Greeley's penchant for exploiting female characters in his own fiction and his persistent defense of clerical celibacy in his nonfiction" (107) and "The perennial aspect of priesthood that Greeley exalts ... is, unfortunately, the vision he shares with other members of the sacerdotal school, a vision that locates the essence of Catholicism in the activities of its priests, affirming the patriarchal structure with its privileged cast of men who have access to the "mysterious dimension" denied to others" (107–108).

Greeley's novels as lacking literary quality—the novels are designated "potboilers"—the reason many give for not liking them. Of course, anyone is free not to like a particular book, and all are free not to read what they do not like. (They, however, ought not to criticize books they have not read!) Indeed, much of the criticism remains a matter of literary taste, but many critics of Greeley's fiction attack his novels for saying what they do not say.[168] In other words, it often seems the case that either Greeley's critics do not read him or they do not read him with the open mind necessary for valid criticism. The question is why?

The short answer to this, why? is that much of the negative criticism of Greeley's fiction comes from those who dislike his characters' experience of how the Catholic Church has existed in time, both positively and negatively, or their criticism is of a version (Greeley's)

---

[168] See, for example, Ingrid H. Shafer's "Odd Man Out: A Modern Morality Play: Andrew Greeley, Joseph Cardinal Bernardin, Eugene Kennedy," and her critique of Eugene Kennedy. In part, she writes,

> When Kennedy discusses Greeley's fiction his account becomes wildly inaccurate. Consider the following passage: "His first novel, *Blue in Chicago*, had appeared but had not attracted the readership he had hoped for. He was finishing a second novel as 1980 dawned, one in which he would combine his knowledge of Rome and Chicago as well as his previous research into sexual intimacy. Warner Books thought that with intrigue in high-church places flavored with sex he had at last found the ingredients of a bestseller. They planned to publish it in the spring of 1981 under the title *The Cardinal Sins*." All of this is pure fabrication. In fact, *The Cardinal Sins* was Greeley's third novel. It was preceded by *The Magic Cup* (1979) and *Death in April* (1980). Both were published by McGraw-Hill, and Warner's would not even bid on the manuscript until Bernard Geis, Greeley's agent, auctioned it off upon completion. Greeley never wrote anything called "Blue in Chicago."
>
> Whenever possible, Kennedy ridicules, patronizes, and maligns Greeley's literary work. Concerning *The Cardinal Sins*, for example, he writes that "Father Greeley claimed later to have selected personally the photograph of a naked woman viewed from the rear that would decorate its bright red cover. For good measure, he decided that the sex scenes should appear in italics." The "naked woman viewed from the rear" evokes images of graphic *Penthouse* buttocks, when in fact the image Greeley picked is of an elegant, chaste, almost Grecian back, nude from shoulders to hips, against the burgundy folds of flowing drapery. In addition, Kennedy fails to mention that the photograph is an artist's self-portrait, and that the italicized scenes are portions of the novel written from a perspective other than the first-person narrator's."

of how the Catholic Church ought to exist. These critics dislike the alternative versions of the church presented in the novels, or they think such versions ought not to be portrayed by a priest of that church. Another way to put it is to say that Greeley's fictional world represents something these critics do not want to admit as possible, or if possible, oppose it on ideological grounds. When, for example, Greeley writes about pedophilia and the Catholic hierarchy's cult of secrecy,[169] he exposes a possibility the reader is forced to confront. This is Kundera's notion that in good fiction all characters demand to be heard, even the antagonists. When Greeley's characters discover God's presence in their lives through their very human sexuality, especially through married love, readers are forced to confront both their own understanding of God and of how well or how poorly they have integrated sexuality into their own personalities. Every good novel presents characters and plots that draw us in or repulse us. Many of Greeley's readers might say they wish their world and their church were more like the world he has created. That is why these versions of the world and of the church entertain; that is why they are good stories.[170]

Negative criticism of Greeley's fiction involves the rejection of his imaginary world and the characters who populate it. Again, the question is why these occasion such negative responses. What is it about this fictional world and these characters that critics find so repulsive? Again, the short answer: we ought to reject Greeley's world because it is a world created by a priest![171]

Sometimes the best answer is the simplest, but even so, its simplicity rests on a very complex reality. An illustration may help. In a 1992 article,[172] A. W. R. Sipe and B. C. Lamb take Greeley to

---

[169] See the discussion of *The Priestly Sins* above.

[170] See the discussion in Chapter 1 about storytelling, religion, and meaning.

[171] While writing this book, I often came upon a kind of critic who frustrated my attempts to understand the animus against Greeley as an author of popular novels. When learning of my interest in Greeley's fiction, I would be informed of how very disappointed my interlocutor was in Father Greeley for writing novels. "Which novels?" I would ask, "Oh, I never read them!" Such disappointment comes from the rumor that Greeley is a dirty-minded priest who writes about sex.

[172] Sipe, A. W. R. and B. C. Lamb, "Chesterton's Brown and Greeley's Blackie: Two Very Different Detectives." *Commonweal*, 14 August 1992:18–19; 25–25.

task because one of his characters, Father Blackie Ryan, does not compare favorably to Chesterton's Father Brown. The article renders many insights about Chesterton and Greeley, but the net result is that Greeley's character comes off poorly when compared to Chesterton's character. Of course, this might be a valid conclusion, except that what is written about Blackie Ryan cannot be supported by the texts. The authors contend that the comparison of Brown to Blackie results in an understanding of "divergent sacramentalities" (18). This understanding, we are informed, begins with the common problem of detective fiction involving members of the clergy. Why would priests be involved in solving crimes? The answer might be in order to help those who have sought their help. But, the authors claim, whereas Brown's help is attached to his office—the hearing of confessions and the reconciliation of the sinner with God (18), Blackie's is "as part of an elaborate web of kinship or power involving patronage and obligation" (18).

Clearly, these critics like Brown better than Blackie—which is their perfect right—yet, they also seem to ignore the sociology and politics involved in inventing an English Catholic priest modeled upon a real person[173] and an Irish-American priest who is a fiction. Aside from the problem of presentism—the application of values relative to one time to those of another—the question becomes why Ryan comes off as less than Brown.

As a boy translating the *Aeneid*, I was instructed not to read its fourth book, which outlined the "sinful" love between Dido and Aeneas. This instruction, I suspect, was given as a way to ensure my reading of that book. The priest who gave these instructions had been told by his teachers to avoid the temptation the fourth book might have presented in his own time. But his time was not mine. No matter how disappointed I was when I finally found the suspected text—"first both Earth and bride-escorting Juno, give the signal; the lightnings flash forth, and the heaven (is) witness to the nuptials, and the nymphs shout from the topmost height" (*Aeneid* IV. l. 160)—my teacher had achieved his goal. Different times approaching the same text for very different reasons.

---

[173] Fr. John O'Connor (1870–1952).

Does any of this obtain? It seems so. At work in the negative criticism of Greeley's fiction is a view of church and of God—therefore of the world—at odds with the reality of the church and the ways Greeley helps us imagine God. St. Thomas tells us that in naming God (i.e., imagining), we necessarily get it wrong. God is not self-evident, nor can creatures of their own accord truly tell who God is. The best we can do is come up with images that do not contradict what God is not. Where Greeley's fiction respects this negative way,[174] his critics often seek to disown the images that seem possibly to articulate a God who escapes their theological formula. They seem to insist that because the God of Chesterton and of Greeley is the same God, that God must appear in the same ways in each author's fiction.

Indeed, Blackie Ryan responds to those who ask for his help by using the power of his relationships and the authority[175] that he has been entrusted with as a priest and later as a bishop. As such, he is a model steward. What his critics insist upon, however, is that because he has been entrusted with authority, i.e., because he is neither powerless nor is he poor, there is something lacking in him as a witness to God's grace in this world. One might ask, isn't the purpose of authority and the power it represents to serve those who are in need? That certainly has been the teaching of the church and the Catholic tradition going back (at least) to Aquinas. Just as Chesterton's world would have been a better one if individuals had found the reconciliation the church offers all men and women, wouldn't the world be a better place and the church much more like what Jesus intended, if its power and authority were truly in the hands of people like Blackie Ryan.[176]

Why Blackie is suspect where Father Brown is not reveals something about the ideology of those critics who raise the suspicion.

---

[174] "Having recognized that a certain thing exists, we still have to investigate the way in which it exists, that we may come to understand what it is that exists. Now we cannot know what God is, but only what he is not; we must therefore consider the ways in which God does not exist, rather than the ways in which he does" (*ST* I q 2).

[175] See Chapter 4 above on the necessity of community to the existence of power and authority and the limits on both required for human (humane) authority.

[176] He certainly is the kind of priest I would want my sons and daughters to be, were they to be called to such a vocation; and more importantly, he certainly is the kind of priest who has helped me in times when I have needed help.

Whereas Father Brown lives in the world of the individual—a particularly English, Protestant idea and one Chesterton remains the great proponent of—Father Ryan is portrayed, as one criticism put it, "as a kind of Chaplain to one powerful Chicago clan ..." and turns up whenever that clan is threatened (19). And, indeed, this is true. But the question remains, why is this character not to be recommended whereas the individualist is?

At issue are (at least) two conflicting ideas about what the church is supposed to be; just as there are conflicting views about what sex is supposed to be when critics see Greeley's novels as the sexually inappropriate work of a celibate priest. Such critics miss the point of celibacy, which is to allow the persons vowed to celibacy the opportunity to be generous to many with their love and gifts, rather than to only one other person, as would be the case in marriage. Celibacy is one way to allow some the freedom to love broadly. Whether or not it should be for life, or for a term, is not the immediate issue. What is at issue, however, is whether love can be plurally expressed. Such is the question human sexuality raises too. Just as it would be incorrect to assume that different generations of teachers would approach the fourth book of the *Aeneid* in the same way, it seems to be an error in criticism to assume that authors from differing times and circumstances would approach their fiction in such same way.

Yet, we need to return to the differences in ideology between those who favor Greeley's fiction and see in it a real witness to the Gospel and those who oppose that same fiction because they see it as opposed to that same Gospel. It is here that the Catholic imagination becomes important.[177]

The Catholic imagination, which Andrew Greeley has written of so convincingly, sees community—family, school, state, church, economic enterprise, and culture, to name only the largest of categories—as an extension of the person. This, too, has been the constant teaching of the Catholic Church and its natural law tradition. In such an imagination, there is no divide between individual and society, even as there are essential distinctions to be made. Thus, one's political community is part of a life that involves the person in the

---

[177] See the discussion in Chapter 2 above.

process of guarding the common good and ensuring that the allocation of goods and services among members of society be just, and when possible, fair. Ethnicity, or the manner in which culture is embodied in a particular time and place, then, becomes a definitive historical reality, and in a pluralistic society, acquires importance, as it requires respect. Again, as Arendt and others have persuasively argued, if power and authority are to be understood properly, another distinction is imperative. Power is always, for good or ill, a communal reality, while authority serves as the rubric by which that power is limited or not.[178] Thus, with Lord Acton, we might agree that power corrupts and absolute power corrupts, absolutely. In constitutional governments, laws, customs, and norms govern and limit the role power plays in social, economic, and individual life.

Because of these understandings, the Catholic imagination is properly suspicious whenever it notices a lack of respect for the social manifestations of community. So, when we read, for example,

> The attractiveness of the [Irish-American romance] for America at the present time [1982] may be more than merely a nostalgia for a lost culture of shared values, it may be, more seriously and distressingly, a nostalgia for a simplified world of easy solutions and unexamined bromides that was false to begin with. This at any rate is the impression one gets of the culture of Irish-American Catholicism from Greeley's [novels]. (McConnell quoted in Sipe and Lamb 19.)

These become fighting words! First, because anyone who has read Greeley's fiction knows them to be insulting, and second, they impugn American Catholicism by inference. The fictional clans created by Greeley mark a rich and varied experience that like the history of black slavery and civil rights, proves essential to the historical narrative of the American experience. The immigrant church with its Irish cohort, along with the success of those immigrants, is and will always be part of the American story. Greeley's novels use this history to imagine lives

---

[178] See Chapter 4 above as well as Arendt's *On Violence* and her essay "What is Authority?"

as they might have been, as they are now, and as they might be; hence, the great popularity of Greeley's stories.

More importantly, however, is that Greeley employs these fictions and this history as a metaphor for the church as it is and as it can be—both positively and negatively. To dismiss this literature as false nostalgia for a simplified world indicates either a failure to have read the texts or, more sadly, a dismissal without cause of part of our human experience and of our nation's history. Any reader of the Blackie Ryan mysteries knows, first of all, they are stories first and foremost. They are popular with many because the characters reveal a verisimilitude either to the way things were and are, or to the way things might have been or might yet be. They are exercises in imagination of a certain type.

Whether or not they should be dismissed seems to involve a sociological and historical set of arguments. That set of arguments is beyond the scope of this writer, but not beyond the scope of Greeley himself. Readers need only refer to what has been said in preceding chapters about the connections between Greeley's sociology and his fiction. But something else is afoot here. Blackie is dismissed because he has a place of power in a "powerful Chicago clan." Why might it be advantageous to some elites to dismiss as inauthentic the power of other elites? Either powerlessness, as *per* poor Father Brown, is a virtue to be imitated, or power itself may be something good. At root in Greeley's characters is a view of the created order that argues that all creation is, in fact, good, coming as it does from the hands of the Creator. If it is not, the argument goes, we need to find out why it is not. Has it been somehow corrupted, and if so, does that corruption destroy its very goodness once and for all?

Robert Bellah and his associates have worked very hard to explicate the various languages at work in American culture.[179] Are we without any goodness and left alone in a world of chance—thus, really without power, save what we can impose through violence from time to time—or are we, though flawed in nature and weakened in will, nonetheless capable of reason and meaning? Are we pilgrims on a journey in this vale of tears, or are we at home on this earth, entrusted with its stewardship and loved by its maker? Greeley's characters would say that it is the

---

[179] See Chapters 2 and 3.

latter they want to believe in because they have more evidence that such a world is worthy of them than the former. But they also know that the former is a world that human beings have created and have the power to reform if they understand it correctly. This is the Catholic (analogical) imagination at work. What Greeley's characters do is insist that the march of history is in some sense about God in the world, but not exactly as we read it or as we might wish it to be—and certainly not as Georg Wilhelm Friedrch Hegel understood it. The analogical imagination is one which realizes that the exercise of freedom, however limited by historical and social choices, is the way to create an authority that uses power in ways worthy of human beings in their best sense. Blackie may well be "a Chaplain to one powerful Chicago clan." It is good to know that one of them has a chaplain!

Rather than using the issue of how Blackie Ryan gets into the action—always as a response to someone's need for help—the issue should be, what does he see along the way and what does he give witness to in terms of the Gospel. This assumes, as many critics today will not allow, that the Gospel still has something to teach us. More to the point, it is not true that Greeley's criminals are "truly evil" and "damned by their very nature," so much so that they can be known by their appearance. (See Sipe 19.) Nature, weather, architecture, art, natural and human beauty, sexuality, marriage and family, and the Roman Catholic understanding of theology are all used to proclaim what God might be like. That Greeley's characters enunciate these realities in specific, though not exclusive, cultural forms means only that his characters take on the natures he needs to tell the story. If evil has a role in Greeley fiction, it is as the antagonist to his main character, who is always God. In Greeley's novels, evil warns us of what we are capable.

We have only to note the cultural differences between the England of the first three decades of the twentieth century (Chesterton died in 1936) and the last three decades of the twentieth century to be cautious of any comparisons between Blackie Ryan and Father Brown. Greeley's treatment of evil takes cognizance of the fact that evil has defined the twentieth century and still threatens the future of the twenty-first century. If Greeley's characters perform differently than those of other writers who have gone before him, such as Chesterton or Flannery

O'Connor, it is because of the advances in our knowledge of the human sciences—psychology, political science, sociology. It is just not true that Blackie "knows who is truly evil" (19); he and his sister, Mary Kathleen Ryan Murphy, MD, know the effects of psychological diseases and their physical and social causes; his cousin Mike Casey knows how criminals generally think and how civilized societies ought to treat those charged with crime; and it is knowledge such as these possess that helps readers mitigate the judgments they might make regarding the evil that imperfect men and women, and sometimes societies, involve themselves in. It means we might be able to condemn the sin but still love the sinner, even get him or her some help. It means we are not to be vengeful in the presence of evil, but it is also to name evil for what it is and does. It means, too, we might learn how to forgive.

We must return to the differing views of the church and the sacramental and non-sacramental understandings that have such powerful holds on the human imagination. Neither magic nor mere sign, a sacrament involves the affirmation that *things* when touched by the Spirit, are the agencies of grace, i.e., signs of God's life in the world and in each person. Father Brown could hold as his major theme "the discourse on confession" because he lived at the end of the Tridentine age: an age in which merit and grace had been very carefully measured so that the Catholic Church could hold on to its temporal as well as its spiritual powers. Thus, the theology of penance became the avenue of conversion. But it has not always been so. Witness St. Augustine and his profound *Confessions*. In his meaning, the very term that primarily meant reconciliation to Chesterton represented to St. Augustine a hymn of praise. Yet, both were working toward the same good. Greeley's characters live at the beginning of the age of Vatican II, wherein the church declares that the hopes and joys of this age, along with its anxieties and griefs, are the joys, hopes, griefs, and anxieties of the people of God.[180] If a priest in a Greeley novel behaved according to the theology and mores of any age other than his own, such a character would live in the imaginations of the readers but probably as an antagonist to Greeley's message. Critics ought to grant, at the very least, that an author has a point of view. Of course, the theology is different; it is supposed to be! What Blackie does that so outrages his critics is to insist that all things—even the criminal and the reprobate—are open to

---

[180] *Gaudium et Spes* in *The Documents of Vatican II*.

God's grace, and moreover, that grace is abundantly channeled through both the church's sacraments and through all other things as sacramentals, even human sexuality. The claim that this leaves an undifferentiated mass of things competing for human attention falls before the differentiating judgments of Blackie and other Greeley characters. It is their informed judgments, thinking for themselves that makes sense out of the mass of things and gives to that mass the form that makes sense to them. This is God working through the human heart and mind. This is a God who respects human freedom. And it is this respect that many of Greeley's critics resent. The question remains—and it is the question of Greeley's fiction—if we, like God, respected human freedom, how different might this world be?

Before using Greeley's most recent novels[181] to illustrate why his critics oppose his characters so consistently, it might help to be reminded of the theoretical structure[182] that gives rise to a defense of these characters. In a 2002 article, Mark S. Massa, SJ, explores anti-Catholicism, both old and new, in relation to David Tracy and Andrew Greeley's use of the analogical imagination.[183] Massa's task is to discern the cause of American anti-Catholicism and explain why it remains, in the words of Arthur Schlesinger, Sr., "the deepest bias in the history of the American people ..." (in Massa 1). Writing of the various attempts to account for this bias,[184] Massa suggests that such attempts share with their antagonists a sense that Catholicism

---

[181] As of January 2008.

[182] Certainly, this theoretical structure informs much of the discussion in preceding chapters.

[183] Massa, Mark S. (SJ) "The New and Old Anti-Catholicism and the Analogical Imagination." *Theological Studies* 62.3 (2001): 549.\

[184] Massa writes, "Some interpreters of this contemporary anti-Catholicism (Andrew Greeley) would say that, to begin with, the new anti-Catholicism is not all that new. Indeed, Greeley argues that recent anti-Catholic displays simply represent a contemporary form of an animus that never really went away. Other interpreters (George Weigel) have offered a gloss on the secularization theories of Peter Berger and Martin Marty, arguing that in North America (unlike, say, Germany) "secularity" does not mean the disappearance of religion, but rather its privatization—its removal from the public sphere into domestic quarters. Thus, so this interpretation goes, a resolutely public religion such as Catholicism—a very large institutional religion that refuses to keep silent on neuralgic public issues such as abortion—opens itself ineluctably to cultural criticism and derision" (1).

is countercultural in contemporary America and suggests an important tension between theological perspectives. Massa contends,

> [...] Catholicism offers a quite distinctive way of seeing the world, a pre-rational lens, if you will, identified by David Tracy as the "analogical imagination." That imagination, according to Tracy, differentiates Catholics from other Christian believers (most obviously, from Protestant Christians who make up the majority of U.S. citizens), and might help to explain why guardians of institutional Catholicism can be seen, and in fact probably are, more prone to worry about group loyalty and theological orthodoxy than protecting the rights of individual believers and guaranteeing the free expression of religious belief. (2)

It follows, then, that charges of authoritarianism and blind obedience (negative readings of "group loyalty and theological orthodoxy") do not fit well into the representative democratic system that is believed by many to have been realized in the American state. Characters like Greeley's who argue for this representative democratic system as at least a possibility in Catholic thought and tradition, are open, then, to charges of disloyalty and religious disobedience. In fact, such characters are seen as manifestations of anti-Catholicism in the priest who creates them.

When American Catholicism's countercultural stance is combined with a virulently ideological reading of American history, the result is a stereotypical view of Catholic culture that belies its reality. Massa encapsulates this ideological view of history by quoting William Warren Sweet's claim in 1947 that "all the great concepts for which American democracy stands today—individual rights, freedom of conscience, self-government, and complete religious liberty—are concepts coming out of the left wing of the Reformation" (Massa 6). Greeley's characters, on the other hand, having read the social teachings of the church since 1891, and as immigrants on the receiving end of the "realities" of American democracy, often suggest a different reality, one that seems to be heresy in light of that dogmatic view of history. These characters refuse to be either authoritarian, often by rejecting that characteristic in their hierarchy and culture, or blindly obedient, often by demonstrating the ability to think for themselves. Greeley's fiction rejects both stereotypes and suggests that being Catholic and being American may be done in multiple ways.

Massa is on to something much more implicit and important, however. By juxtaposing the "analogical language" of Tracy and Greeley with the "dialectical language of mainstream Protestant theology, Massa points to an essential tension and complementarity between both languages. To understand this tension and this complementarity, I submit, is to understand Greeley's project as a writer of fiction. Read what Massa says. Quoting Tracy, he writes,

> The "conceptual language" supporting the Roman Catholic theological tradition Tracy dubs "analogical language," a "language of ordered relationships articulating similarity-in-difference." In this language tradition, the Incarnation of Christ represents the focal event, the "primary analogue for the interpretation of the whole of reality." And because of this incarnational focal point in interpreting reality, "the entire world, the ordinary in all its variety, is now theologically envisioned as sacrament—a sacrament emanating from Jesus Christ as the paradigmatic sacrament of God, the paradigmatic clue to humanity and nature alike"(27). While Tracy posits that the distinctions and dissimilarities between "God" and "world" remain as real and tensive as the similarities in this analogical language, the emphasis in this Catholic tradition remains on "analogies in difference," which are expressed in a whole series of "ordered relationships ... all established in and through reflection on the self's primordial experience of its similarity-in-difference to the [Incarnation] event." And the articulated analogues, based in the revelatory power of the constitutive event and its disclosure of radical, all-pervasive grace, are further developed into a literally, cosmic wide pattern of sacramental, analogical relationships between God and creation. With this all-pervasive grace, a fundamental trust and confidence in the goodness and sacramental nature of matter and history ultimately emerges, even in the face of absurdity and chaos: the created world embodies and sacramentally discloses the Holy, that same Holy who came fully and definitively in a human nature, Jesus. (8)

Massa continues, Protestant theology is essentially in tension with this conceptual language, which insists on the necessity of radical negation in distinguishing the Holy from human culture in all authentically Christian language. That is, this language system [the dialectical] posits a "rupture" between God's revelation of salvation and the human condition, a "rupture at the heart of human pretension, guilt and sin—a rupture disclosed in the absolute paradox of Jesus Christ proclaimed in the judging, negating, releasing word." This "word," of course, refers to both Jesus and to the secondary means of disclosing the Holy: over against "sacrament" in the analogical language system, this conceptual language focuses on the "preached word"—the word of judgment and of grace. And this "word" emphasizes not analogical similarity in difference, but rather Kierkegaard's "infinite qualitative difference" between this world and God's kingdom, between the human and the divine, between the historical Church and Christ's true disciples. Human communities utilizing this conceptual language tend not to emphasize their worship as the locus of God's sacramental presence; on the contrary, they rather tend to fear that they are always, potentially, an idolatrous source of oppressive power and overweening pride that must be resisted. (8–9)

Greeley's contribution to this insight is succinctly summarized by Massa:

As sociologist of religion Andrew Greeley has argued, using the definitions of anthropologist Clifford Geertz, if all human religions are, at their most basic level, cultural systems that inspire certain moods and feelings in believers, feelings that offer explanations regarding the ultimate meanings of personal and collective human life, then the world views shaped by these cultural systems represent something like the hardware on which the software of creeds and liturgies operate. In Greeley's own words, "religion, both in the life of the individual and in the great historical traditions, was then experience, symbol, story (most symbols were inherently narrative) and community before it became creed, rite, and institution. The latter were essential, but derivative" (31). For Greeley then, glossing both Geertz and Tracy, the symbols and stories of the great religious systems, including Christianity, inspire distinctive "religious imaginations" that see the world through the lens of the narratives or symbols of the tradition. Onto this primary template of the imagination, institutions (derivatively if essentially) build theological systems, doctrines, and church structures. For Greeley, as for Tracy, the underlying "religious imagination" of any tradition remains primary (both in terms of epistemology as well as of chronology) to institutional forms:

"Therefore, the fundamental differences between Catholicism and Protestantism are not doctrinal or ethical. The different propositional codes of the two heritages are but manifestations, tips of the iceberg, of more fundamentally differing sets of symbols. The Catholic ethic is "communitarian" and the Protestant "individualistic" because the preconscious "organizing" pictures of the two traditions that shape meaning and response to life for members of the respective heritages are different. Catholics and Protestants "see" the world differently" (9).

Now, I have quoted so extensively from the Massa article both to indicate an intellectual debt to his scholarship as well as to make obvious again, perhaps too starkly,[185] these different ways of seeing because they can explain why critics often misread Greeley's characters.

---

[185] Massa points out, "At the same time, however, Tracy has pointed out that the two conceptual languages he adumbrates are not in competition with each other. Still less did he want to imply that either was theologically superior to the other in disclosing the Holy. They are, rather, complementary conceptual languages, that complete and enrich each other. In his view, dialectical language needs the analogical to disclose and name the presence of the Holy in the world and in the community, and to off-set a dangerous tendency to valorize the individual; and analogical language needs the dialectical as a "firewall" against the idolatry of confusing human power plays with the activity of the Holy Spirit, or running roughshod over individual rights in the name of communal identity. For Tracy, the analogical language of the Catholic tradition needs the healthy negations of the dialectical imagination to offset an idolatrous tendency toward univocally identifying the institutional symbol with the mystery celebrated. For as Tracy reminds us, "negations of any claims to full adequacy (for example, any attempts at exhaustive, univocal meaning in any analogue) are negations to assure that the similarities remain similarities-in-difference. The negations function as principles of intensification constituted by the tensive event-character of the focal meaning to negate any slackening of the sense of radical mystery" (36). Indeed, any attempts to force out all tensions from analogical language ends in destroying that conceptual language. This insight is especially important for an institution claiming such a sacramental/communal language as its own, for the iron law of bureaucracy tends toward heightening the similarities between the Church and Christ's true flock, and flattening out the tensive quality of sacramental revelation" (10–11).

They see the world differently and think Greeley should see it the same way they do. Greeley's characters, on the other hand, constitute a world in which these different ways of seeing are accommodated and criticized.

In his most recent novels,[186] we again meet the O'Malleys through Thomas Moran, senator from Illinois and husband of Mary Margaret O'Malley, daughter of that family's most recent "patriarch,"[187] Ambassador Chucky O'Malley; Nuala Anne McGrail and her "spear carrying" husband, Dermot; Joseph Ryan Murphy Jr., nephew to Archbishop Blackie Ryan, who is "jularker"[188] to Margaret Anne Nolan of the dysfunctional family from Nolan Landing, and Donna Teresa Maria Romero y Avila, duchess of Sevilla and Huelva. Together these characters and their stories represent a snapshot of the late twentieth-century church refracted through the political challenges that church has faced both successfully and unsuccessfully. Taken together, which one need not do, these four novels move from the most general of Catholic practical concerns to the most specific of human expressiveness: from politics to sexual intimacy. *The Senator and the Priest* is about the need to respect human politics as part of the sacramental order; the stories in *Irish Linen* are about our duty to attend to the state before it usurps God's place in our lives; *The Bishop at the Lake* reflects our need to respect the family, no matter how flawed; and *The Archbishop in al-Andalus* is about how God gets into the locked room which is our very self, it is about sexual love as the sacrament of God. None of these novels presents anything new to Greeley's body of fiction, but their recurring themes helps us understand how critics often get this fiction wrong.

The requirement of civility in politics involves more than the claim that we should be nice to our political opponents. At the very core of civility is the recognition that politics has a positive role in the

---

[186] *The Senator and the Priest.* New York: Tom Doherty Associates, 2006; *Irish Linen.* New York: Tom Doherty Associates, 2007; *The Bishop at the Lake.* New York: Tom Doherty Associates, 2007; and *The Archbishop in al-Andalus,* manuscript, 2007.

[187] Consider the development of this character throughout these novels as both a critique of the evil of patriarchy as well as a treatment of genuine authority, especially through marital love.

[188] Sweetheart and potential intended.

development of the person because it is an essential part of human nature. As persons, we are social beings who develop (for well or ill) depending upon the health of the political process that supports and sustains the interconnecting network of relationships that make us who we are. In Catholic thought, government has a positive role to play in defending, protecting, and augmenting the common good. That good is our good; what is harmful to the common good is also harmful to persons who depend upon it. It follows, therefore, that determination of the common good involves many interests and should entail as many viewpoints as possible. The health of the civil polity depends, then, upon a willingness to compromise our interests in light of the needs of the common good. No matter how positive political life might be, it is never simple. It is our understanding of justice, then that should inform both the complexity of political life; that very same understanding makes generalizations difficult when considering questions of public policy. Difficult, but not impossible.

At the very core of political life, then, is a recognition of the need for balance, openness, and compromise. We work in the world because we recognize that though embodied we are not completely of this world. Catholics must become political because they are called to hope, the virtue that connects faith to love. The one thing that ought to be obvious from history, both secular and ecclesiastical, is that where civility fails violence results. The question that worries *The Senator and the Priest* is whether American politics has stepped beyond civility.

In this novel, we meet two brothers, Senator Thomas Moran and Father Anthony Moran. The opening scene finds the priest deriding his politician brother and in the process deriding political life as antithetical to ethical principle. As the older brother, Father Moran assumes the role, which churchmen have often assumed, of preaching the necessity of doing what is right even if the heavens fall. The younger brother, like Joseph in the Old Testament, must find a way to do what is right amid the circumstances in which he finds himself. His is the task of giving witness to the Gospel in a system that both formally and informally dismisses that Gospel as, at best, a private mode of belief like every other, or at worst, not applicable to the realities of power. Thomas Moran stands for the person who cares enough to engage in political life because he takes his faith seriously when it teaches him to be leaven in the lump. He cares enough to find effective means to protect the weak from the strong. He knows when to compromise. His virtue is prudence. In rejecting the moral compromises said to be "necessary" to win in political life, Thomas Moran stands for Catholic social principles in political action. He assumes that education—he has written and even read books—when added to moral decency constitutes the reformed politics that American civility requires. (See 133.) And he refuses to engage in negative campaigning to win, or even to defend himself and his family from calumny. He does know, however, how to use the law and the police to protect his family and himself from physical violence.

The novel is an exposé of the difficulty of doing social justice in American politics. But his greatest hurdle is not those who lie and slander his good name. Rather, his greatest obstacle to keeping his integrity is his priest brother who insists that good Catholics cannot be part of a flawed political system without selling out to the devil. The issue of bishops ordering priests to deny Holy Communion to "excommunicated" politicians they morally oppose stands as the most recent misuse of religion for political purposes. Such moral judgments of others are evidence of a political system near collapse, not from the moral evils that social justice should address but from the demise of civility as a working virtue in that system. By identifying a person's moral state with that person's politics,[189] bishops enact a judgment that makes politics impossible.

The grace of matrimony, the love of Tom and Mary Margaret (258), enables the protagonist to stand up to the violence of his church and his family. Notice that it is Tom's community, his O'Malley family, and his political constituency that frees him to act with personal integrity. It is also the community, through the police, that protects him and his family. In the end, forgiveness marks the relationship of the two brothers. God's grace is even open to the self-righteous Father Moran; this is perhaps the most important, though least developed, theme of this novel. And this grace comes though the agency of a woman, Mary

---

[189] We might say, too, that by identifying an author's moral state with those of his characters, critics make fiction something more than it really is.

Margaret, who will have none of the priest's authoritarian bluster, but who knows grace when she sees it.

Critics will claim that these characters belie the Catholic commitment to the right to life. This has been the priest-character's claim until the end of the novel, and it is the issue that haunts American political life. How could a priest write a novel in which his characters stand in opposition to the hierarchy's clear teaching on the dignity of the human person? In the dialectical language of either/or, he ought not to have done so; in the analogical language of both/and he could do nothing else but point out how difficult it is for the laity to do the work of justice. That Tom Moran does not vote in favor of abortion legislation while still being able to affirm and augment other legislation that advances human dignity and respect for life is exactly the point of the importance of having moral men and women in political life, the military, the police, and even, the academy. But it is also true that some moral evils must be confronted for what they are; this truth entails the question of how, and thus, the place of prudence in the order of civil virtues.

What moral persons might do when faced directly with participating in moral evil is the subject of Greeley's next novel, *Irish Linen* (2007). It is a novel about tyrannicide and the moral requirements leading to it. Before discussing these, however, I wish to draw attention to a 2004 criticism of Greeley for an analogy he made in the *Chicago Sun-Times* between the cultures that produced President Bush and Hitler. It indicates again two different ways of viewing the world. Defending himself from readers who think he is too soft on Greeley, Richard Neuhaus excerpts the following from Greeley's column,

> [Bush] is not another Hitler. Yet there is a certain parallelism. They have in common a demagogic appeal to the worst side of a country's heritage in a crisis. Bush is doubtless sincere in his vision of what is best for America. So too was Hitler. The crew around the President—Donald Rumsfeld, John Ashcroft, Karl Rove, the "neo-cons" like Paul Wolfowitz—are not as crazy perhaps as Himmler and Goering and Goebbels. Yet like them, they are practitioners of the Big Lie—weapons

of mass destruction, Iraq democracy, only a few "bad apples." Hitler's war was quantitatively different from the Iraq war, but qualitatively both were foolish, self-destructive, and criminally unjust. This is a time of great peril in American history because a phony patriotism and an America-worshipping religion threaten the authentic American genius of tolerance and respect for other people[...].

Neuhaus goes on to comment,

George W. Bush as Adolf Hitler? A reader asks how Fr. Greeley can still be a priest in good standing. That is a question best addressed to the Archbishop of Chicago, but I expect his answer would be that, if he kicked out every priest who is a political nut case, there would be a lot of empty altars in Chicago. The problem is not unique to Chicago, although it is no small blessing that Fr. Andrew Greeley is.

The issue is why Greeley's analogy is thought to be inappropriate in discussing the weighty matter of war and peace, and why Greeley's uniqueness in making this analogy might be a blessing. Why are those who see in twentieth-century history certain dangerous parallels between the activities of other states and our own foreign policy dismissed in the their right to be taken seriously ("political nut case"). Isn't this the essence of incivility?

"This is a time of great peril in American history because a phony patriotism and an America-worshipping religion threaten the authentic American genius of tolerance and respect for other people [...]" (Greeley in Neuhaus). I suspect that it is this phony patriotism that infects critics who deny to others the right to use images as they see fit. And it is this false patriotism that Greeley's *Irish Linen* addresses.

As is his practice, Greeley's Nuala Anne McGrail novels involve two stories, one a fiction about a case Nuala and her husband Dermot are given, and a second, a story that is rooted in history, which the fey Nuala and her daughter discover. The McGrail fiction always illuminates history. *Irish Linen* involves the fictitious Desmond Doolin who is lost somewhere in Iraq, perhaps dead. He is neither a soldier nor a mercenary, and his function in the novel is as exemplar of Catholic ethical concerns, especially about the moral use of force. The novel also tells in fictional terms the story of Timothy Patrick Clarke, Lord Ridgeland, the Irish ambassador to the Third Reich. Through his love story and neutral eyes,[190] we learn the historical tale of Claus von Stauffenberg's failed tyrannicide against Hitler. Through the juxtaposition of these stories, the reader is asked to use history to address the real issues that confront moral persons when their society has ceased to be a polity and become a state dependent upon violence for its continuation. What are moral men and women called to do when violence replaces politics, when the state has assumed the place of God in their lives?

Two stories, both of them true. One is fiction the other is history. Both have heroes made in God's image through Greeley's imagination (347), and both are lovers in pursuit of a great love. Both Doolin and Ridgeland, however, place their loves in a larger context, one that is no surprise to readers of Greeley's fiction. That context is the love of God for his people defined by the dignity of the image in which they are made. In Doolin and Ridgeland's cases, this context will call forth two very different ways of acting in the world: Doolin's will be the way of pacific resistance, Ridgeland's will be through aiding and abetting tyrannicide (56, 72). These stories indicate two ways to love: Doolin's story is about how to fight war fever and its false patriotism, along with its claims to vengeance, (all evident in 1914, 1939, and 2003) by being a fool for Christ (26) and going to Iraq to help end the war through prayer and good works. Ridgeland's story is about what must be done when society has passed the threshold of politics and entered into the realm of violence and war. Together they give us the moral options open to reasonable men and women living at the beginning of the twenty-first century.

Grim as these options might seem, throughout the book, the love of Nuala and Dermot calls forth the power of memory and the power of beauty to renew our hope (63). This is required not only because of the narrow range of options open in times of great violence, but also because an underlying question throughout the novel—never

---

[190] See Greeley's "Afterword" on the demonization of von Stauffenberg in US propaganda.

definitively answered to Greeley's credit—involves whether or not the Secret Germany of von Stauffenberg—the noble ideas of German culture as found in its art, music, literature, and philosophy opposed to the paganism of the Nazis—might not parallel the Secret United States of America, if not in content, at least in ideals ("American genius of tolerance and respect for other people …").

Ultimately, the book presents the question of how a polity might defend itself from the death that comes with every commitment to violence, even violence used in the good cause. Killing the tyrant is not merely a utilitarian act to save many lives, rather it involves the principled decision to remove the source of violence in society, recognizing as it does the reciprocal to the notion that grace comes into the world through the use of things; evil also comes into the world through the use of good things. It takes us close to the Manichaean view of good and evil—itself a grave danger. Like all acts of self-defense, it is an extraordinary act, one not lightly engaged in; it is an act required when all else has failed. Greeley's characters are designed both to critique the conditions of violence in our world and to raise questions about how those conditions might be prudently and morally addressed. Doolin's role is that of the prophet acting to stave off violence, of speaking truth to power before it is too late, Ridgeland and von Stauffenberg's actions are those of the prophet perishing with his people in witness to their love. The readers' role is to say where their understanding of both history and current events situates them and what their moral response might be.

In the last two novels, both of which are Blackie Ryan mysteries, we are confronted with the locked room conundrum. Used many times in his mystery stories, we might ask what it conveys. My contention is that the locked room in which an evil has been committed, wherein a mystery must be solved before order is restored, stand for the human heart.

In *The Bishop at the Lake* (2007), Blackie Ryan is sent by the cardinal archbishop of Chicago to investigate Bishop Howard-Nolan, a character who for his own interests uses gossip and innuendo to distort the Vatican's understanding of conditions in the Chicago archdiocese. Through Bishop Nolan, we meet the dysfunctional Nolan family, scions of the World War II hero, Spike Nolan, and his wife, Lady Anne Howard. How two such well-developed and well-endowed people could produce such children is one of the great mysteries known to anyone who has raised children. The only one who has escaped being a failure as a person is the granddaughter Margaret Anne, who may become romantically attached to the young Joseph Murphy. Blackie's involvement with these two young people indicates an old priest's wisdom: we always need to listen to our children.

Through the inept investigation of some of the local authorities and the professional behavior of others, through reliance upon the requirements of due process and the correct civil and criminal procedure, and by naming the dysfunctional dynamics of this very wounded family, we discover not only who committed the crime, but in the process of solving the mystery of the locked room, something in the very heart of every one of us. The attempted murder of Bishop Nolan, the ineptitude of the police, the mental illness of the culprit, and the attempted murder of Margaret Anne and Joseph are all explained, it seems to me, through the metaphor of the locked room. This mystery device is always solved by figuring out how the evil was committed when all the ways into the room are locked. And the answer is always that such evil gets into the room before it is locked. Someone has the key or knows how to use those who have one. It very well might stand for the mystery of the Fall.

Like St. Augustine, the characters in this novel discover that they were infected by hatred and misunderstanding long before they come to the evil within the locked room. It is selfishness (treated here as a form of mental illness) that locks into each character something of the evil that will lead to attempted murder. Paradoxically, this selfishness is also the means by which the characters might be healed. This is "the restless heart" of Augustine: the very instrument by which we are called back to God. Loretta Nolan, mother of Margaret Anne, hates her child because that child represents everything she is not. Loretta thinks she should run the family's company even in the face of Margaret's superior gifts. She therefore attempts to kill her bishop brother-in-law as a way to frame Margaret, and later, attempts to kill her. Loretta Nolan has a very "good" reason to do what she thinks best for herself and her family. It is as though her disease has closed her to her very self thus, the resulting selfishness. The ineptitude of the investigators, too, is the result of the closed heart. They are certain about who is guilty and want that view of reality imposed, just as the ineptitude of Bishop Nolan resides in his certainty about what is good for the church of Chicago. Their means to achieving the good are merely instrumental to their point of view. Every one of the characters who cause the problems in this family relies on their point of view without caring for those of anyone else.

In the end, procedure and intuition—dare I say faith—solve the mystery of the locked room. We might think of these as keys to open human hearts. When investigators and lawyers use procedure and rules to do their work, such work prospers. When Blackie, Margaret, and Joseph trust their best selves, they figure out what went wrong and discover ways to overcome that wrong. In the end, the love of two families, Joseph's Ryan-Murphy clan and the Nolan family, carry the day. The family is essential to well developed persons because it is the first society into which we are placed. Its health is the health of both individuals and society.

The Archbishop in al-Andalus, soon to be published, is set in Spain, and uses that country's fascinating history to continue the metaphor of the locked room. Without giving away any of the surprises in this novel, we find Blackie Ryan working at the behest of a philosopher, Don Diego, the cardinal archbishop of Seville, to solve another locked room mystery. This mystery is used to introduce the tragic history of Spain—Greeley is especially good at using large sweeps of history to tell this story—as the backdrop for the tale of the redemption of the main character, Donna Teresa Maria Romero y Avila, duchess of Sevilla and Huelva. In the story, we learn what we owe to Islamic civilization, especially as an antidote to the anti-Muslim ideology that today scars the American trait of tolerance. In this regard, we are again presented with hope as the virtue best to address the cynicism and fatalism of a religious community marred by the Inquisition and anti-Semitism. Hope is the virtue most needed in cultures near the Manichaean abyss. That hope comes to live in the locked heart of Donna Teresa through the erotic passion—God's image. We read, for example, "Hope ... is structured into our brains so every act of human love contains within it organically an act of hope even [if] the lovers don't intend the hope or accept it." This is God's way into the human heart.

I shall allow the readers of this novel its newness and not give away the plot, but I also shall affirm that its plot reveals how those who admire Greeley's fiction might want to be Catholic. Others may reject it, but they ought not to deny it to those who want it, for it has been, in the past, an historical possibility and that possibility may just save the church from further ruin. Donna Teresa's scruples about going to hell because of sex may be the way God saves us from our own negative illusions about our sexuality as distancing us from him. Again, Greeley's God lurks everywhere, and we see this especially in his scramentality of the body. It is a very clever God who lurks so, even having incarnated himself into that sexuality. In a sense, this is a novel about getting our bodies back; it is about sexual love as sign of resurrection. In the process, it retells the story of the Cronins—a family that Greeley gave to us long ago. It reminds us that locked hearts contain both the potential for good and for evil, and that it is love that distinguishes the two. It is a story that gives flesh to Augustine's greatest advice, "Love, then do as thou will."

Some concluding thoughts on the criticism of Greeley's fiction.

The following thoughts on the criticism of Greeley's fiction range from criticism that is impossible to answer, to criticism raising substantive questions that may be answered by the novels themselves. The first involve *ad hominem* arguments that make the author the target of deeply felt emotions over which he has no control. These are the arguments that spring from the vice of envy—the emotion that diminishes the accomplishments of others precisely because they are the accomplishments of others. These involve criticisms that begin with an unstated assumption: that priests who write successful novels (and who enjoy their success and the resources that come with such success) really ought not to be heard or read because they must not be very good priests. Envy destroys the souls of those who suffer it.[191] But

---

[191]See the treatment of the culture of envy in Chapter 2.

part of this destructiveness is that those who are the object of envy's sad gaze are almost without defense. Without judging the interior motives of the envious—something we are not morally permitted to do in most cases—the person who is envied is silenced and forced to suffer envy's attacks.

Another *ad hominem* argument found in some of the criticism of Greeley's fiction involves the claim that authors who are dirty-minded priests infect their stories by using human sexuality for prurient reasons. Apart from the absurdity of proscribing an essentially part of our human being from fiction that hopes to be credible in terms of today's experiences, this criticism would remove from Greeley's novels one of their most important characters, the character of God, whose dialogue often is constituted through human sexuality. It is one of the ways God speaks with us; it is a way that is so important that Roman Catholics believe it to be a special kind of sacrament, one that if taken seriously, transforms those who live It and may serve to found the family, which is the foundation of all other social institutions. To silence God on such important subjects would seem to be a new form of blasphemy.

More substantively, however, Greeley's critics often take him to task for what they label elitism, especially an Irish-American form of elitism. His characters use the law and civil procedure as a means of helping God "delivery us from evil." For this, he is castigated as a representative for successful men and women who are engaged in this world. What is often overlooked in this charge is the fact that these characters are almost always helping someone in need by using their expertise and experience to make the system work. What is also often ignored is that such characters call forth one of the great success stories of the twentieth-century US life, that of immigrant groups rising to take part in the opportunities of American society. Underneath this criticism is a fundamental misunderstanding of the structure of human groups. All societies include the composite of elites; democratic societies are those that allow a plurality of elites into the system and which construct their legal and political systems to hear their voices. To condemn elites as elites is like condemning the rain. Both are part of the nature of things, both can create problems. Greeley's reliance upon law and civil procedure is textbook good civics. As James Madison wrote in the Tenth Federalist: there are two ways to address the problem of factions (with their consequent elites) in society; one is to destroy their cause, which is liberty; the other is to control their effects through law and procedure.

What is often at stake in critiques of Greeley's characters is a new kind of Catholic layperson, one unlike the illiterate immigrant Catholics of the first half of the twentieth century. These are characters who have learned to think for themselves, using the expertise of their educations as the means to make informed moral, psychological, political, and social judgments, which are based on sound evidence. They read the "signs of [their] times" and are open to the working of the Holy Spirit, whose presence is confirmed, in traditional theological terminology, by the seven gifts[192] and their fruits.[193] These gifts and their fruits might be said to constitute a liberally educated, well-integrated person. What such characters do is open themselves to others and resist the misuse of power and authority by holding both accountable to law and to their traditions.

At their best, Greeley's characters have experienced the Church of Christ as it subsists in the Roman Catholic Church and to which all-sincere Christians are said to belong. They are also witness to the possibility that all men and women of good will belong to this communion in some mysterious way. These are the Ryans, the Murphys, the Coynes, and the O'Malleys: Chicago democrats all! These are also characters who confront evil, name it—whether in its psychological manifestations, or as actively embraced by The Outfit. They have learned how to forgive, and therefore, how to change.

Such characters reveal the tension and the complementarity of analogical and dialectical languages, which both seek to address the Great Mysteries. Both languages seek to speak the unspeakable. Through their vocations, these characters give witness to the good news of Christ. They know they have a right to be happy here and now

---

[192] Wisdom, understanding, counsel, fortitude, knowledge, piety, and fear of the Lord.

[193] Charity, joy, peace, patience, benignity, goodness, long-suffering, mildness, faith, modesty, continency, and chastity.

just as they hope, without presumption, for happiness in the next life; they affirm in the everydayness of their lives the manifesto of human rights given by John XXIII in *Pacem in Terris*. They are characters who learn how to listen to God through their traditions and cultures, to the Holy Spirit, especially, through discovering their very selves, and perhaps most importantly for the church today, they have learned to listen to each other: through human sexuality, through psychologically healthy relationships, through those who are in need of being heard—the least in society—and through the planet as it calls us to be stewards of its well being.

The substantive question critics must answer is why they might oppose such characters!

Epilogue

At this point, our question might be what do we have after having read Greeley's novels and my analysis of them? In the beginning, I began to study Greeley's fiction as an exercise in political philosophy; in the end, I have learned a theology of grace. Good enough! might be the reply, yet it is not enough to notice that politics leads us to religion; rather something seems amiss if politics and God are not, at least, allied. If this is so, and I think it is, we should find ideas embedded in Greeley's fiction—the vehicle of his theology of grace—which are of practical, political value in the real world. Here again, we might object: why does everything necessarily need to be practical? Isn't this merely the echo of a utilitarian ethic, something that distorts humanity and serves to diminish its value? Could not the theoretical—the concept that comes closest to the idea of the contemplative—be *in se* of value? Why require practical justification? Why do we need "a political" if we have an adequate theological view of the world?

Answers to these questions would require another book, but the short answer seems to involve the failure of modernity, what Evelyn Waugh brilliantly notices as the Age of Hooper in *Brideshead Revisited*. Waugh begins Captain Charles Ryder's melancholic remembrances—the story that has made him who he has become—with a description of his subaltern Lieutenant Hooper: a person unfamiliar with poetry and with no sense of duty. Indeed Hooper has nothing of the romantic about him. Everything is business and efficiency, even as he lacks competence in everything. In short, Hooper symbolizes the person without imagination, and therefore, one lacking in the capacity to be human (8–10).[194] We might see Hooper as a person without grace. At the end of the novel, having taken memory as his theme (225) and reliving the grace that he had once discovered but failed to see, Ryder's story ends after he has toured the remains of Brideshead. Having revisited its chapel and saying a prayer—"an ancient, newly learned form of words" (350)—he returns to his unit and his subaltern with this thought.

> The builders did not know the uses to which their work would descend; they made a new house with the stones of the old castle; year by year, generation after generation, they enriched and extended it; year by year the great harvest of timber in the park grew to ripeness; until, in sudden frost, came the age of Hooper; the place was desolate and the work all brought to nothing; *Quomodo sedet sola civitas.* Vanity of vanity, all is vanity.
>
> And yet [...]. Something quite remote from anything the builders intended had come out of their work, and out of the fierce little tragedy in which I played; something none of us thought about at the time: a small red flame—a beaten copper lamp of deplorable design, relit before the beaten-copper doors of a tabernacle; the flame which the old knights saw from their tombs, which they saw put out; that flame burns again for other soldiers, far from home, farther, in heart, than Acre or Jerusalem. It could not have been lit but for the builders and the tragedians, and there I found it this morning, burning anew among the old stones.

Between Hooper and his age, at the heart of the novel, we find Cordelia—a sort of union of every character in the novel—describing part of Brideshead's fate.

> They've closed the chapel at Brideshead [...]. Mummy's requiem was the last mass said there. After she was buried

---

[194] Evelyn Waugh. *Brideshead Revisited.* Boston: Little, Brown and Company, 1945.

the priest came in [...] and took out the altar stone and put it in his bag; then he burned the wads of wool with the holy oil on them and threw the ash outside; he emptied the holy water stoup and blew out the lamp in the sanctuary and left the tabernacle open and empty, as though from now on it was always to be Good Friday[...]. I stayed there till he was gone, and then, suddenly, there wasn't any chapel there any more, just an oddly decorated room (220).

Hooper is Cordelia without memory or imagination, but it is "the lamp of deplorable design" that guides Ryder to his final "And yet." What "burns anew among the old stones" is the possibility that God's being with us makes a difference in how we live. This is, in both Waugh and Greeley, the theological part of their messages. But in the Catholic intellectual tradition in which both are located, what remains dependent upon the theological is living as though the theological makes a difference: practicing what we preach. This is the political part.

Part of what? Throughout this study the supposition has been that the theological and the political are essential dimensions of our humanity. Ignore or exclude either and we have the Age of Hooper. Without both dimensions, we merely inhabit oddly decorated rooms. Imagination is the faculty that unites the theological and the political. This is the basic conclusion to be drawn from the work of Andrew Greeley. His fiction testifies to the unity of body and soul, and to the proposition that this unity constitutes the moral anthropology of Catholicism from its beginning. We are neither our body nor our soul, but the union of the two; their separation is what we call death. By understanding cultural images as the basis of religion, and by relying on stories as the means of communicating these images, Greeley creates—perhaps recreates—a method of preaching that joins the theoretical to the practical. In his fiction, God becomes human being and human being becomes divine. This is, perhaps, the most important message in Greeley's novels, and his novels are his means of making this message known in the Age of Hooper. His argument through his characters is that this world is more than oddly decorated rooms.

From this conclusion and through this message, his characters and their worlds convey several important ancillary ideas. This study notes three clusters of concepts.

The first is overtly political: imagination is our way to create our freedom and it is only that freedom which can limit authority. Character after character in Greeley's fiction involve themselves in and learn how to create their own freedom. They find ways to transform their talents and their histories into a definition of self that creates unique and personal power. This power becomes their means of holding authority of all types accountable to its reasons for being. But the fact that these strong characters never accomplish their freedom alone is of equal political importance. Community—what Catholics theologically understand as the Communion of Saints—is the context in which Greeley's characters create freedom and limit authority.

Embedded in Greeley's conception of community, moreover, is a means of explaining how persons come to be part of communities. Greeley's characters very often come to understand their lives and their situations by moving from what they know particularly (their cultural images) to what everybody knows or should know (different yet connected cultural images) generally. In this process, their movement to understanding also reveals how they are tethered to this world and to each other.

Freedom, authority, and community constitute the core of Greeley's political and social philosophy. To these we might add that Greeley's theory of imagination is also a theory of change: images change the way we think, the way we believe, and the way we behave. This means there is good news and there is bad news depending upon the content of our imaginations. Greeley's villains[195] are formed by the circumstances of their lives, just as his protagonists are by theirs. The redemption of both kinds of characters is accomplished through alteration of their images. Nowhere is this more obvious than in the anthropology of sex which emerges from the portrayal of the relationships between his characters, and ultimately, between them and God.

---

[195] To the extent that there are villains in his fiction, they are mostly victims of abuse, addiction, or illness.

The second cluster of concepts found in his novels is overtly theological. Greeley's novels insist that there is the possibility of a Reality behind the real and that this possibility gives us permission to be paradoxical. There may be more than meets the eye and not to live accordingly is to miss most of what is humanly valuable in life. Nowhere is this more important than in the realm of religion. If religion is about the relationship of human beings to the divine, and if faith is about understanding this relationship to be real, then how we imagine the Reality behind the real has consequences that are personal, aesthetic, moral, and therefore, social, economic, and political. An example is in how Greeley uses time and seasons. If time and seasons are sacramental as well as salvific—as the structure of Greeley's novels contends—our stewardship of them and of all that derives from them will be of a certain kind. We will attend to the world as though it is sacred, rather than treating it like an aggregate of things less worthy than we are. The theological reading of time and seasons implies both a moral and political accountability. Moreover, we are aided in bearing this accountability precisely as we understand its sacred source. Noticing Greeley's use of time and season makes it very difficulty to miss his comedic understanding of this world.

The third cluster includes concepts that unite the political and the theological and help us see their complementarity. Greeley's metaphysical system emerges from these unities. For example, whether or not we see creation as good and as sacramental makes all the difference in how we act in this world, because how we live in this world reveals what we care about. In this sense, religion implies politics because both are constitutive of the images that give us meaning. So it is important, then, how we answer basic questions: Does life trump death? Is life a comedy or a tragedy? Do we lose what is good or merely misplace it by the decisions that make up our lives? Do we get second chances? Is God a hanging judge whose justice is revealed in his anger? Or, is justice also mercy? Could God be a great lover who pursues us unrelentingly and seduces us unto himself?

Is this God in heaven most of the time, or does God lurk in this world—sometime in its darkest corners—to be reveled in friendship, especially that of lover and beloved? What does God's silence reveal?

Does it leave us free to account for ourselves? Is this kind of silence like the locked room mysteries we find so intriguing? What does sex tell us about what God might be like? Each answer implies a mode of being in this world.

So we end where we began, with a fiction and a set of characters that carry these political and theological concepts. If this book has been correct in its analysis, then we can read Greeley fairly and with insight. That the political precedes the theological is significant—I started it as an exercise in political thought and ended learning a theology of grace—because that order and connection bring us to wonder about why it might be so. I do not have a story for this yet. But blessedly Andrew Greeley keeps writing novels!

Greeley References
(From the Andrew Greeley Web page)

Fiction

The Magic Cup. New York: Warner Books, 1975.
Death in April. New York: McGraw-Hill, 1980.
The Cardinal Sins. New York: Warner Books, 1981.
Thy Brother's Wife. New York: Warner Books, 1982.
Ascent into Hell. New York: Warner Books, 1983.
Lord of the Dance. New York: Warner Books, 1984.
Virgin and Martyr. New York: Warner Books, 1985.
Angels of September. New York: Warner Books, 1985.
Happy are the Meek. New York: Warner Books, 1985.
God Game. New York: Warner Books, 1986.
Happy are the Clean of Heart. New York: Warner Books, 1986.
Patience of a Saint. New York: Warner Books, 1987.
The Final Planet. New York: Warner Books, 1987.
Happy Are Those Who Thirst for Justice. New York: The Mysterious
    Press, 1987.
Rite of Spring. New York: Warner Books, 1987.
Angel Fire. New York: Warner Books, 1988.
Love Song. New York: Warner Books, 1989.
St. Valentine's Night. New York: Warner Books, 1989.
Andrew Greeley's Chicago. Chicago: Contemporary Books, 1989.
    (Photographs)
All About Women. New York: Tor Books, 1989.
The Cardinal Virtues. New York: Warner Books, 1990.
The Irish. Chicago: Contemporary Books, 1990. (Photographs)
The Search for Maggie Ward. New York: Warner Books, 1991.
An Occasion of Sin. New York: G. P. Putnam's Son, 1991.
Happy Are the Merciful. New York: Jove/Berkley Publishing, 1992.
Wages of Sin. New York: G. P. Putnam's Son, 1992.
Happy Are the Peace Makers. New York: Jove Books, Inc., 1993.
Fall From Grace. New York: G. P. Putnam's Son, 1993.
Irish Gold. New York: Forge/Tom Doherty Associates, 1994.
Happy Are the Poor in Spirit. New York: Jove Books, Inc., 1994.
Angel Light. New York: Forge/Tom Doherty Associates, 1995.

Happy Are Those Who Mourn. New York: Jove Books, Inc., 1995.

White Smoke. New York: Forge/Tom Doherty Associates, 1996.

Happy Are The Oppressed. New York: Jove Books, Inc., 1996.

Irish Lace. New York: Forge/Tom Doherty Associates, November 1996.

Summer at the Lake. New York: Forge/Tom Doherty Associates, May, 1997.

Star Bright! New York: Forge/Tom Doherty Associates, October 1997.

The Bishop at Sea. New York: Berkeley, November 1997.

Irish Whiskey. New York: Forge/Tom Doherty Associates, March 1998.

Contract with an Angel. New York: Forge/Tom Doherty Associates, May 1998.

A Midwinter's Tale. New York: Forge/Tom Doherty Associates, October 1998.

The Bishop and the Three Kings. New York: Penguin Putnam, Inc., October 1998.

Irish Mist. New York: Forge Books, 1999.

Younger Than Springtime. New York: Forge Books, 1999.

Irish Eyes. New York: Forge Books, 2000.

The Bishop and the Missing L-Train. New York: Forge Books, 2000.

A Christmas Wedding New York: Forge Books, 2000.

Irish Love. New York: Forge Books, 2001.

September Song. Thorndike, ME: Center Point Pub., 2002, c2001.

Irish Stew. New York: Forge Books, 2002.

Second Spring. New York: Forge/Tom Doherty Associates, 2003.

The Bishop Goes to the University. Thorndike, ME: Center Point Pub., 2004.

The Priestly Sins. New York: Forge Books, 2005.

Emerald Magic: Great Tales of Irish Fantasy. New York: Tor Books, March 2004.

Golden Years. New York: Forge Books, 2004.

The Bishop in the Old Neighborhood. New York: Forge Books, 2005.

Irish Cream. New York: Forge Books, 2005.

Irish Crystal. New York: Forge Books, 2006.

The Senator and the Priest. New York: Tom Doherty Associates, 2006.

Irish Linen. New York: Tom Doherty Associates, 2007.
The Bishop at the Lake. New York: Tom Doherty Associates, 2007.
Irish Tiger. New York: Forge Books, 2008.

Nonfiction

Religion and Career: A Study of College Graduates. New York: Sheed
    & Ward, 1963.
The Education of Catholic Americans, with Peter H. Rossi. (NORC
    Monographs in Social Research, No. 6.) Chicago: Aldine
    Publishing Co., 1966.
The Hesitant Pilgrim: American Catholicism After the Council. New
    York: Sheed & Ward, 1966.
*The Catholic Experience: A Sociologist's Interpretation of the History of
    American Catholicism.* New York: Doubleday and Co., 1967.
The Changing Catholic College. (NORC Monographs in Social
    Research, No. 13.) Chicago: Aldine Publishing Co., 1967.
Uncertain Trumpet: The Priest in Modern America. New York: Sheed
    & Ward, 1968.
The Crucible of Change: The Social Dynamics of Pastoral Practice. New
    York: Sheed & Ward, 1968.
What Do We Believe? The Stance of Religion in America, with Martin
    E. Marty and Stuart E. Rosenberg. New York: Meredith
    Press, 1968.
The Student in Higher Education. New Haven, CT: The Hazen
    Foundation, 1968.
*From Backwater to Mainstream: A Profile of Catholic Higher
    Education.* New York: McGraw-Hill, 1969.
Religion in the Year 2000. New York: Sheed & Ward, 1969.
A Future to Hope in: Socio-religious Speculations. Garden City, NY:
    Doubleday, 1969.
Life for a Wanderer. Garden City, NY: Doubleday, 1969.
Recent Alumni and Higher Education: A Survey of College Graduates,
    with Joe L. Spaeth. New York: McGraw-Hill, 1970.
Can Catholic Schools Survive? with William E. Brown. New York:
    Sheed & Ward, 1970.
Why Can't They Be Like Us? New York: E. P. Dutton, 1971.

The Denominational Society. Glenview, IL: Scott Foresman & Co., 1972.

Unsecular Man. New York: Schocken Books, Inc., 1972.

Priests in the U.S.: Reflections on a Survey. New York: Doubleday, 1972.

That Most Distressful Nation: The Taming of the American Irish. Chicago: Quadrangle Books, Inc., 1972.

The Catholic Priest in the U.S.: Sociological Investigations. Washington: United States Catholic Conference, 1972.

American Priests. Chicago: National Opinion Research Center, March 1971. (Prepared for the US Catholic Conference.)

Ethnicity in the U.S.: A Preliminary Reconnaissance. New York: John Wiley and Sons, 1974.

Building Coalitions. New York: New Viewpoints Publishing Co., 1974.

The Sociology of the Paranormal. (Studies in Religion and Ethnicity, Vol. 3.) Beverly Hills, CA: Sage Publications, 1975.

Ethnicity, Denomination, and Inequality. (Sage Papers in the Social Sciences, Vol. 4.) Beverly Hills, CA: Sage Publications, 1976.

The American Catholic: A Social Portrait. New York: Basic Books, 1977.

No Bigger Than Necessary. New York: New American Library, 1977.

Neighborhood. New York: The Seabury Press, 1977.

Crisis in the Church: A Study of Religion in America. Chicago: The Thomas More Press, 1979.

Ethnic Drinking Subcultures, with William C. McCready and Gary Theisen. New York: Praeger Publishers, 1980.

The Religious Imagination. New York: Sadlier, 1981.

The Young Catholic Family. Chicago: The Thomas More Press, 1980.

Young Catholics in the United States and Canada, with Joan Fee, William C. McCready, and Teresa Sullivan. New York: William H. Sadlier, Inc., 1981.

The Irish Americans: The Rise to Money and Power. New York: Harper and Row, 1981.

Catholic High Schools and Minority Students. New Brunswick, NJ: Transaction Books, 1982.

Parish, Priest and People, with Mary Durkin, David Tracy, John Shea, and William C. McCready. Chicago: The Thomas More Press, 1981.

The Bottom Line Catechism. Chicago: The Thomas More Press, 1982.

Religion: A Secular Theory. New York: Free Press, 1982.

The Catholic Why? Book. Chicago: The Thomas More Press, 1983.

The Dilemma of American Immigration: Beyond the Golden Door, with Pastora Cafferty, Barry Chiswick, and Teresa Sullivan. New Brunswick, NJ: Transaction Books, 1983.

Angry Catholic Women, with Mary Durkin. Chicago: The Thomas More Press, 1984.

How to Save the Catholic Church, with Mary Durkin. New York: Viking Penguin Inc., 1984.

American Catholics Since the Council. Chicago: The Thomas More Press, 1985.

Confessions of a Parish Priest. New York: Simon and Schuster, 1986.

Catholic Contributions: Sociology & Policy, with Bishop William McManus. Chicago: The Thomas More Press, 1987.

An Andrew Greeley Reader: Volume One. Chicago: The Thomas More Press, 1987.

The Irish Americans: The Rise to Money and Power. New York: Warner Books, 1988.

When Life Hurts: Healing Themes from the Gospels. Chicago: The Thomas More Press, 1988.

God in Popular Culture. Chicago: The Thomas More Press, 1988.

Sexual Intimacy: Love and Play. New York: Warner Books, 1988.

Myths of Religion. New York: Warner Books, 1988.

Religious Change in America. Cambridge, MA: Harvard University Press, 1989.

The Catholic Myth. New York: Charles Scribner's Sons/Macmillan, 1990.

The Bible and Us with Jacob Neusner. New York: Warner Books, 1990.

Faithful Attraction: Discovering Intimacy, Love, and Fidelity in American Marriage. New York: Tor Books, 1991.

Sex: The Catholic Experience. Chicago: The Thomas More Press, 1995.

Religion as Poetry. New Brunswick, NJ: Transaction Publishing, 1995.
Sociology and Religion: A Collection of Readings. New York: HarperCollins College Publishers, 1995.
Common Ground with Jacob Neusner. Cleveland: Pilgrim Press, 1996.
Forging a Common Future with Chilton, Green, Neusner. Cleveland: Pilgrim Press, 1997.
I Hope You're Listening God. The Crossroads Publishing Co., 1997.
FURTHERMORE! Memories of a Parish Priest. New York: Forge Books, 1999.
Book of Love. New York: Tom Doherty Associates/Forge Books, 2002.
The Great Mysteries: Experiencing Catholic Faith from the Inside Out. Lanham, MD: Sheed & Ward, 2003.
Catholic Revolution: New Wine, Old Wineskins, and the Second Vatican Council. Berkeley, CA: University of California Press, 2004.
Priests: A Calling in Crisis. Chicago: University of Chicago Press, 2004.
The Making of the Pope. New York: Little, Brown, 2005.

References

Arendt, Hannah. *Between Past and Future.* New York: Penguin Books. Reissue 1993.
------. *The Human Condition.* Garden City, NJ: Doubleday Anchor Books, 1959.
------. *The Promise of Politics.* New York: Schocken Books, 2005.
Augustine's Confessions. New City Press; New Ed edition, 2003.
Becker, Allienne. *Andrew M. Greeley: The Mysteries of Grace.* New York: Writers Club Press, 2002.
Bellah, Robert. "Religion and the Shape of national Culture," *America.* July 31, 1999.
------. *Habits of the Heart: Individualism and Commitment in American Life.* Berkeley, CA: University of California Press, 1985.
------. *The Good Society.* New York: Knopf, 1991.
Cast, David. *The Calumny of Apelles: A Study in the Humanist Tradition.* New Haven: Yale University Press, 1981.

Catholic Higher Education: Practice and Promise. Washington, DC: Association of Catholic Colleges and Universities and the University of St. Thomas, 1995.

Cernera, Anthony J. and Oliver J. Morgan. (Ed.), *Examining the Catholic Intellectual Tradition.* Fairfield CT: Sacred Heart University Press, 2000.

Charles, S. J. Rodger. *Christian Social Witness and Teaching: The Catholic Tradition for Genesis to Centesimus Annus.* Vol. 1. *From Biblical Times to the Late Nineteenth Century.* Herefordshire: Gracewing Fowler Wright Books, 1998.

Colish, Marcia. *Catholic and Intellectual: Conjunction or Disjunction.* Dayton, OH: University of Dayton, 2002.

Clark, Kenneth. *Civilization: a Personal View.* London: British Broadcasting Corporation, 1971.

The Document of Vatican II. Walter M. Abbott, SJ (Ed), New York: Guild Press, 1966.

Ex Libris: A Selected Reading List of Books in the Catholic Intellectual Tradition. Interdisciplinary Program in Catholic Studies of the University of St. Thomas, n.d.

Farlie, Henry. *The Seven Deadly Sins Today.* Washington: New Republic Books, New York: Simon and Schuster, 1978.

Justice in the World in *The Gospel of Peace and Justice.* Maryknoll, New York: Orbis, Books, 1976.

Gandolfo, Anita. *Testing the Faith: The New Catholic Fiction in America.* New York: Greenwood Press, 1992.

Grasso, Kenneth L., Gerard V. Bradley, and Robert Hunt. *Catholicism, Liberalism, and Communitarianism: The Catholic Intellectual Tradition and the Foundations of Democracy.* Lanham, MD: Rowman and Littlefield, 1995.

Hawley, John C., ed. Through a Glass Darkly: Essays in the Religious Imagination. New York: Fordham University Press, 1996. Questia. 14 Oct. 2007 <http://www.questia.com/PM.qst?a=o&d=72535756>.

Hellwig, Monika K. "The Catholic Intellectual Tradition." *Examining the Catholic Intellectual* Cernera, Anthony J. and Oliver J. Morgan. (Ed.), Fairfield CT: Sacred Heart University Press, 2000.

Ignatieff, Michael. "Modern Dying." *The New Republic*. Vol. 199: 26: 28–33 (December 26, 1988.)

Kundera, Milan. "Man Thinks, God Laughs," Milan Kundera. *New York Review of Books*, June 13, 1985.

McClory, Robert. Turning Point: The Inside Story of the Papal Birth Control Commission. New York: Crossroad Publishing, 1995.

Massa, Mark S. (SJ) "The New and Old Anti-Catholicism and the Analogical Imagination." *Theological Studies* 62.3 (2001): 549.

Marsden, Michael T. "The Fiction of Andrew Greeley: The Sacramentality of Storytelling." *U. S. Catholic Historian*. Vol. 25: 3, Summer, 2005.

Novak, Michael. *The Experience of Nothingness*. New York: Harper and Row, 1970.

Neuhaus, Richard John. *First Things: A Monthly Journal of Religion and Public Life*, No. 147, November 2004.

Pasquariello, Ronald D. *Conversations with Andrew Greeley*. Boston: Quinlan Press, 1988.

Ple, Albert. *Duty or Pleasure?: A New Appraisal of Christian Ethics*. Translated by Matthew J. O'Connell. New York: Paragon House Publishers, 1987.

Russello, Gerald R. "A Different Discipline: the American Catholic Novel." *Renascence: Essays on Values in Literature*, 51.3 (Spring 1999: 205–215.)

Schillebeeckx, Edward. *Christ, the Sacrament of the Encounter with God*. Translated by Paul Barrett, revised by Mark Schoof and Laurence Bright. New York: Sheed & Ward, 1963.

Shafer, Ingrid H. Ed. *The Incarnate Imagination: Essay in Theology, the Arts, and Social Sciences*. Bowling Green State University Popular Press: Bowling Green, OH, 1988.

------, "Odd Man Out: A Modern Morality Play Andrew Greeley, Joseph Cardinal, Bernardin." Eugene Kennedy (July 1995 Draft) <http://www.usao.edu/~facshaferi/SALIERI.HTML>

Shaw, Bernard. *Saint Joan*. New York: Penguin Books, 1978.

Sparr, Arnold. *To Promote, Defend, and Redeem: The Catholic Literary Revival and the Cultural Transformation of American Catholicism, 1920–1960*, New York: Greenwood Press, 1990.

Tilley, Terrence. *Inventing the Catholic Tradition*. Maryknoll, New York: Orbis. 2000.

Tracy, David. *The Analogical Imagination: Christian Theology and the Culture of Pluralism*. New York: Crossroad Pub. Co., 1989.

Thompson, Francis. "The Hound of Heaven." *The Oxford Book of English Mystical Verse*. Nicholson and Lee. Editors. Oxford: The Clarendon Press, 1917.

Villa, Dana. (Ed) *The Cambridge Companion to Hanna Arendt*. Cambridge: Cambridge University Press, 2000.

Waugh, Evelyn. *Brideshead Revisited*. Boston: Little, Brown and Company, 1945.

Wolin, Sheldon S. *Politics and Vision: Continuity and Innovation in Western Political Thought*. Boston: Little Brown, 1960.

INDEX

P

Papacy

authority of, 23, 138

on birth control, 137

elections, 22, 137

encyclicals, 130, 137, 229

politics of, 239

Passover Trilogy, 190

Patience of a Saint, 223–229

Patriarchy, 243

as different from hierarchy, 34, 244

faith in, 47

and family, 116

Paul VI, 137

Pentecost, 110, 151

Ple, Albert, 46

Pleasure

versus duty, 47

and morality, 48

Pluralism

in catholic church, 10

and freedom, 94–95

intellectual, 12, 32

Political action, 95, 96, 136, 261

Politics

authentic, 96–99, 133

and authority, 86, 87, 116

civility in, 260

envy in, 11

and equality, 12

freedom in, 12, 91, 92, 133

and friendship, 118–119

of liberation, 232

Machiavellian, 102, 103, 185

and morality, 97, 98

obedience, 87

of papal government, 137

radicalization of, 139

and religion, 51

role of church, 38

and social disorder, 120

of violence, 101, 265

Power

absolute, 241

versus authority, 90, 91

corruption of, 210, 239

of individuals, 239

and mercy, 208

Predestination, 59

Pride, 145, 147, 148, 179, 204, 227

The Priestly Sins, 94, 103–109, 231

in others, 66

in ourselves, 154, 167

place in social order, 209

result of distrust, 72

in use of truth, 173

Truth, 11–12, 29

courage of, 188

versus facts, 105

God as, 34

and trust, 173

understanding, 39

205, 221

of the past, 34

sources, 155

X

Xenophobia, 37

Y

Younger Than Springtime, 121–126

U

Universality, 35

V

Vices, 11

Virgin and Martyr, 98, 232

Virtues, 132, 175

W

The Wages of Sin, 148–153

"What is Authority?" (Arendt), 85

White Smoke, 236, 239–241

Wisdom, 110

"higher," 157

integration of knowledge, 35,